FRAM

CHERRYL SMITH

FRAMING ISRAEL

A PERSONAL TOUR
OF MEDIA AND CAMPUS RHETORIC

RVP Press
New York

RVP Publishers Inc.
Roslyn, NY 11576

RVP Press, New York

cover photo: David Stein Potache
author photo: Jeremy Zev Smith-Danford

The publication of this book is supported by International Center for Western Values, Amsterdam.

RVP Press™ is an imprint of RVP Publishers Inc., Roslyn.
The RVP Publishers logo is a trademark of RVP Publishers Inc., Roslyn.

Library of Congress Control Number: 2019948791

ISBN 978 1 61861 343 1

www.rvppress.com

This book is dedicated
to my parents, Warren and Frances,
of blessed memory

Table of Contents

chapter 1

Berkeley to Jerusalem and Back

A young woman walking along a sunny beach and a young man sitting by himself on the sand notice each other. The young man gestures toward the space next to him, inviting the woman to sit down. She declines and continues walking but also continues glancing back as he encourages her to join him; he smiles at her, offers her a bottle of soda. Smiling back, she walks into a wooden post! We hear the recorded voiceover: "Indeed, Israel *can* be a dangerous place. If you thought you knew all about Israel, think again."[1]

Many countries and cities embark on campaigns to encourage tourism and to impact their image abroad. Although the historic and religious sites of Israel are always a draw for tourists, its image has never focused on the miles of sparkling Mediterranean seashore or included the slightest hint of Israeli humor. When the Israel Ministry of Foreign Affairs began consulting specialists in "country positioning" or "nation branding," the first goals were to highlight Israel's extensive contributions to science and technology, its medical advances, and its humanitarian aid around the world.[2]

Israel might have had some advantages for this kind of image building given its accomplishments from a population of only 8.5 million. Just listing a few of its many inventions might have been impressive: the technologies for solar power plants, cell phones, voice mail, computer virus protection, instant messaging, personal computer operating systems, and micro-imaging cancer detection. Israelis invented drip irrigation, lead the world in waste water recycling, and pioneered desalinization of sea water.[3] They have more start-ups and more medical device patents per capita than any country in the world and only the US and China have more companies on the NASDAQ.[4] Israel's humanitarian aid teams are often the first to set up field hospitals at disaster sites and they have brought medical and emergency help to 140 different countries.[5] Less well-known is that Israel consistently ranks among the top countries of the world in measures of life satisfaction and happiness.[6] Accordingly, in 2014 the Tourism Ministry began promoting "Israel: Land of Creation," highlighting Israeli arts, music, fashion, foods, cultural diversity, and the natural beauty of the country.

Explaining the need for Israeli country positioning projects, their director, Ido Aharoni said, "We researched worldwide and it came up almost universally that Israel's image is identified with the conflict."[7] Given the conclusions of academics such as Eli Avraham, who study public diplomacy, Aharoni understated the situation:

> The result of the activity of Israel's opponents and the media coverage was the total omission of any non-conflictual/political characteristics from the country's image and its perception as a dangerous and menacing place in which no 'fun' or normal life was to be found.[8]

Although branding efforts likely have led to many international business successes and to encouraging more tourism, it doesn't seem that there have been major shifts in Israel's image. Rated the third best country in the world to raise children,[9] Israel is also "the only nation of the world whose right to exist is constantly questioned and challenged."[10]

Though it is a tiny country of 8,367 square miles—only four US states are smaller and New Jersey is pretty much the same size—the news coverage it receives makes Israel seem enormous. English language media give Israel attention vastly disproportionate to that of other countries. And yet, with hundreds of reporters' microphones and photographers' lenses directed toward the Jewish state, we actually learn very little about it. Perhaps this contrast is to be expected; bad news always seems to be most newsworthy. Yet the intense media focus on what is labeled "the conflict," to the near exclusion of any other aspect of Israel, does not appear to give a clear picture even of the conflict.[11] By blocking out nearly everything else about the country, reporting on the conflict itself becomes distorted.

If you follow the news about Israel and observe closely how it appears in mainstream US and UK media, you are likely to see repeating patterns, phrasings, and images, even, one can reasonably say, slogans that recur regardless of the particular events described. You may begin to identify the Israel-connected complexes of words, the language we most often hear when media tell us what is happening—or what to make of what is happening—in and in relation to Israel and you will readily encounter the frameworks of reporting outlined in this book. These influence the way news stories and opinion pieces are shaped on the subject of Israel. Certainly, not every mainstream report fits these patterns. But over time the topics and key words repeated during years of media exposure, the messages promoted by this cumulative attention, create an Israel constructed by language, a kind of shadow to the real, living country.

And a dark shadow it is.

Yet I barely noticed until I actually visited Israel in the summer of 2000 and returned home to Berkeley that September. I began to observe what had been nearly invisible to me before, that particular patterns of anti-Israel rhetoric are entirely commonplace—in the media, on university campuses, and most directly on the world stage in places like the United Nations—that distortions, even fictions posing as facts, are an everyday occurrence.

For years after my first trip to Israel, I thought what I was seeing in mainstream media, and in a more abstract version on college campuses, was a lack of information. I imagined that Israelis' stories just weren't getting out. I wanted to explain, point by point, what news reports and campus speakers seemed to be missing. I didn't know that the Hebrew word, *hasbara*, which is often translated as Israeli "public relations," actually means "explanation" or "information" but I did think that these were most needed, that if there were better spokespersons from Israel or if the books that offer information about Israel's history and situation were widely read,[12] the prevalence of what I now saw as one-sided discourse would disappear. I even thought that "rebranding" would have worked. And sometimes, people do have a change of heart when they learn that there is more to a story or that they have been misinformed.

However, the impetus for this book is not the need to get out a set of facts, though factual information is important—and, in this case, readily available—but to address why even factual information often has no impact on discussion of Israel. What I have come to understand is that although, like all countries, Israel has many problems and limitations, the language and rhetoric about Israel has framed it unfairly, unlike any other country of the world.

Welcome to Israel

That first summer was exhilarating, as living in a different country can be. My then nine-year-old son Jeremy and I swapped our Berkeley apartment for a small studio in Jerusalem. We explored the city, walking up and down the hilly streets of our neighborhood between Rasco and Katamon—just uphill from the big park, Gan Sacher. We got to know the winding alleyways of the Old City and we visited the rest of the country by taking public busses, often on day trips from Jerusalem, for Israel's size (and population) is not much larger than that of the San Francisco Bay Area.

We knew no one in the country and on the fourth night of our trip this was a worry, for when we hurried off a crowded bus, I discovered too late that I had left my small backpack. We were without passports, credit cards, the key to the apartment—and our copy of *Harry Potter and the Prisoner of Askaban*. I knocked on apartment doors in our building until, in spite of the late hour, a door opened. Without understanding my English explanation of who we were and what was our problem, we were invited in, served cake, coffee, and Coca-Cola and offered a place to stay. From then on we became fast friends with our neighbors, the Kimchi family, who lived on the top floor of our four-story building, Gin and Israel and their four children, the youngest of whom was five years older than Jeremy, and the oldest who had already completed her military service. One of the sons climbed up from the balcony and managed to unlock our apartment. We never recovered our lost items but eventually we did replace them, a detail I usually forget to include when I have retold this story, since the losses that evening were so trivial in comparison to gaining an instant, essentially family, connection.

Gin speaks only Hebrew, and though the rest of the family could translate if necessary, language wasn't the barrier I would have expected. Throughout the summer they invited us for delicious and plentiful Friday night dinners, their table expanded to fill the small livingroom space, crowding in as many as 12 or 13 chairs to include frequently visiting relatives, and the two of us, whom they simply welcomed into their boisterous family. The table was very crowded, too, with trays of roasted beef, beans in bubbling sauce, bowls of spiced eggplant, crispy cubed potatoes, enormous quantities of chopped salad, and warm pita with hummus and tehina—great food being one of the major attractions in Israel. Besides the hospitality of our new friends we ate very well everywhere; even the small falafel stands that Jeremy especially liked served fresh pita and salad. And we encountered many welcoming people. Later in the summer, at a swimming pool in Eilat, we met an artist with her also nine-year-old son, and we were immediately invited to stay with them in their apartment in Tel Aviv, which we did for several days.

In all, Israel seemed to be a perfect tourist destination, full of pleasant cafes, outdoor markets, gardens and parks, and sized small enough to encounter ancient history, beautiful beaches, and an overload of cultural attraction all in a single day. The people: friendly, welcoming, exuberant, and extremely direct, were for me the best bonus.

Several days a week I volunteered as a tutor in English for native speakers of Arabic, Israeli Hebrew University students who were preparing to take the English reading exam required at Israel's universities and who were the beneficiaries of special programs to help them with the difficulties of reading academic work in English. On my own campus, besides teaching courses in rhetoric and composition, I directed the university Writing Center, training and supervising tutors. So, at Hebrew University, I kept notes on my experiences, collecting data, planning to write an academic article about reversing the director and tutor roles and, I realized later when we were back in California, somehow imagining that the particular country in which I was doing this was all but immaterial.

Jeremy came with me when I tutored, sat in the classroom reading *Harry Potter* or drawing while I met with students, and then wandered around the sprawling Humanities complex on his own. He got to know the staff at the busy lunch kiosk on the second floor and had more freedom as a nine-year-old than he ever had in Berkeley.

It was the summer of the Bill Clinton–Yasser Arafat–Ehud Barak peace talks and as Jeremy and I rode the busses in Jerusalem or on our excursions to Tel Aviv and farther destinations like Haifa or Safed, the drivers usually had the radio blaring. We would hear the word "Clinton," with Israeli accent, among the Hebrew words we did not understand, and then the bus would quiet down because everyone wanted to listen to the latest news. Indeed, at homes we visited and in public places, news broadcasts seemed to be the soundtrack of the country.

And the mood of the country, it seemed, was hopeful. Among the people I was getting to know, the political leanings were mixed like the Israeli newspaper options in English.[13] Yet there seemed to be general consensus that a peace agreement was likely. Prime Minister Ehud Barak, who in May had unilaterally withdrawn Israel's last troops from Lebanon, would agree to a Palestinian state that included all of Gaza, nearly all of the West Bank, and even a divided Jerusalem. And with nothing further to argue for, Yasser Arafat would agree to lead a Palestinian state. Bill Clinton seemed especially convincing as a broker of this deal, lobbying also for his own legacy at the end of his presidency. There was wariness, certainly; I'm not sure that I met anyone who was comfortable with the concept of a divided Jerusalem. Neighborhoods in Jerusalem are close and entangled and no two countries in the world actually share a capital. But the possibility that there could be peace—like the peace that treaties with Egypt and Jordan have maintained—was powerful. There was hope that a settlement between the Israelis and the Palestinians was finally near at hand.

Cognitive Framing

Writing this now, years later, that summer hopefulness feels like a fantasy, a naïve dream. And yet the same kind of talks, and talks about the possibility or futility or urgency of such talks, go on.

Our tiny Jerusalem apartment belonged to a Hebrew University doctoral candidate, who now teaches at Bar Ilan University, needing housing near the Berkeley campus in order to complete her research on the novelist, Raymond Carver. It was a coincidence that Ayala was an academic and in a related field to mine (Raymond Carver even had once, famously, been a student in my department) and that Jeremy and I were temporarily living close to UC Berkeley while waiting to move into a new house. The next morning after sending her an email, in which I had only said that yes, I have an apartment near campus, I received a one-line email back: "Where shall I send my key?"

The other fortuitous timing was that I had chosen to go to Israel for the summer rather than for the fall semester, the actual time of my sabbatical. If not for this, had I waited until September, there is no chance that we would have taken a first trip to Israel. For the second Intifada began shortly after we got home.

And I am not sure that I would ever have got around to visiting Israel at all.

Given that my political life began as a Berkeley undergraduate in the late 1960's/early 1970's and has continued pretty much on the same general path, in the mainstream of the university, I could easily have viewed the issue of Israel through the frames that are the subject of this book. For, known only from a distance, especially the distance of an American university, Israel is more an issue than a country. I might have read the newspapers, watched the TV coverage, and observed the campus response to Israel and the Second Intifada[14] without the sudden cognitive dissonance—more jolting, really, than mere cognitive dissonance—a feeling that my worldview, if not my world itself, had flipped upside down when we returned to Northern California, while peace most definitely was not occurring in Israel.

There is nothing unique about this observation. We can't investigate every issue for ourselves and so must categorize, to some degree, just to get though each day. Whole complexes of unexamined information are catalogued in our consciousness; our minds are very busy and very full and we clump information into manageable pieces, adding more to already established categories, reshaping categories as needed. Psychologists have labeled humans "cognitive misers"; that is, we don't create a new category or adjust an old one unless we are absolutely forced to by the dissonance between what we already know and the appearance of some new informa-tion.[15] Certainly, the trip to Israel had created new categories. But the return to California created even more.

Without any change in my own politics, my grounding seemed to have slipped away. My trusted sources of information: CNN, *The New York Times*, the *San Francisco Chronicle*, seemed inadequate on this topic of Israel, missing what was for me essential information about the "conflict in the Middle East." Much of mainstream media seemed strangely uninterested in historical background and yet very interested in finding and empathizing with "root causes" for suicide bombing. Campus communities, even my own quiet, nonpolitical campus in Sacramento, experienced great demand for speakers about Israeli military "oppression" and "Palestinian resistance" and "The Occupation," topics that I considered worth discussing, but here they were decontextualized and one-sided. Where was concern for Israeli citizens who were reeling from deadly bombings in their busses and cafes?

And then one day when I happened to be walking through the university quad at lunchtime, there appeared a marching group of students. This, in itself, was rare on our campus; yet there they were: marchers shouting, "Sharon is Hitler!" and carrying signs painted with swastikas. Swastikas? On my easy-going campus? Next to each huge, black swastika were white equal signs connecting to big, blue Jewish stars, dripping with red, as with blood.

Something was deeply wrong. Surely we don't allow hate speech on campus. Calling Jews "Nazis" is offensive and cruel. And, in any case, American universities are exceedingly sensitive to speech that could offend minority groups.

Freedom of speech protects the marchers, their swastikas, and a whole range of deeply offensive speech. But regarding sensitivity to minorities, Jews are not a "protected" minority on campus. Without protected status, there has been no recourse for Jewish students at schools where extreme anti-Israel rhetoric and Jewish star/Nazi swastika equations have become commonplace, campuses where students (and faculty) have felt the environment to be hostile, where intimidation, including physical intimidation, has occurred.[16] In fact, there has been an effort to make a legal status change that would include Jews among "protected" minorities.[17]

That this legal path has been necessary is significant, for the usual way of regulating speech at universities is not legal, but informal. As an English professor, I require that students do not write in ways that may be interpreted as sexist or racist or homophobic, and teach them how to do this if the need arises. If another minority were shouted out as Nazis, a group, for instance, for whom the term, Nazi does not connect to their own people's genocide in the Holocaust, campus expectations for non-racist, non-offensive language would quickly stop this from recurring.

Notice that we set out to talk about Israel and here we are talking about Jews. Yet, you will be told that the star dripping with blood and equated to a swastika should not be interpreted as a Jewish star, that it represents the flag of Israel. It doesn't refer to Jews but to Israelis, though I am assuming only to Jewish Israelis. Indeed, the suggestion that there may be something at least vaguely antisemitic about this image will be met with outrage, with the counterclaim that such suggestions are meant to silence objection to Israeli policy. The star, you will be told, merely refers to the Israeli government, like the American flag, when it's burned or trampled on, does not refer to Americans (except, perhaps, to those who would be offended by the burning of an American flag) and is fair game. This is an apt analogy, for political reactions to Israel most often are consistent with political reactions to America. Ideology is a most powerful inspiration for framing.

chapter 2

War and PC

My heart is in the East, but I am in the farthest West[1]
—Yehuda Halevy (1075–1141),
Spanish Jewish philosopher and poet

I am talking with a neighbor, a congenial neighbor with whom I often talk about gardening. She has caught me just as I am leaving the house, just after I have read on *Haaretz* online that there was another suicide bombing in Jerusalem.

Have I heard? The Israelis are cutting down olive trees! In the West Bank!

"Why are they cutting down trees?"

"It's collective punishment," she says darkly.

I don't know what to say.

"There's a rally on Saturday," she says, "I was thinking you would want to go with me."

"Oh, uh no, thanks, not at all . . ."

She is genuinely surprised. "I mean, since you're interested in Israel. My friends who told me about it are Jewish," she offers.

Why, I want to ask her, of all the horrors taking place in the world at this moment, including the murder of children in suicide bombings in Israel, the vast genocide going on in Darfur, slavery still in existence in Yemen, does the thought of these particular trees inspire her to take to the streets in protest?

"I think," I say carefully, "that the rally is probably not so much about trees."

She considers this. I like my neighbor. She has been friendly and hospitable. Her politics have always been the same as my own. We vote the same way, criticize the same politicians; we hold the same positions on the issues of importance in Berkeley. "I guess, that's true," she says. "It's about the whole Occupation. Cutting down the trees. The checkpoints. The Oppression."

"You know there was a bus bombing today in Jerusalem?"

She doesn't know. Nor why I have mentioned it. Nor does she ask.

Maybe if I could talk with her about the history of Israel, of the Jews, about the Balfour Declaration, the Partition plan, about the fact that no one called the 19 year annexing and naming of the West Bank by Jordan an Occupation, about defensive war, about the rights of Jews to self-determination, about the opportunities for Palestinians to have a country for the first time in their history. Maybe if she read some of the books I've been reading. Or, if she visited Israel. Maybe if she knew Israelis who would also object to cutting down trees for no reason. Or maybe if the possibility were more prevalent here for an interest in Israel not necessarily to mean wanting to rally against it nor believing that Israel is always in the wrong.[2]

It feels overwhelming.

I have many conversations like this. Most of the time I don't know where to begin; much of the time, I don't.

I tell her that her agave plants are looking really good, and I walk out to my car.

Jeremy and I didn't get back to Israel for five years, until the summer of 2005. The news of terrorist attacks on civilians kept me away: deadly bombings targeting people in the cafés we had been to in Jerusalem, on the busses we had ridden, and even killing students at Hebrew University, where Jeremy had wandered so freely and I had tutored English in a setting of more diversity than the universities of California. There, Hamas terrorists killed nine students and staff, six of them American, and wounded nearly a hundred other people. One of the students murdered while eating her lunch in the Hebrew University cafeteria was Marla Bennett, age 24, from San Diego, a recent UC Berkeley graduate who was studying in Jerusalem and was, I learned later, a friend of my eldest niece. No one took to the streets of Berkeley to protest against the murderers of Marla Bennett.[3]

The news didn't stop having an impact on my travel plans until some time after the summer of 2006, the summer when we experienced being in Israel during a war. After that I began to feel that the political situation, whether there was war or only threats of war, was not the consideration it had been to me. And by the time we left Israel in January of 2008, after a four-month sabbatical when I taught a seminar at Hebrew University, I felt that the next time I went there, it would be without paying much attention to "the situation." After all, I had already seen all the tourist sites. I didn't need to go anywhere in particular. Just to be there had started to become my purpose in going to Israel. But before that, and especially in the years between our first trip and the second, I was scared away by terrorism. So, we stayed in California where the war I was experiencing was only one of words.

I found it very hard to participate. It was as if people were speaking in sound bites and to explain why their soundbites were distorted or completely inaccurate I wanted to speak in big books of history, volumes of information, of facts, and maps, and declarations. I noticed that many words—Zionism, occupation, apartheid, human rights, nationalism—had been redefined, Alice-in-Wonderland-like, to mean something new in terms of Israel.

Of course, language is a living thing, evolving over time. There were no existing words to name the unique traumas of the Jews and those that have been invented—diaspora,[4] genocide,[5] holocaust, ghetto—have taken on generalized meanings rather quickly. I remember that my grandmother and my father found it disturbing, even offensive, that "ghetto," the word invented to name the locked, enforced enclosures of European Jews, came to name free but poor US city neighborhoods and big portable "blasting" radios. Now there's a neighborhood of upscale restaurants in Berkeley called the "gourmet ghetto."[6] Even the word Holocaust translated from the Hebrew *shoah* has shifted meaning from its original focus on the Nazis' relentless mission to annihilate the Jews, regardless of an individual's religious belief or country of citizenship but determined by bloodline, by having one quarter Jewish ancestry, one Jewish grandparent. At the same time, the Nazis also murdered millions of other civilians. The word, Holocaust was not a term for all of the Nazi atrocities and perhaps new words are needed to encompass all the victims and all of the evils of the National Socialist German Worker's Party while also identifying the uniquely horrific focus of the Nazi machine on destroying the Jewish people.[7]

Far more disturbing is that the words holocaust and Nazi get used so often and so frivolously. By 1988, Elie Wiesel had stopped using the term, holocaust at all: "First," he said, "because there are no words and also because it has become so trivialized that I cannot use it any more. Whatever mishap occurs, they call it a holocaust."[8] I admit I am unnerved every time I hear traditional English teachers called "grammar Nazis." I understand Elie Wiesel's reaction to casual uses of the word, holocaust, and my father's and grandmother's sense of diminishment to the people who experienced real Nazis and locked ghettos.

But if words morph naturally into new meanings over time, they also can be artificially revised. And these strange usages signaled that whole frames of reference about the Jewish state were askew, though it took me years to reach that conclusion.

The Z Word

During this time I give a talk on campus, as part of a panel presentation that takes months to arrange, with a retired professor of business, a local rabbi, and the Israeli Hillel director from the nearby research campus, University of California, Davis. I believe it is the only presentation that year that is not from an anti-Israel perspective.

The lecture hall fills up and a group of around ten students each wearing a keffiyeh (I assume that they are students) stands at the back of the room. We invite them to sit down but they remain standing. The rabbi outlines Jewish history, moving quickly from biblical times all the way to the establishment of the state of Israel; the retired professor talks about Israeli innovations. I am the only member of the panel to read from a prepared talk; I'm too uneasy to do otherwise. I tell about my experiences on my summer sabbatical. I describe the vibrancy of Israel, its democratic values and laws, its progressive, open culture—the only place in the Middle East with equal rights for all its citizens, with freedom of religion, and of the press, and free speech, with gay rights and acceptance. We are informative. Positive. The Hillel director talks about Zionism. He says that it is the Jewish movement for self-determination. There is shouting from the group at the back of the room. "Free Palestine! Free, free, Palestine!" For a few minutes, he is drowned out in spite of the microphones: "Colonialist!"

I'm struck by the oddity of calling the only person the whole room knows to have been born in Israel a colonialist. I didn't understand during that panel presentation that the term, "colonial," like many other words, had changed meaning in the case of Israel and the Jews. I even thought that "free Palestine" referred to the West Bank and Gaza.

The Hillel director and then the rabbi do their best to respond, speeding through complicated history in a few minutes. Jews have always lived in Israel. They had lived all over the Middle East for millennia, until they were driven out by local mobs and state governments. In its 4,000-year history, Jerusalem has been made a capital only by the Jews.[9] In fact, the land of Israel is not only the birthplace but the center of Jewish nationhood. The Jewish communities of Jerusalem, Safed, Hebron, Tiberius, and other places are thousands of years old. The Jews who came to Israel in the 19th and early 20th century, before the establishment of the state, were escaping centuries of persecution. They didn't conquer or colonize or steal land.

In the years between 1517 and 1917 the land was a district of the Ottoman Empire. When the Ottoman Empire and Germany were defeated in World War 1, the French and British held mandates for administering parts of the Empire until the areas would become autonomous. Areas that became Syria, Iraq, and Lebanon were administered by the French and areas that became Israel, Jordan, the West Bank and Gaza by the British. Even before that, in 1917 the British and Allies had already committed to a reestablished Jewish home within the Mandate. In the 1920s, the British turned over 78 percent of their Mandate to the Hashemite King who created the Kingdom of Transjordan. At around the same time that Pakistan was established to divide it from India (and for similar reasons), the British suggested a partition of the rest of the mandate in order to form a second, new Arab country and the Jewish country. The Arab leadership did not agree so no country of Palestine was established. The day after the British left in 1948, Israel declared its independence. The next day, five Arab armies invaded with the stated purpose of destroying the new state.

After the presentation a colleague whom I was surprised to see in attendance shakes my hand and says in his blustery way, "Well! You sounded pro-Israeli *and* pro-Palestinian!" Yes, of course I am. I was surprised this was so surprising.[10] Another, much closer colleague, gives me a hug. She says, actually whispers in my ear, she agrees with me about Israel. And a lecturer I had met on a university committee tells me very quietly, "I'm a Zionist, too, but I'd never say it."

Judea Pearl, UCLA professor and father of Daniel Pearl, *The Wall Street Journal* reporter who was kidnapped and beheaded by al-Qaeda terrorists, has written eloquently about the co-opting of the term Zionist and the acceptability of anti-Zionist rhetoric at universities. He explains that anti-Zionism is inherently racist, for it denies to Jews the rights of all other peoples to nationhood.[11]

The murderers of Daniel Pearl proudly videotaped his beheading and dismemberment; they sent the gruesome video to his family and out to the Internet. Review of the video revealed that it was filmed in two parts: the second part in which Daniel reads propaganda and then is brutally murdered and the first part, spliced on from an earlier taping when likely he had been told he would be released after the film was finished. This part records his last freely spoken words: "My father's Jewish, my mother's Jewish, I'm Jewish. Back in the town of Bnai B'rak there's a street named after my grandfather, Chaim Pearl who was one of the founders of the town."[12]

Academic Freedom

A week or two after the panel presentation, a former graduate student comes to my office. "I've really been wanting see you," she says. "I heard your talk about Israel. I always thought you were so leftwing!"

"Wait, and now you don't?"

"Well, I mean, you know what other professors say about Israel, right? It's even worse than America!" And she stays in my office for an hour telling me how she learned in graduate school to keep her own political views to herself: "I like the professors here. Just, I would never say what I think. I mean, you can't really go around being all patriotic USA and still be thought of as smart, right?"

Although from outside the university it may seem unfair or even unseemly, ethical responsibilities at universities do not include "equal representation" of ideas. Faculty members are expected to treat students equitably but there is no expectation of political diversity or of offering multiple political perspectives. Some professors and some whole disciplines teach from particular political positions.[13] Indeed, positioning oneself against the nonacademic mainstream, which in the Humanities can often mean against the American center/right majority, is valued, even, assumed. In my own field of Rhetoric and Composition it is a given that there are no neutral teaching attitudes, that we are always advocating, even implicitly, for or against something. And the usual way to understand this is that one is either advocating for or against the status quo.

Since academic knowledge depends on the ability of scholars to criticize each other's theories, to add new research that may discredit previous studies, the institution of "academic freedom" is a protection of professors' right to say what we know without fear of reprisal in terms of tenure and promotion decisions or otherwise. At the same time, we are free to speak or write as individuals rather than as representatives of the university. The university can take credit or even disavow responsibility as it chooses. But academic freedom does not mean that we have an obligation to tell all sides of a story. Of course, it also does not mean that students or faculty should find themselves intimidated into keeping their values or politics quiet. If, for example, anti-Zionism were acknowledged as a racist ideology, as Judea Pearl suggests, the possibility for such intimidation would be diminished or even eliminated.

There are organized weeks and countless events against Israel at universities. At some schools an anti-Israel platform is common for student-government elections. While a student can easily graduate from college never having had a course in which one of the subjects is Israel, when students do hear of Israel, the odds are very much against hearing something positive or even neutral.[14] What will be familiar on many campuses are calls for boycott.

The movement for Boycott, Divestment, and Sanction (BDS) is linked to a NGO forum held during the 2001 UN World Conference Against Racism from which the US delegation withdrew because the event became filled with "hateful language" against Jews and against "only one country in the world—Israel."[15] The conference was overshadowed by the non-governmental groups and their "NGO Declaration" that condemned Israel and demanded its boycott. In 2005, these same demands showed up as if original to the BDS movement and as if originally "called for by Palestinian civil society, a group that is never defined."[16] In fact, as Harvard professor

Ruth Wisse points out, BDS is simply a recent form of the Arab boycotts of Israel that began decades before the founding of the modern state.[17]

At universities in the US, UK, Canada, Australia, New Zealand, and Europe there are demands to divest from Israeli companies and even to remove Israeli hummus from cafeterias, but the major agenda of campus BDS is boycott of Israeli academic institutions. Though the term "institutions" suggests that people aren't involved, BDS, which is funded mainly by European governments and privately supported NGOs,[18] targets only Jewish-Israeli academics—essentially for being Jewish and Israeli. Resources for understanding BDS that were not available when it began include the AMCHA Initiative that since 2011 has been tracking BDS and conducting research into its impact on American students[19] and the first collection of essays by academics arguing *The Case Against Academic Boycott of Israel* published in 2014.[20]

I think it can be argued that the biggest impact of BDS so far has occurred outside Israel. For BDS generally has been unsuccessful in terms of actually accomplishing boycotts (or divestments and sanctions) but it has been quite successful at creating anti-Israel noise and agitation on campus. This noise is daunting. It is extremely hard to go against what appears to be the dominant discourse.

At this point, anti-Israelism seems simply part of the uncontroversial politics valued in the humanities and social sciences, in the way that environmentalism and multiculturalism and Marxism are valued.[21] It was shocking to find myself on the "wrong side" for the first time in my life and for a while I didn't take seriously the accusations against Israel—of comparisons to apartheid and full blame for the conflicts of the Middle East.[22] I treated these views as mere theorizing, as I had in graduate school when we joked that our theoretical Marxist professors did live in actual, luxurious homes in the southern California hillsides. I thought that these were simply abstractions that, like other theories, could be argued against with other abstractions.

But in conversation after conversation, I began to feel that the distance between what I had experienced in Israel, what I knew and was learning of Jewish and Middle Eastern history, and what was being said on campuses— the speakers and demonstrations, the academic rhetoric in which Israel is deemed an example, even the worst example, of "imperialist oppression"— was so enormous that I certainly would not be able to bridge it on my own.

For years, I struggled to understand why this was the case. Why would progressive sympathies be expected to lie with only one side of "the conflict"? Why did university speakers insist that suicide bombers had been driven by "poverty and oppression" as if there were no alternatives to killing civilian women, men, and children on busses and in cafés and as if the bombers were poor and had not been trained and supported by anti-Israel governments and terror groups?[23] Why was this violence so acceptable and any Israeli response a cause for outrage? I remember one particular conversation vividly; it occurred nearly seven years after our first trip, after two more summers and a semester-long sabbatical in Jerusalem. I remember the room and the atmosphere, and the feeling of having reached a low point of frustration.

At a conference of English professors, a few of us are gathered around one of the major scholars. He has recently become interested in the Middle East and he is telling us that Israel is "really reprehensible."

I jump in to say that I've just been there and that I was impressed. "But you can't be OK with what Israel is doing?"

"What exactly?"

"The settlements, the refugee camps, the Occupation. You're not OK with that, surely."

I give it a try. I say that I hope the Israelis will have a chance to have peace there. And that I hope the same for the Palestinians.

"So, the Occupation needs to end."

"Well, yes, and Israel needs to not have to defend its existence."

"They . . . are . . . colonialists," he says this slowly, as if he can't believe what he's hearing or as if he is speaking to a slow-to-catch-on student.

"No, it's their country. They took their small part of the British partition and the Arabs leaders didn't. They still won't."

"I don't see how you can excuse Israeli behavior."

"Sure, I don't like everything that happens there; I don't like everything that happens here. But they have a right to their country."

A younger woman professor in the group interjects, "What about the wall, the apartheid wall?" She gives it two syllables: wa-all.

"Ah, the whole nationalism thing," the famous professor continues, "you see how destructive it is. I think nationalism is pretty much over. Does it really make sense to have a specifically Jewish country?"

And then I just get angry. "So every other group in the world, Palestinians, new countries in Africa and Asia, and everyone, everywhere, all except the Jews, for them it's too late to be nationalistic?"

"Ah, this is an emotional thing for you."

"Yes, of course. I spent my sabbatical there. I loved it."

"So, maybe you're just not thinking clearly about it."

As clearly as suggesting some kind of national suicide for Israelis? I imagine this rejoinder but in fact, his comment stops me, stops me maybe the way my "patriotic" graduate student felt stopped from saying what she thought in her classes. Or the way one simply does not say aloud in this setting, "I am a Zionist."[24] Or because here, emotion for a thriving democracy is so suspect. What strikes me most is that there is no dialogue to have, even among specialists in language. Israel is at fault and illegitimate. And this position, lodged securely in the mainstream discourse of the academy, is unassailable. I can't marshal an argument because the entire framework confronting me precludes it. No other country in the world is talked about this way.

It was a low point, but it also was a turning point. If I were going to feel angry nearly every day because of what I saw in the media, and overwhelmed by the non-controversial stature of anti-Israelism and anti-Zionism in academe, if my neighbors and even some friends had become impossible to talk to, I determined to unravel the dissonance I was experiencing.

chapter 3

Why Citing the Facts
Has So Little Impact

We hold to a standard of academic free speech, where any view that wishes
to be heard must also submit to rational, empirically-grounded criticism.
To that end, we combat the increasingly politicized scholarship in Middle
East Studies programs and related academic areas of study which obsess
over denouncing Israel, the only democracy in the region, while silencing
any effort to either counter misinformation or provide context.[1]

—Scholars for Peace in the Middle East

Looking back, it seems surprising that it took as long as it did for me to make
use of my own academic discipline. Rhetoric surrounding Israel in the settings of my California life had become a daily battle, yet only after that last
conversation at the conference did I begin to investigate. I also know that
I did not want to look further, to be on the other/wrong side, to examine
positions that in my familiar world lie outside the norm.

Rhetoric is not only the overblown statements of politicians, though this
everyday use of the term is relevant to Israel or to any political topic. It's the
ancient and contemporary study of the persuasive elements of communication. Once the center of a liberal arts education, rhetoric now crosses into
a number of academic fields including Communications, Media Studies,
Philosophy, Speech, Linguistics, and my own field, Rhetoric and Composi-

tion. The tools of rhetorical analysis proved useful as I struggled with what I was hearing about Israel.

Rhetoricians most often analyze public discourse: writing or speaking in the public sphere, though it's possible to look at the rhetorical elements of any communication, at how speakers or writers—or the creators of visual or multimedia communication—influence or attempt to influence audiences about any subject matter.

Rhetoric has had a bad name since ancient Greece and for pretty much the same reason it has a bad name now. Words can be persuasive even if what is argued is not true. Persuasive discourse does not necessarily lead one to know the truth, just to discover what is most convincing, and in that way to make a best judgment about what is true. Rhetorical study tells us what distinguishes various kinds of speech or categories of discourse from one another, how arguments are made, where they break down in errors of logic, how speakers may lack credibility, where appeals to emotion may distract from other convincing evidence, and so on. It cannot claim to lead directly to "the truth" but when words alone are the means of persuasion, rhetoric is actually all we have.

Normal Academic Discourse

I've found that in trying to talk about Israel, the biggest stumbling block has been the certainty that since so many educated and progressive people find such unlimited fault with the country, their claims must be valid. The very measured and understated findings of a 2012 comprehensive study, *Israel on the Campus,* includes this: "Israel is the only country in the world that is routinely attacked by faculty and students on college campuses."[2] Such distinction alone suggests that we have moved into areas beyond reason and logic.

In the vocabulary of classical rhetoric, it demonstrates the impact of the two "appeals" other than logic that speakers and writers use to persuade an audience or reader. We are convinced as much by an appeal to our emotions, from a speaker who conveys authority, as we can be by the information presented. Citing of the facts and logical reasoning are often no match for drawing sympathy from an audience and speaking authoritatively. *Who* makes a claim and how emotionally the listener or reader is affected, can matter more than *what* is being argued. These features of persuasion operate even if a speaker or audience does not consciously pay attention to them. However, we also can find that an argument dependent mostly on the stature of the speaker and the emotional reaction of the audience may slide into fallacies in terms of logic.

It's hard to counter such argument since facts have not been the primary means of persuasion in the first place, though they may have appeared to be. In that conference conversation I was the one labeled "emotional" (and I was) but even without having worked it out clearly at that time, I knew I was responding to fallacious argument and that on this topic my colleagues were not interested in discussing information or facts. The whole concept of "facts" has been challenged to such a degree that the conventional meaning of "the facts" as we use this term in every day life does not necessarily hold within academic fields in the humanities and social sciences.

Different rhetorical settings create differing expectations for what is appropriate in speaking or writing. Scholars in my field have described "normal" as opposed to "abnormal" discourse[3] to account for how we learn new terminology and, more broadly, how we are socialized into what is expected and acceptable in the various, often overlapping, large and small "discourse communities" that we move among each day, those formed by our households, workplaces, interests, activities, professions, subcultures, and so on. We know what topics are usual or appropriate, what kinds of jargon or slang are common, what values are shared. These create the normal discourse in different situations and it is always hard to speak outside the norms of what is considered mainstream in any setting.[4] I began to see that where anti-Israel rhetoric has been normalized, it is not simply that alternative views have a hard time being heard but that they can be considered "abnormal" speech. This is at least in part why dialogue is so hard to come by. Abnormal speech is so far outside the mainstream in a particular setting that you sound silly, kooky,[5] fanatical, uninformed, or irrelevant. In other settings the same comment might be unremarkable or valued. I think this is why a kind of numbness set in for me during the years between our first trip to Israel and the time I began researching this book, an exhaustion and frustration from trying unsuccessfully to redefine the terms of normal discourse about Israel and from finding myself on the outside of my familiar academic discourse community.

Communication is also influenced more generally in academic settings by the worldview of postmodernism. Postmodernist theory permeates most academic fields in the humanities and social sciences. It is an interesting and powerful theory and I'm used to teaching graduate students that postmodernism is a "given" of current academic thought.[6] It seems to me that the most basic terms of postmodernism help explain the difficulty of my forays into conversation about Israel, difficulties that face students or faculty who wish to challenge calls for boycott or Israel "apartheid" weeks.

The biggest difference between everyday, modern worldviews and a postmodern one is the understanding that, since things look different from differing perspectives, there are no objective facts nor any reliable truths. Facts are subjective and entirely open for interpretation, so much so that factual accounts can be considered stories, "narratives." Historical reports, our own retelling of experience, even our perceptions, are "socially constructed." That is, they are formed by our social environment and by our beliefs, by our ideologies.

A postmodernist perspective helps explain why there was no curiosity among my conference colleagues about what I had experienced in Israel that led me to see the country differently than they did, why there was no interest in what I had observed, or in what I might know about Israel's history or current situation. For in that setting it was clear that I had moved outside the normal academic discourse about Israel.

I am not saying that academics are in agreement about Israel or any other subject but that when I asserted that Israelis "had a right to their country," and even suggested that the British plan had validated this, especially when I indicated my approval of nationalistic sentiment in a first world country, I had aligned myself with ideologies—Zionism, nationalism, first-worldism and, disregarding Jewish history, apparently even with British imperialism—that made my commentary irrelevant, beyond the pale (to use another term taken from Jewish experience).[7] For in postmodernist thinking, it is ideology that allows us to make sense of and to interpret the narratives of history or of our own lives. Ideologies that are considered oppressive—like those with which I had seemed to identify—cannot provide valid interpretations in the way that progressive ideologies can.

Since facts are unstable rather than objectively verifiable, we settle on one interpretation over another as part of a particular discourse community. The "social construction of knowledge" makes sense in that we know what we know because we have learned in a social setting rather than, for instance, by independently discovering "the truth." Yet, the application of this theory does rest on a majority rule about what is valid and, perhaps even more importantly, about what is acceptable. As is often the case, it is in the application of theory to life outside the seminar room that the limitations of theory show up.[8]

The major theorists of postmodernism were Marxists, so even though postmodernists argue that we can't trust any particular values over any others, that value systems themselves are oppressive, a particular political action agenda is built into many fields of the humanities and social sciences. A starting point for scholarship, and therefore coursework, is the victimization of various groups at the hands of Western oppressors and Western values. Underlying courses in a wide variety of disciplines is a focus on victims and oppressors.

Even within this focus, there is a real sense that postmodernism doesn't allow for a case to be made primarily with facts. Facts are unreliable because their validity is really just a matter of power-relationships. That is, the structure of social systems determines who are the victims and who are the oppressors.

For this reason, although the Israelis and the Palestinians are said to have "competing narratives" there really is no competition. Since Israel has been deemed an example, usually the worst-case example, of "first-world oppression of third world peoples," what happens to Palestinians is of necessity more compelling than what happens to Israelis. Advocating for self-determination for both Palestinians and Jews in the postmodern view appears impossible; for one side must be victim and one must be oppressor.

Nationalism (or too overt patriotism) for a first-world country is unacceptable because Western countries are so tainted by oppression and colonialism. This emotional response to Israel, and to America, along with the status of these theories, holds sway on many campuses especially in the humanities. It has actually become difficult to speak outside of these dominating academic ideologies, not only about Israel but also about many other topics on campus and several organizations of scholars have formed in response to this situation.[9]

To assert that Israel is the only fully functioning, multicultural democracy in the Middle East, or any other attributes one might offer, becomes irrelevant. Citing information about Israelis' scientific and technological accomplishments or the country's humanitarian contributions becomes simply a political ploy to deflect from its oppressor role. The panel discussion, in which we spoke positively about Israel, or my challenge to the dominant academic view expressed by the professor at the conference were unlikely to have impact because the terms of the discussion were already set.

Extreme Anti-Israel Rhetoric

Yet, as one-sided as this layer of rhetoric may be, things can be much worse. Here, it is not usually socially acceptable to call directly for the destruction of the Jewish state, even if one is, in fact, calling for its destruction. In spite of the failures of the BDS movement to accomplish boycotts or even to get universities and professional organizations to call for boycott, the "apartheid" weeks and boycott threats have to some degree masked the reality that the goal of BDS is "not to change government policy but rather to eliminate the Jewish State."[10]

The academic layer of rhetoric often sounds mostly theoretical, expressing indirect opposition to the country of Israel, as if one may be reluctant to say so but one simply has to admit that Israel is an obvious example of an "oppressive" country. Literary critic Judith Butler even described "Hamas/Hezbollah as social movements that are progressive." Her explanation for this apparent contradiction is instructive. She did not condemn their terrorist agenda but simply noted that Hamas and Hezbollah define themselves as "anti-imperialist" as does the "global left."[11] This alignment was enough to tell her which side to value. Such academic abstractions can and do influence young people who might otherwise learn, at the very least, about both of the "competing" narratives.

The academic layer of rhetoric creates an intellectual justification for the framing of Israel. It forms a bridge between the milder, media language about Israel and the most extreme layer of anti-Israel discourse. To hear the most extreme layer of anti-Israel rhetoric we need to listen to the less abstract and more direct statements of Arab and Islamist political leaders and their advocates in the West (some of whom are academics) who explicitly and clearly call for the end of Israel and often also of America.

The Hamas Covenant, for example, states that both the destruction of Israel and the killing of Jews is a religious imperative. It describes Jews as controlling the world, and the Freemasons, Lions and Rotary clubs as secret Zionist organizations; it rails against Communists, capitalists, "the People of the Book," and "infidels."[12] It may be hard for most Americans to take seriously. Yet, Hamas is the government of Gaza and the Covenant is their official governmental agenda.

Hassan Nasrallah, the leader of Hezbollah in Lebanon, has referred to Jews/Israelis as "the grandsons of apes and pigs." Nasrallah, like the leaders of Hamas, makes clear that he is not talking simply about the state of Israel: "If (the Jews) all gather in Israel, it will save us the trouble of going after them worldwide."[13]

I had paid no attention to this extreme rhetoric; it didn't concern me until I began to notice that it concerned me intimately. If you are willing to read websites like MEMRI (Middle East Media Research Institute) or PMW (Palestinian Media Watch) that translate Middle Eastern political press into English, you notice that slurs like "sons of apes and pigs" are not all that uncommon.[14] It is hard to accept, and I preferred not to accept, that in many places, virulent, genocidal rhetoric against Israel and Jews is unremarkable, even acceptable. This language uses the same tropes, stereotypes, and characterizations of Jews as in traditional anti-Semitism.[15]

The fake *Protocols of the Elders of Zion*, which for more than a hundred years has "proved" the evils of Jews (the *Protocols* served as propaganda for both Hitler and Stalin), provided the material for a popular 41 part Egyptian-made TV series and another 21 part series from Syria. This rhetoric appears as part of the everyday language in various sermons and political discourse in Arab and Muslim-majority countries and even on everyday television broadcasts.[16] Along with the powerful difficulty of speaking outside the accepted rhetoric in any setting, here dissenting voices are further muted or completely silenced by lack of freedom of religion, lack of free speech, and the absence of a free press.

It is acceptable to replace facts with "narratives" where postmodernism is the norm, and in settings where extreme anti-Israel rhetoric is normalized, it is considered acceptable and appropriate to replace facts themselves as needed for the sake of—the greater good of—a political agenda. Names are changed, histories rewritten, indisputable events denied.

The varieties of Holocaust denial, for instance, from claiming the Holocaust never occurred, to claiming that Jews caused the Holocaust, to claiming that Israelis exaggerate its horrors, are widespread in the Middle East in spite of the fact that the perpetrators of the Holocaust made it the most carefully documented genocide in history.[17] This discourse is active at the United Nations where the "nonaligned" countries are the majority. A version of it sometimes shows up in the language of activist groups in the West whose individual members might recoil from the behavior of terrorists, yet who call for measures that would target Jews and make a Jewish state disappear.

We can describe what is mainstream in different settings, but there are no absolute boundaries. These layers of language interconnect and, of course, speakers and writers are not necessarily conscious of all the possible interconnections of our words. In America, we are far less likely to hear the most extreme layer and when we do, we may dismiss what we hear as lunatic fringe, interpreting it from within our own norms.

The language that we experience most is the least dramatic. Rhetoric against Israel is overt at the most extreme layer where political figures shout out that they are enemies of the Jewish state; it interweaves with abstraction in the bridging layer where theories or philosophies or political agendas of intellectuals explain it. But most of what we know about world events we learn from media coverage. In fact, we would expect that if bias against Israel occurred at all in this setting, it would be rare, since the heart of ethical concern for journalists in democratic countries is maintaining fair and reliable coverage. A free press commits to telling us what goes on in the world so that we can come to our own conclusions. So, it is surprising how frequently mainstream media fail to meet their own standards when it comes to political subjects, including the subject of Israel. This milder form of rhetoric offered the clearest way to understand and respond to the framing of Israel.

chapter 4

Media Slant and Rhetorical Frames

*Do the political proclivities of journalists influence their interpretation of
the news? I answer that with a resounding yes.*[1]
—*Jim A. Kuypers,*
in *Partisan Journalism,*
A History of Media Bias in the United States

In some ways it seems a distraction to address media. The extreme layer of
anti-Israel rhetoric from political leaders and even the academic layer of
theory and abstraction seem so much more powerful. Yet, by far the most
influential and wide-reaching distributers of news and opinion are mainstream media. This is our entry point to knowing what goes on in the world.
Western media have enormous impact on public perception and, unlike the
other layers of rhetoric, advocate "balance" and "objectivity" as professional
requirements. At the same time, mainstream media framing of Israel is not
unconnected from the other two layers of rhetoric; rather, the same framing
simply operates more subtly in the media.

Of course, there are many other sources of news outside the mainstream
press. The proliferation of alternative news sites, of unlimited Internet
sources, even of comedy news shows and of following one's own Facebook
feed may be more popular than getting news from traditional media. I focus

on mainstream media, however, because most often they are still our initial source of news. Commentary and political spin take off from news that is first reported in mainstream media, sites that in democracies are expected to work toward unbiased coverage.

The responsibilities of media are daunting: they need to gather information from reliable sources, to assemble material into readable stories, and to provide complete and accurate enough information that they give readers, viewers, and listeners a sound basis for drawing their own conclusions about the news. Central concerns for the profession include how the press should conduct itself, what its ethical responsibilities are, and what makes for a "socially responsible" press.[2] The Society of Professional Journalists (SPJ) has an impressive "Code of Ethics" that includes many "standards of practice" that, if followed, would make slanted reporting on Israel or anything else a rare occurrence:

> Journalists should test the accuracy of information from all sources and exercise care to avoid inadvertent error. Deliberate distortion is never permissible . . . Diligently seek out subjects of news stories to give them the opportunity to respond to allegations of wrongdoing . . . Make certain that headlines, news teases and promotional material, photos, video, audio, graphics, sound bites, and quotations do not misrepresent. They should not oversimplify or highlight incidents out of context . . . Never distort the content of news photos or videos . . . Distinguish between advocacy and news reporting. Analysis and commentary should be labeled and not misrepresent fact or context . . . Avoid misleading re-enactments or staged news events . . . Show sensitivity for those who may be affected adversely by news coverage . . . Avoid conflicts of interest, real or imagined . . . Admit mistakes and correct them promptly . . . [3]

In a democratic society the press is expected to give us the whole story, to provide enough information so that we can make our own judgments, to minimize political slant or to offer balanced coverage. And when this does not happen, the public begins to lose—or feels it is losing—its broad window onto national and world events. According to Gallup, based on their yearly polling since the 1990's, "Americans' trust in the media has been falling slowly and steadily." In 2016, Gallup reported "public confidence in the accuracy and fairness of mainstream media" at an all time low.[4] At the same time, a PEW poll found 74 percent of Americans saying "news media are biased."[5]

From the perspective of media scholarship, "that the media is biased is a rather uncontroversial assumption."[6] For this reason, many Internet news sites and blogs serve as "watchdogs" on the mainstream press, attempting "to offset their monopoly on the news."[7] The two most comprehensive organizations that track English language reporting on Israel are Honest Reporting and CAMERA.[8] Two others focus specifically on coverage of Israel in the UK: BBC Watch and UK Media Watch.[9]

How Framing Works

The fact that we can't encounter the news directly, that media convey news to the public, means that the information we receive has already gone through a selection process before we get the news. Scholars who study this flow of information remind us that news and, of course, opinion are filtered through the eyes and lenses of reporters and photographers, editors and producers, publishers and directors. Decisions about what is newsworthy, about which information should be included, who should be quoted, how prominently any item should be presented, and how much time should be devoted to any story are made by reporters on or close to the scene, by wire services, and by editors or directors at various media outlets.

The language of headlines, for instance, encapsulates what readers take as the major significance of a story; a different headline focusing on

some other aspect or offering a different summary or slant, gives readers a different impression of what the story is about. This BBC headline:
"Deadly Attack on Israel-Egypt Border" does not specify who was killed
(an Arab Israeli citizen) nor who were the attackers.[10] Yet the previous day,
BBC's headline "Palestinian 'attackers' killed by Israeli truck driver" states
who were involved and puts "attackers" in quotes conveying doubt about
whether the Israeli driver really was under attack.[11] BBC's headlines when
reporting on Israel have emphasized the terrorists killed rather than the
victims attacked but reporting on similar events elsewhere have focused
on the victims and have used the term, "terror." Compare "Four Palestinian attackers killed by Israeli troops" with "London Attack: Four dead in
Westminster terror incident."[12]

Media watch groups find such headlines to be typical of reporting on
Israel. Tracking Reuters headlines during the Second Intifada, Honest Reporting concluded:

> . . . when Reuters wrote about Israeli acts of violence, Israel was em-
> phasized as the first word; also, an active voice was used, often without
> explaining that the 'victim' may have been a gunman. A typical headline
> was: 'Israeli Troops Shoot Dead Palestinian in W. Bank' . . . By contrast,
> when Palestinians attacked Israelis (almost always civilians), Reuters
> usually avoided naming the perpetrator. For example: 'New West Bank
> Shooting Mars Truce' . . . In many cases the headline was couched in
> passive voice.[13]

Beyond headlines, rhetorical decisions determining which aspects of a story
should be emphasized, what background information is needed, or what
specific language should be used, all influence the creation of what news we
can read or hear. Every decision, from the choice of stories covered to the
choice of words and visuals included, to the location of a piece in a newspaper or broadcast episode, whether an occurrence becomes top "headline"

news or is relegated to a small space in the back pages or is not conveyed to the public at all is made by individual reporters, editors, and directors. Israel-focused media watchers have long complained that daily rocket attacks on Israel go unreported but if Israel responds it gets wide coverage, a topic of particular significance in the Cycle of Violence frame (chapter 9).

BBC's policy guidelines include "the need to ensure that when we report acts of terror, we do so consistently in the stories we report . . ." Yet when BBC Watch objected that attacks in Tunisia, Kuwait, and France were reported on as terrorism while attacks in Jerusalem around the same time were not, BBC responded that they "didn't believe" that the Jerusalem "murders were comparable to the recent attacks in Tunisia or Kuwait." No further explanation was provided.[14]

Media critics do not expect reporters or editors to be free of bias or of personal perspective but that effort will be made by reporters themselves, or during the editorial process, to offer as complete a picture of the news as possible. This requires painstaking attention and the ethical commitment to fair reporting; it requires work to adjust for and "manage" bias.[15] This effort does not just come naturally because, as scholars explain, reporters and editors need to frame the news, just as any communicator needs to frame information, in order to make sense of it.

Framing is necessary to make streams of information coherent. And it is powerful because it is both a rhetorical and a cognitive process. That is, cognitive framing describes how we make sense of perceptions, the thinking processes whereby we classify observations and experiences into categories; rhetorical framing describes what we do with that information, how we communicate our perceptions to others. Linguist George Lakoff examines how language frames convey political ideas, and his guidebook for progressives, *Don't Think of an Elephant! Know Your Values and Frame the Debate,* set out to "harness the power of language framing for a progressive agenda."[16] He was pointing out that we are rhetorically persuasive when we connect to listeners' already formed cognitive categories.

A narrative pattern using David and Goliath, a storyline that appears especially in the Neighborhood Bully frame (chapter 8), allows readers or viewers to feel empathy with David without the need for much evidence. Simply designating one player David and the other Goliath—or one the Jew and the other the Nazi—makes the case, makes a recognizable story without necessity for a lot of detail or supporting material. Even more powerful is disruption of the familiar pattern wherein the Jew is portrayed as the Nazi.

Think of cropping a picture. What is left outside the frame? What is included? Or compose a scene inside a camera lens. What is the dominant image? What parts of the scene are captured inside the frame? What parts are excluded? What is in sharp focus and what is blurry background? And later on, what gets photoshopped?

Researchers in academic fields including communications, cognitive psychology, rhetoric, linguistics, and politics use the concept of framing to examine phenomena that are of interest to their disciplines. Cognitive psychologists tell us that we make sense of experience and information through a process of classifying and labeling, a kind of filtering system through which we are able to take in vast amounts of sensory input at once because we naturally sort it into categories.

Scholars who study media describe the related process of news framing: how journalists direct the attention of listeners, readers, or viewers to a particular understanding of events, often implying a specific interpretation of what is occurring or a particular solution to problems. Media gather information from sources, and "need their sources' frames to make news, inevitably adding or even superimposing their own frames."[17] Framing does not simply crop reality in varying ways; the framing creates a reality. As it would in the case of an actual picture frame, our attention is drawn to what is enclosed inside the frame and not to the frame itself.

The process of framing works to arrange material so as to present a particular way, over other possible ways, of making sense of what the public is seeing. Media frames "set the agenda" for the news by making some events more significant than others, by giving more time to some stories and downplaying or ignoring others. Then media further "extend" this agenda in that framing implies particular interpretations of the news, suggests ways of defining problems, and indicates possible solutions.[18] Although readers may not necessarily agree with these interpretations, we usually only notice the framing if somehow we are not engrossed in the story or communication, itself, if something takes our attention away from our usual mode of observation, if something happens to disrupt our habitual ways of seeing.

One can experience such a disruption abruptly, as I did upon returning from my first trip to Israel to my familiar Berkeley environment. Going to Israel and coming back at that particular time proved to be transformative; it altered my perceptions and my life. But another way to notice framing is the way scholars who study it proceed, by putting their attention on the borders within which news is presented, compiling the features of frames methodically and empirically, and in this way allowing us to step back from our usual absorption in the flow of rhetoric.

The Frames

Media analysts do not try to get inside the minds of journalists but they do examine how publications or broadcasts present the news. Once writers, editors, and directors sort out events for themselves, they must arrange and edit this material into what will be presented as a news or feature story. At this point they have obligations to their professional standards for unbiased reporting. While slant or bias can be unconscious as well as intentional, professionals do have the conscious choice of meeting or neglecting to meet editorial and ethical standards.

Admittedly, it is much harder to see one's own biases than it is to identify an opposing point of view as biased. And perhaps for this reason, there are two main schools of thought about the causes of media bias or slant, both of which have scholarly support. Some observers attribute media bias to the dominant political leanings of members of the profession; the political positions that are sometimes explicitly stated in editorials color the reporting of news. Others believe that bias results from corporate marketing, from emphasizing news that sells, and that these demands influence reporting and media presentation.[19] Some argue that the corporations that own media naturally bias reporting in a conservative direction while the opposite argument holds that journalists and editors naturally bias reporting in a direction farther to the left than the UK and US majority. Either way, slant is most often implicit rather than directly stated. And either way, the topic of Israel fares poorly.

Whatever the specific causes, by analyzing how the news is framed we can identify the dominant perspectives the media actually offer on any subject. Scholars begin their research with an observation about how media are handling a particular topic often, as I did, with noticing a mismatch between features of the topic and its media presentation. They identify news frames by noticing repeated language and key phrasings; by tracking the implications, focus, and tone of articles on a given issue; by noticing the choice of topics, the sources of information, the emphases of stories, and the metaphors used in covering the news. They look at what is left out, what is implied, where it is that an article or report steers a reader, what assumptions underlie the story.

Following this method of rhetorical framing analysis in reviewing hundreds of news articles and broadcasts, I began to identify the features of interconnected frames used by media to report on and talk about Israel. For about two years I collected reporting on Israel from a selection of mainstream sources including Associated Press and Reuters wire services, *The New York Times*, *Los Angeles Times*, *Time Magazine*, BBC, *The Guardian*, *The Washington Post*, CNN and NBC. Over time, I sketched out both what seemed to be included inside the media framing and what was left outside the limits of these frames.

In the chapters that follow, I cite representative examples from this original collection as well as from older and more current coverage. All the material I cite is available online and is referenced in the Notes at the end of the book as I hope that readers will take a look at the full stories. For the more you read, the more you may see the framing patterns in which rhetoric about Israel occurs.

The six frames outlined in the next chapters overlap, kaleidoscoping together to form particular views of Israel. When these perspectives bolster argument, they have enormous persuasive power and yet they turn out to be rhetorical or logical fallacies. Starting with what media analysts call the spotlight fallacy for the way a spotlight lights up only one point on a stage and the rest vanishes into the dark, the frame of Only Conflict (chapter 5) connects everything about Israel to only the conflict. Four frames together create a distorted picture of the conflict itself. The false premise that the conflict is simply a Struggle Over Land (chapter 6) underlies the other frames and supports the double standard framing of Refugees (chapter 7). Both the bandwagon fallacy of the Neighborhood Bully frame (chapter 8) and the faulty analogy of the Cycle of Violence frame (chapter 9) implicate Israel as fully or nearly fully to blame. The culmination of these perspectives is the framing in which Israel, sometimes subtly in the media and sometimes overtly in public forums, is identified with actions that are the World's Worst (chapter 10).

Limits of Framing

Of course, rhetorical framing analysis does not propose to account for all of the coverage on any topic and the frames I identify are not noteworthy because they always occur but because they occur so frequently. Exceptions to negative framing of Israel apparently so exceed the norm that media watch groups are known to praise balanced or positive coverage of Israel when it occurs. CAMERA identifies such articles with their "thumps up" posts.[20] BBC Watch, for example commended travel writer, Dan Savery Raz for writing "informative and accurate reports without falling into the trap of politicizing his subject."[21]

I have made generous use of mainstream media coverage as a guide to the framing of Israel. This mildest form of public rhetoric about Israel is what is most available to most people. Yet these same frames show up in the much stronger rhetoric of some academics and even in the annihilationist language against Israel that erupts in some political and Middle Eastern venues. If this last were "mere" rhetoric, it might not be worth considering. However, though language can obscure intention, it most often conveys it, and the intentions behind describing Israel as "a cancer" needing to be destroyed are perilous to ignore.[22]

Identifying the frames will not change these intentions. It may not even change media representation of Israel, since one of the characteristics of frames is their "durability, their persistence over time."[23] It is hard for individual reporters or editors to break out of the usual framing patterns with which they present the news. They may have little motivation to do so, whether because like-minded colleagues dominate their workplaces or because publishers and producers who manage their output are satisfied with sales from the usual framing. Though complaints from the public about specific inaccuracies can result in retractions or corrections, research suggests that frames once established tend not to change and this creates much of their powerful impact:

> Frames are most influential when they persist over time. The persistence, or ongoing repetition of frames, creates meanings that are resistant to change. If constantly inundated with information that is framed in a specific way, an individual is likely to treat that framed referent of reality as reality itself.[24]

To explain the limits of the framing of Israel I necessarily address historical information and political topics although my focus remains on language, on its persuasive capacity, on the ways in which rhetoric informs and creates the images of Israel. Noticing the existence of particular framing can change our perception of the news dramatically, and students may react differently to campus discussions of Israel when they are familiar with the way the country is being framed. Paying attention to the ways a rhetorical picture is cropped, seeing what lies outside the framing, naturally changes our perspectives. And perhaps from my own experience a word of caution is needed, for my changed perspective on the topic of Israel did impact my perspective on media coverage of other topics as well. In fact, reporting on Israel does not appear to be an anomaly. Instead, it seems to be an especially clear example of the slant or bias that critics and the public have been identifying for some time.

Framing is the "most frequently utilized theory in top mass communication journals."[25] Professor of Communications, Jim A. Kuypers, who pioneered scholarship in the field of rhetorical framing analysis and conducted numerous studies into "how the press frames controversial issues," reaches a grim conclusion as a result of his research:

> . . . in its role as provider of objective, balanced information for the American polity, the press fails miserably. As it now exists, the mainstream press is clearly an anti-Democratic institution. The media have evolved into a partisan collective which both consciously and unconsciously attempts to persuade the public that their interpretation of the world is true.[26]

I am aware that without that first trip, I would not have found myself so at odds with mainstream media coverage (or campus discussion) of the controversial issue of Israel, nor would I have set out to analyze "their interpretation" of what goes on in that part of the world..

chapter 5

Spotlight Fallacy:
Frame of Only Conflict

*Peace for Israel means security and we must stand with all our might
to protect its right to exist, its territorial integrity. I see Israel, and never
mind saying it, as one of the great outposts of democracy, and a marvelous
example of what can be done, how desert land almost can be transformed
into an oasis of brotherhood and democracy.*[1]

—Dr. Martin Luther King, Jr.

When Israel's national airline, El Al, started flying from Tel Aviv to Los
Angeles in 1988, it broke the current record for longest commercial flight:
7,000 miles in just under 14 hours.[2] But there were no direct flights from San
Francisco so Jeremy and I never took El Al; it was easier and less expensive to
fly with other airlines out of San Francisco to New York and then to Tel Aviv.
Gradually, El Al's prices became no worse than other airlines and though it
has received low ratings, at times even the worst, for on-time departures, El
Al has another distinction that I decided makes it the best possible choice: it
is the world's safest airline.[3] With air marshals on every flight and more careful
check-in screenings than other airlines, El Al is the only commercial airline
outfitted with anti-missile technology.[4] It's true that in flight, I've found that
there does tend to be more standing in the aisles and general noise than one
encounters on other airlines; before boarding, the gate waiting area will often

seem unusually chaotic. You start your trip with a bit of Israeli experience and the slogan lets you know: "It's not just an airline. It's Israel." The slogan in Hebrew translates literally to: "the most at home in the world."

At the gates for flights I've taken from the US to Israel, I've usually seen armed guards. Any flight to Israel from the US has additional layers of security. But when you land at Tel Aviv's Ben Gurion Airport, you find the airport calm, though often busy at four a.m., and the security invisible. Yet Ben Gurion is the safest airport in the world.[5] Is it widely known that Israel is home to the safest airline and the safest airport? Certainly, nothing at Ben Gurion suggests you've landed in a Middle Eastern hot spot, except of course, a literal one in summer when you walk out the doors into the sauna-like air. In Tel Aviv, contrasts between the framing of Israel and the Israel that one sees, lives, and effortlessly can document run very much at odds.

Tel Aviv is the "bubble," the center of "the center," Israel's dynamic but laid back "city that doesn't stop." It's high tech, increasingly high rises and high prices, and a world-class city, the arts and culture center of the country. A tourist can spend time at the sea, the busy shops, the art galleries and museums, or choose among the hundreds of sidewalk cafes; it is not an exaggeration to say that good restaurants are everywhere. The surrounding sounds and sight of Hebrew tell you it is Israel, though it's also simply one of the great cities of the world, an exciting yet easy going, Mediterranean destination.

Yet some tourists miss out on Tel Aviv entirely; it took me many trips before I began to appreciate the energy of Tel Aviv, the way it embodies the progressive culture of modern Israel. Like the bubbles of San Francisco or New York, Tel Aviv's bubble builds from the arts, finance, nightlife and city diversity, but Israel's second largest city also reflects its contrast with Jerusalem.

A good number of religious people live in Tel Aviv and the majority in Israel's capital is not religious; however, the two cities pull at the oppositions of secular and religious, new and old. Jerusalem sports many new buildings, parks, modern hotels and contemporary cultural offerings, and the new light rail looks like it comes from a future part of the 21st century. But most powerfully Jerusalem is the spiritual center, the ancient and modern Jewish capital, home of the Western Wall and, at the same time, the Church of the Holy Sepulcher and the golden Dome of the Rock. The layers of a 4000-year history are built literally on top of each other. In Jerusalem I felt the urgent need for a longer skirt, in Tel Aviv, for skinny jeans and thin-strapped sandals. What I didn't feel was a need to think about the conflict.

In fact, on each return visit I was relieved to be in Israel instead of far away reading news about it. Visitors to the country will notice how much is going on and the intensity combined with an ease and casualness. No "office casual," just all the time casual. When I rented an apartment in Tel Aviv near some of the foreign embassies, for the first time I saw someone wearing a suit. And in Israel generally, there seemed to be much less reservation making or planning ahead than I'm used to in California.

Throughout the country, entrances to shopping malls, museums, theaters, most public buildings as well as some restaurants include a security guard to check your bag or you. Any public event, concert, game, or festival requires entrances with security. And given that soldiers go to and from their bases on public busses and trains, you see young, uniformed, very good-looking women and men everywhere, walking along with their rifles dangling across their backs. At the start of the weekend the bus and train stations are crowded with soldiers hauling their big duffle-bags, like but unlike their college-aged US counterparts going home with the laundry.

I found the relaxed atmosphere combined with the care for security quite comfortable once I adjusted to it. The Old City of Jerusalem, where the Muslim, Jewish, Christian, and Armenian Quarters together fill only .35 of a square mile, bustles with tourists (especially in the summer and in December) staying protected by the many, mostly hidden security cameras, and the soldiers strolling through. The conflict is a fact of life; there are some people in close proximity who really do want to kill you. At the same time, Israeli security measures stop the vast percentage of would-be terrorists.[6] Truthfully, I feel safer in Israel than in the big cities of America.

But the small-scale size and the sense of interconnectedness take some getting used to. You see the West Bank in some places simply across the street or highway. Tel Aviv is only 44 miles from Jerusalem but it is even closer to Gaza. And those 18-year-olds, of necessity in uniform, are the norm for what one's sons and daughters do after high school; if we lived there, rather than going off to college in the beautiful far north of California among the redwood trees, Jeremy would have been drafted. Everyone in the country connects intimately to the conflict. Nevertheless, Israelis manage a high standard of living, enormous contributions to science, medicine, technology, the arts, and humanitarian efforts, and a ranking among the top countries of the world in terms of personal happiness—though most of Israel's achievements and everyday life occur outside its framing.

The Spotlight Fallacy

When a spotlight shines on a stage, the rest disappears in darkness, creating an illusion; we see only the object under the light. A spotlight fallacy overgeneralizes from what may be faulty information in the first place; it assumes that what draws our attention, what we hear most about, in fact represents the most significant aspect of the whole. The spotlight on conflict serves to block out, distort, or represent with varying degrees of suspicion the rest of Israeli life. Certainly, what we hear about most when we hear about Israel is "the conflict." For many people, it may be impossible even to hear the word Israel without thinking simultaneously of the "Middle East," or "Arab-Israeli" or "Israeli-Palestinian" conflict. And our concept of "conflict," the images in our minds, likely link to what we've seen in the media or to what we have heard on campus.

A spotlight fallacy occurs when we take media coverage at face value, for media necessarily focus our attention on only a few big news events at a time. Perhaps a hurricane dominates all the networks for a day or two and then a political coup in another part of the world becomes the major story. Though the hurricane survivors still struggle with their situation, the coup suddenly takes precedence. As savvy consumers of news we know that these particular events and shifts of our attention do not really represent the major "news of the day." But we can't research all the news ourselves and, even within the particular events described, we may hear mainly about one area where the hurricane hit or one primary cause for the political coup leading us to take these points of focus as representative of the whole story. News rises and falls in and out of our attention along with media emphasis; celebrities seem briefly important simply because they get coverage. It can even be argued that media create celebrity and notoriety.

In the case of Israel, a fascinating and also disturbing result of the spotlight on Only Conflict is the limiting angle, how the country appears through boundaries in such a way that normal life doesn't merely disappear; it becomes suspect, even sinister or disallowed. The spotlight sweeps all aspects of Israeli life into the Only Conflict frame so pervasively that even in feature stories where conflict is insignificant, it dominates nonetheless. Framing establishes itself implicitly. No one comes out and says, "If we mention Israel, it will be only through our focus on and interpretation of the conflict." Instead, for example, *Time Magazine* offers the cover story: "Why Israel Doesn't Care About Peace."[7]

No Everyday Life?

The bold black letters of the cover story title are enclosed by a big Jewish star made of daisies on a thin wire, an image that seems to resemble the crosshairs of a target.[8] A newsstand display in the Los Angles airport with a dozen copies of this issue confronted me as I hurried to my gate. Who is making this accusation? Based on what? The story, with photos of young, hookah-pipe-smoking Israelis relaxing at the beach, tells us that everyday life in Israel, and especially in Tel Aviv, provides the damning evidence.

Notice that Israel, the whole state, is implicated, not merely some individuals. Even as applied to the specific people mentioned in the piece, the claims are farfetched and this particular article drew many, outraged responses.[9] Yet in the context of *Time Magazine*'s excessive coverage of Israel, this story's stance is routine. Examining the "73 articles, photo galleries, and quotes of the day" about Israel that the magazine fit into its pages in just one year, Honest Reporting produced a report on the "opinions cited as facts," the "omission of key context" and the "lack of balance" recurring throughout *Time*'s "anti-Israel bias" in their coverage.[10] Here's how this one begins:

> Heli and Eli sell condos on Exodus Street, a name that evokes a certain historical hardship in a neighborhood that suggests none at all, the in-gathering of the Jews having entered a whole new realm here. The talk in the little office is of interest rates and panoramic sea views from handsomely appointed properties on the Ashdod waterfront selling for half what people are asked to pay in Tel Aviv, 18 miles (29 km) to the north.
>
> And sell they do, hand over fist—never mind the rockets that fly out of Gaza, 14 miles (22.5 km) to the south. "Even when the Qassams fell, we continued to sell!" says Heli Itach, slapping a palm on the office desk.[11]

Realtors and clients, in a real estate office, talking about real estate! This is newsworthy only because the one allowable topic is the conflict. "Condos on Exodus Street" does have a ring to it. Most Israeli street names commemorate events or people significant to the state, creating all kinds of possibilities for strange juxtapositions, but as we read on we notice the implication; it seems there *should be* an exodus from Ashdod's Exodus Street instead of a surprising normalcy disrupting the writer's focus on conflict. Success, going on with life in spite of dangers close at hand, even happiness, is turned against the people cited in the article. The Only Conflict frame through which the reporter views

Israelis leads him not simply to denigrate the other aspects of their lives but also to mishear their comments about the conflict, itself:

> 'Listen to me,' says Eli Bengozi, born in Soviet Georgia and for 40 years an Israeli. 'Peace? Forget about it. They'll never have peace. Remember Clinton gave 99% to Arafat, and instead of them fighting for 1%, what, Intifadeh.' Another whack for the desk.
> 'The people,' Heli says, 'don't believe.'
> Eli searches for a word. 'People in Israel are indifferent,' he decides. 'They don't care if there's going to be war. They don't care if there's going to be peace. They don't care. They live in the day . . .'[12]

The realtor points out that peace offers, even the Bill Clinton-negotiated one, have been met with terrorism, so with an uncertain future people focus on the present. Yet in articles like this, rockets simply "fly out of Gaza" as if no one is firing them and as if they aren't intended to kill civilians.[13] Neither Hamas terror tactics nor Israeli resilience is newsworthy; instead, the article focuses on the incongruity between Israel known "only from the headlines" and real life. In this contrast, *Time* seems to prefer the headlines:

> In a 2007 survey, 95% of Israeli Jews described themselves as happy, and a third said they were 'very happy.' The rich are happier than the poor, and the religious are happiest of all. But the broad thrust, so incongruous to people who know Israel only from headlines, suits a country whose quality of life is high and getting better . . . Don't they realize that only peace with the Palestinians will ensure a lasting happiness?"[14]

The Hamas government broadcasts its goal of eliminating the Jewish state and fires rockets indiscriminately at civilians across the border; yet here, the people targeted, who apparently try to live their lives as normally as possible under these circumstances, are accused of not noticing that peace would make life happier. Only within this framing can such illogic sound reasonable. For, the frame blocks out all the other dimensions of the conflict except Israeli responsibility: the support of Iran for Hamas, the involvement not only of Israelis but also Palestinians, the history of the region, and so on.

More than anything, the people interviewed here seem to be realists. Apparently they lead fulfilling and, for many, spiritual lives. In fact, they seem remarkably well adjusted. A young man interviewed later in the article says, "We concentrate on what we can do, on how we can improve our lives," in spite of the fact that another interviewee reminds the reporter of her first concern when buying an apartment in Ashdod: does it have a good bomb shelter?

The story presents no evidence that "Israel does not care about peace" and plenty of evidence that, well-aware of their precarious location in the range of lethal rockets directed at them, people work to have productive and satisfying lives—in spite of the conflict. While the conflict certainly exists, its reality is nothing like the image presented in the article. In fact, the absence of focus on conflict becomes the story. When the reality of Ashdod does not match the writer's expectations, he accounts for the discrepancies by accusing Israelis of apathy and even of sinister motives, turning financial successes into shades of the traditionally anti-Jewish trope of moneygrubbing. Rather than reporting on what he actually finds in Israel, he frames the story around "the conflict" even disregarding what his interviewees say.

This habit of spotlighting only conflict shows up most peculiarly in feature or human interest stories like this one; the conflict isn't there and yet it appears as the emphasis of the story. A different framing of the people in the article would create a different focus. For example, in a Reuters article "West Bank High Life Masks Deepening Economic Crisis," writer, Noah Browning, like *Time Magazine*'s Karl Vick, observes a scene that does not match the standard narrative, in this case that all Palestinians live in poverty.[15] Upon noticing wealthy areas of downtown Ramallah, the "trendy" shops, and an attitude of live for the day among Palestinians, the reporter describes a land sale boom in the West Bank as "more mirage than miracle" as opposed to examining the actually booming real estate. When an owner of a thriving, upscale restaurant chain says "If you're immersed in troubles, why not try to live well, have night life and good coffee?" there are no accusations leveled against him for lack of concern about peace, and the disparity between the wealth in parts of Ramallah and the poor economy in other West Bank areas is attributed to Israel.[16]

Although the Palestinian Authority receives one of the highest per capita amounts of foreign aid in the world,[17] a single quote mildly hints that there may be problems other than the conflict: "Palestinian ministry admits that his government is also to blame . . . 'though we don't control the means of production we could have encouraged more foreign investment and interest in the private sector.'"[18] Apparently uninterested in offering any details about the "high life" he sees in Ramallah, the writer focuses almost entirely on the usual framing of Israel, touching on most of the connected frames we will examine.

No Pride?

Portraying everything about Israel as part of the conflict, like all the connecting frames, usually does not originate with the press but often is propelled by it. So those who criticize Israel frequently get a bigger and more sympathetic hearing than they might were the country viewed neutrally or favorably. Another offering from *Time Magazine* illustrates this so well that outside the Only Conflict framing the title of the piece reads as a non sequitur—like a headline in the parody news site *The Onion*. Imagine, "Is the US using major league football to excuse its policy on the environment?" or "Are the Swiss talking about their ski resorts to distract from all the money in their banks?" *Time Magazine* asks: "Is Israel using gay rights to excuse its policy on Palestine?"[19]

The story mentions no "policy" at all but does quote Columbia Professor of Modern Arab Politics, Joseph Massad, who has equated Israelis with Nazis and written about "international Zionist Jewish brigades of baby killers."[20] In the *Time* article Massad asserts that Israel and its "propaganda organs" are trying to deflect from "international condemnation" when they promote gay events and rights in Israel. The story reports on some activists (there is no mention of how many) who protest the inclusion of Israeli films in LGBTQ film festivals, Israeli marchers in Pride parades, and an Israeli Consulate sponsorship of a film festival in San Francisco.

Although it might be newsworthy that there are supporters of gay rights who protest against the one country in the Middle East where gays have rights, writer David Kaufman focuses on the lack of Jewish/Israeli counter-protest to the accusation of "pink-washing." Invented by academics, this term in the context of framing Israel means that if Israelis take public pride in their social norms that are inclusive of LGBTQ people, it's actually a trick to get us to look outside the Only Conflict frame, a "pink-wash" to distract from the conflict.

"The critics of Israel in the LGBTQ community are a small, fringe movement," writes Jayson Littman,[21] founder of New York's, Hebro "the largest gay party and event scene for Jews outside of Tel Aviv":[22]

Are anti-pink-washing activists really suggesting that the richness and diversity of pro-Gay life in Israel is all a conspiracy by the government to distract the world from other issues within the region? It would be hard to make up the reality that is Gay life in large swaths of Israel.[23]

Time Magazine doesn't seem interested in this "richness" but only in talking about "pink-washing":

Over in Israel, meanwhile, community leaders seem to view the debate as a problem for their country's image abroad that has little to do with LGBT issues at home. "Rather than openly opposing international anti-Israel LGBT groups, the gay community in Israel has essentially ignored the pink-washing issue," says filmmaker Yair Qedar, whose recent movie *Gay Days* is the definitive history of the Israeli LGBT civil rights movement. "This is a real shame because LGBT rights are something Israelis should be proud of—for ourselves, our neighbors and all peace-seeking people.' By making Israel out to be a 'pink leper,' says Qedar, the anti-pink-washing movement 'ultimately serves homophobia far more than dialogue and peace."[24]

Proud of gay rights in Israel, Yair Qedar objects to the "anti-pink-washing" group and says it works against gay causes. But the *Time* article fits his words to the standard framework: "As Qedar suggests, the real danger of both pink-washing and the anti-Israel opposition is their potential to distract both camps from the long-term goal of peace."[25] Qedar says no such thing; he certainly does not suggest that "pink washing" is a "real danger." The article takes the accusation of the headline (and the protesters) and enshrines it as fact, concluding:

> Each side fails to recognize core—and perhaps, constructive—truths about the other: Israel does have some of the world's most progressive LGBT policies, yet it's also mired in an illegal, militarized West Bank occupation.[26]

These "sides" are nonsensical. The West Bank description is hardly a "truth," though it is an opinion held by numbers of people both inside and outside Israel. Little known and left out of the article almost entirely is the extent to which Israel has "some of the world's most progressive LBGT policies."

Israel is not merely the safe place for LGBTQ people in the Middle East, hosting Pride parades in Jerusalem, Haifa, Eilat, and a week-long event with 200,000 participating in Tel Aviv;[27] it is so welcoming that the city of Tel Aviv has been named the best gay tourist destination in the world.[28] In an enthusiastic article in *The Boston Globe* titled "Welcome to Tel Aviv, The

Gayest City on Earth," Christopher Muther writes:

> Tel Aviv is, for lack of a better description, super gay. It could even be
> characterized as post-gay. Most urban centers have a concentrated epi-
> center affectionately called a gayborhood or a gay ghetto. Tel Aviv doesn't
> need to bother with such a dated concept.

Muther gives plenty of praise and attention to the night life in Tel Aviv but
also describes its lesser known qualities:

> Tel Aviv is the most gay friendly city in the Middle East. It's a welcoming
> destination for residents of less hospitable territories. The government
> funds the massive Pride celebration, along with the Tel Aviv Municipal
> LGBT Community Center. The center hosts a gay parents support group,
> a queer cinema workshop, painting lessons, a kindergarten, a medical
> clinic, performance space, and nearly any other service you can imagine
> . . . There is a gayby boom happening here, and there are plenty in the
> LGBT community who have no interest in staying up until daylight . . . [29]

However, *Time Magazine* writer, David Kaufman seems to go out of his way
to minimize discussion of real life in Israel and, while emphasizing critics of
the Jewish State, says nothing at all about the stark contrast between Israel
and its neighbors.

Further, calling "anti-pink-washing" protesters a "pro-Palestinian"
group is deeply questionable. What possible help are they to gay Palestinians who, under the Palestinian Authority, have no protected rights and
cannot live openly as gay? What impact can the charge of "pink-washing"
have on gays in Gaza where homosexuality is illegal—as it is in 76 countries
of the world? The punishment for being gay in Gaza is 10 years in prison. In
14 other Muslim majority countries the punishment is death. In Iran, gays
have been thrown off rooftops by order of the government.[30] This does not

mean that Israel, or the US, may have no further progress to make in terms of LGBT equality but that the accusation of "pink-washing" is far more an anti-Israel slur than a pro-gay rights or pro-Palestinian claim, regardless of the serious treatment it gets in op-eds by academics in *The New York Times*[31] and *The Guardian*.[32] Arthur Slepian, founder of A Wider Bridge, a LGBTQ organization in the US and Canada dedicated to "equality in Israel and for Israel"[33] writes one of the clearest and most useful rebuttals I've seen in "An Inconvenient Truth: The Myths of Pink-Washing."[34]

Let me reiterate that I am interested in exposing general patterns in the framing of Israel. Stories that fall too far outside the usual frames, where no ready angle for negative spin appears, may not show up in world news at all. For example, tracking stories of positive Israeli-Palestinian interaction, Michael Ordman found 60 significant stories in one year not covered in the press outside Israel. In medical news, these included such events as the establishment at Hadassah Hospital of the first bone marrow registry in the Middle East for Arab donors and the work of Israel's Save a Heart Foundation, more than half of whose patients live in Palestinian controlled territories.[35] Ordman, who manages a site called, *"Good News From Israel,"*[36] and writes a blog in *The Jerusalem Post* where he "highlights Israel's latest achievements in the fields of technology, health, business, coexistence and building the Jewish state"[37] writes:

> There are occasions when I think that the international media must possess a device comparable to Harry Potter's "cloak of invisibility." It hides Israel's achievements so skillfully that most of the inhabitants of this planet must be under the illusion that some unseen magician is responsible for half of the world's innovations.[38]

Another site, *No Camels*, describes itself as focusing on "breakthrough innovation from Israel for a global audience . . . drawing attention to innovative solutions not just the challenges that so often make today's headlines."[39] The site does seem to demonstrate Michael Ordman's point about the wide reach and largely underreported amount of Israeli innovation. To take just one example, a recent article notes that New York City taxis come equipped with four Israeli inventions: WAZE, the GPS system; Gett, the app for calling a taxi; Mobileye that lets drivers see behind them; and Nexar that detects dangers while driving.[40]

And since 2004, an Internet news site, *Israel 21C*,[41] has sought to provide non-political coverage outside the usual framing of Israel with information on Israeli arts and culture, medical research, alternative energy, and social activism among other topics:

> Focusing beyond the Middle East conflict, ISRAEL21C offers topical and timely reports on how Israelis from all walks of life and religion, innovate, improve and add value to the world . . . The site redefines the conversation about Israel, offering a fair and balanced portrayal of the country, and focusing media and public attention on Israel's vibrant diversity, humanity, creativity, innovative spirit, and responsiveness.[42]

For although media critics generally identify a bias toward bad news, one must search even to find stories about Israeli arts and culture that do not focus on anti-Israel claims or make a connection, no matter how strained, to an anti-Israel interpretation of "the conflict." Of course, the press has much to choose from in this regard. A continual flow of what anywhere else would be good news or non-news, in the case of Israel, descends into the spotlight on conflict.

Rock and Roll and BDS

Major musicians scheduling appearances in Israel generate news, not because of their upcoming performances but because of the possibility that they may cancel at the last moment. I have always wondered about this phenomenon. How does it happen that musicians book shows, arrange venues, sell tickets, excite their fans, and then, at the last minute, become "anti-Israel" enough to boycott their own show, their own fans? Of course, unlike arranging to perform in any other country, musicians planning to come to Israel subject themselves, their crews, and entourage to well-publicized demands to cancel from organizers of BDS (Boycott, Divestment, and Sanction). After some research, I was surprised to learn that in spite of the intensity of this heckling, only a few well-known performers ever have cancelled shows in Israel and, significantly, even fewer apparently did so as a protest; there's a difference between giving into pressure and supporting the BDS agenda.[43]

The biggest music legends: the Rolling Stones, Bob Dylan, Paul McCartney, Elton John, Paul Simon, and the late Leonard Cohen all performed in Israel. So have The Black Eyed Peas, Red Hot Chili Peppers, Madonna, Lady Gaga, Aerosmith, Metalica, Justin Beiber, Alicia Keys, Linkin Park, Jethro Tull, Ziggy Marley, Deep Purple, Depeshe Mode, Morrissey, Rod Stewart, Britney Spears, Adam Lambert and Queen, and many others. In fact, every genre from punk, metal, and alternative, to reggae, rock, and pop is well-represented by major artists who perform in Israel—much to the credit of the musicians themselves. Israel can be an expensive venue to get to and it has a small population; often only a single night performance in Tel Aviv is the norm for many famous acts. So, the gains from a show in Israel may not offset what can become a huge psychological strain put on the performers and their crews who are pressured not to play there.

The spotlight on Only Conflict means that news stories rarely focus on the harassment—even death threats—against musicians, or portray as outrageous the tactics of BDS supporters. Nor have I seen stories outside media watch sites and the Jewish press that spell out how few musicians actually cancel or how many perform in Israel every year. *Tablet Magazine*'s Liel Leibovitz published "The Rock Star's Guide to Eating, Praying, and Loving in the High Security State of Israel," an insider's perspective in which one can see that rather than boycotting Israel, A-list performers especially like playing there.[44]

Major news services and, of course, the anti-Israel websites focus on BDS demands. Even once a show has happened, it is cast in light of the boycott that never was, as in "In Tel Aviv, Alicia Keys Performs Concert That Had Drawn Protests."[45] Rather than describing musicians who cancel as the exceptions they are, spotlight framing, because it connects anything about Israel to the conflict—much like BDS, itself—makes a cancelled concert seem likely. At the same time, it treats any cancellation that does occur as if this represents support for boycott.

However, by reading musician websites and tracking down what stars actually have said I learned, for example, that Marc Almond wanted to make it "absolutely clear" that he did not cancel "for any political reason";[46] that Carlos Santana had a scheduling problem that "forced the postponement" of his show;[47] and that The Pixies sent their "deepest apologies to the fans" for "events beyond all our control."[48] All three acts are routinely cited as boycotters. I learned from a BBC celebrity interview (and the interviewer learned too) that Jon Bon Jovi, another name included in boycotter news, simply had not been to the Jewish state. When asked, "Is there anywhere in the world you'd like to play but haven't yet?" Bon Jovi immediately answered, "Israel."[49] Santana, The Pixies, and Bon Jovi all have since played in Israel.

Nowhere outside the Jewish and Israeli press was there a headline like this one that titled Salif Keita's Facebook posting: "Salif Keita forced to cancel Jerusalem Festival due to dangerous threats by BDS."[50] The post explained that the Afro-Pop star and his agents were "bombarded with hundreds of threats, blackmail attempts, intimidation, social media harassment and slander stating that Mr. Keita was to perform in Israel, 'not for peace, but for apartheid.'" Although the fans and organizers of the Jerusalem Sacred Music Festival missed out on hearing "the golden voice of Africa," Keita made a contribution with a donation to Hadassah Hospital of Jerusalem and also by publishing a clear statement written with his management:

These threats were made by a group named BDS, who also threatened to keep increasing an anti-Salif Keita campaign, which they had already started on social media, and to work diligently at ruining the reputation and career that Mr. Keita has worked 40 years to achieve not only professionally, but for human rights and albinism.

Of course, we do not agree with any of these tactics or false propaganda, but management's concern is to protect the artist from being harmed personally and professionally. Although, we love Israel and all his fans here, and the fantastic spirit of unity of the Sacred Music Festival, as well as the important work your hospital is doing for albinism, we did not agree with the scare tactics and bullying used by BDS; therefore management decided to act cautiously when faced with an extremist group, as we believe BDS to be.

Keita's candor—like Paul McCartney's when Sir Paul's Tel Aviv concert not only prompted boycott demands from the BDS movement but death threats from Islamist Mohammed Omar Bakri—offered the press opportunities to shift their framing away from boycott as a seemingly reasonable possibility to examining its dangers and absurdities.[51] Yet Keita's revelations about why he cancelled were not a major story. Death threats against Paul McCartney may even have been underplayed.[52] So, while BDS fails to attract adherents to its cause among well-known performers, within the spotlight framing "scare tactics and bullying" are presented as mere "protests." Media emphasis on whether or not a star will cancel sweeps stories about boycott into celebrity news, and avoids investigative reporting on attempts to harm famous musicians or "ruin the reputation and career" of the many more vulnerable performers who are less famous than The Beatles.

Lost in the coverage, too, is the fact that BDS calls for boycotting Israel—regardless of Israeli policy. "If the Occupation ends, let's say, will that end the call for BDS? No it will not," says founding member of BDS, Omar Barghouti adding, "I clearly do not buy into the two-state solution." As we'll discuss in the next chapters, the goal is to get rid of the Jewish state. Here, Barghouti explains how this would occur were there to be an influx of Palestinian refugees into Israel, a demand that he considers "non-negotiable": "If the refugees were to return you would not have a two state solution, you would have a Palestinian state next to a Palestinian state."[53]

BDS leaders rarely explain their goals so clearly and even some supporters of BDS may believe that they are actually working toward "two states for two peoples." Curiously, for many years Omar Barghouti conducted his activism for "academic and cultural boycott of Israel" while at the same time going to graduate school at Tel Aviv University.

Because the spotlight on Only Conflict, like BDS, disallows cultural events or everyday occurrences in Israel to be appreciated or even accepted as they would be anywhere else, this framing helps obscure the goals of BDS. It begins to seem unremarkable, and just the way things are, that famous performers are harassed when they book shows in Israel or that only Israeli universities are threatened with boycott.

"Rants, Rhetoric, and Biased Resolutions"[54]

The spotlight on conflict as presented in the news, distorting or erasing everyday Israeli life, takes on a more extreme and disturbing appearance in its raw form on the world stage. Nowhere is this more obvious than at the United Nations whose spotlight on Israel can be accurately described as "an obsession."[55] Certainly, this was not always the case. By the 1970's the "Non-Aligned" member nations along with the USSR had grown to dominate the UN, and in 1975 the UN passed resolution 3379 declaring "Zionism is a form of racism and racial discrimination."[56] There was bipartisan outrage from the US Senate and shock from Civil Rights leaders including Cesar Chavez and Eldridge Cleaver. "To condemn the Jewish survival doctrine as racism is a travesty upon the truth," said Cleaver.

More than 200 leading African Americans signed an advertisement rejecting the racism charge including athletes like Hank Aaron, Roy Campanella, and Arthur Ash, politicians like Los Angeles mayor Tom Bradley and congressman Andrew Young, and civil rights icons like Coretta Scott King and the Reverend Martin Luther King, Jr.

Influential author and co-chair of the Democratic Socialists of America, Michael Harrington remarked, "If one preposterously charges that Zionism is racism, then so are all nationalisms which joined to condemn it at the UN."[57]

The language of Resolution 3379 does not discuss "the conflict" but simply and "preposterously charges" racism, framing Israel as the "World's Worst," the last frame we will address. But this is also a powerful instance of spotlight framing, for only the conflict and Israel's full responsibility for it is visible from the vantage point of such a resolution. At the United Nations, the one country constantly in the negative spotlight is Israel. Although Resolution 3379 was repealed in 1991, hundreds of resolutions since then have also sought to delegitimize the Jewish state.

Daniel Patrick Moynihan's impassioned speech as US Ambassador to the UN in 1975 predicted what the UN has become in regard to human rights and Israel:

A terrible lie has been told here today. Not only will people begin to say, have already begun to say that the UN is a place where lies are told, but far more serious grave damage will be done to the cause of human rights itself. The harm will arise first because it will strip racism from the precise and abhorrent meaning it still precariously holds today. How will the people of the world feel about racism and the need to struggle against it when they are told it is an idea as broad as to include the Jewish national liberation movement?

As the lie spreads it will do harm in another way . . . There will be new forces, some of them arising now, new prophets and new despots, who will justify their actions with the help of just the sort of distortions of words we have sanctioned here today. Today we have drained the word, 'racism' of its meaning. Tomorrow words like 'national self-determination' and 'national honor' will be perverted to serve the purposes of conquest and exploitation . . . how will the small nations of the world defend themselves . . . when the language of human rights, the only language by which the small can be defended, is no longer believed and no longer has a power of its own.[58]

Gil Troy writes in *Moynihan's Moment: America's Fight Against Zionism as Racism*, that Patrick Moynihan was animated by the power of words, "frequently proclaiming 'Ideas are important and words matter.'" Like many resolutions, 3379 did not call for particular action but its false accusation, dependent on words "drained" of their meaning, exerted wide-reaching influence. Even after its repeal "the claim slandered Israel, slowing progress toward peace. It effectively kept the Jewish state on probation, shifting debate from Israel's policies to its very existence"; this anti-Israel focus has damaged the UN's mission to uphold human rights.[59]

The UN Human Rights Council formed in 2006 to replace the original Human Rights Commission that UN President Kofi Annan said had "developed a credibility deficit . . . States have sought membership not to strengthen human rights but to protect themselves against criticism or to criticize others."[60] However, the newer Council has not done better than the first one. Its membership has included some of the worst human rights violators: China, Saudi Arabia, Cuba and Algeria[61] and the most criticized country in the world—by far—continues to be Israel.

During its first year, the Human Rights Council passed 10 resolutions condemning Israel and passed no resolutions addressing any of the other 191 countries of the world. It made Israel the only country that is a permanent agenda item (Item #7) even though the Council had promised to drop "the Item targeting Israel." Hillel Neuer, who represents UN Watch at the UN General Assembly, explains:

No other country in the world is subjected to a stand-alone focus that is engraved on the body's permanent agenda, ensuring its prominence, and the notoriety of its target, at every council meeting. The council's credibility and legitimacy remains compromised as long as one country is singled out while serial human rights abusers escape scrutiny. No one has ever explained how Item 7 is consistent with the council's own declared principles of non-selectivity and impartiality.[62]

Speaking at the opening session of the 2011 UN Human Rights Council, Secretary of State Hillary Clinton said:

The structural bias against Israel—including a standing item for Israel whereas all other countries are treated under a common item—is wrong. And it undermines the important work we are trying to do together.[63]

Moreover, this "structural bias" is not limited to the Human Rights Council. From 2012 through 2016 the UN General Assembly passed 83 resolutions against Israel and only 14 among all the other countries of the world. The World Health Organization that makes policy about global health issues singles out only Israel. Similarly, the International Labor Organization "produces a single country-specific report castigating Israel." And UNESCO (The UN Educational, Scientific, and Cultural Organization) "adopts around 10 resolutions a year criticizing only Israel" with one exception in 2013 when UNESCO produced a resolution on Syria.[64]

Forty-two years after Patrick Moynihan's speech, apparently nothing had changed, and US Ambassador to the UN, Nikki Haley, decried the same "outrageously biased resolutions":

The prejudiced approach to Israeli-Palestinian issues does the peace process no favors. And it bears no relationship to the world around us. The double standards are breathtaking.

When we have so much going on in the world, why is it that every single month we are going to sit down and have a hearing where all they do is obsess over Israel?[65]

Seeing beyond the framing of Israel, Ambassador Haley objected not only to its biased treatment at the United Nations but to the way the UN's goals are neglected as a result; for the constant spotlight on Israel creates a distortion that "bears no relationship to the world around us."

chapter 6

False Premise:
Frame of Struggle Over Land

Jews who have lived continuously in Biblical Canaan and Judea for three thousand years might well wonder how they can be accused of occupying their own land.[1]

—Khaled Abu Toemeh,
Israeli Palestinian journalist

With so much attention going to this particular conflict—in press coverage, on campuses, in response to arts and cultural events in Israel, and routinely at public forums such as the United Nations—we might expect the question to arise: what is the reason (or reasons) for the conflict? But I'm not sure this question is often asked. The frame that gives the answer offers so simple and so widely accepted an explanation that we're likely to hear only rhetorical questions for which answers are already known: What is the reason for the conflict? There's conflict because there is no Palestinian state. It is a conflict over territory.

Through this frame we see Israelis and Palestinians in a struggle over the same land. Within the frame, it is still possible to see both peoples as having claims to land but the Struggle Over Land frame makes it very difficult to value the Jewish along with the Palestinian claims. This framing makes it nearly impossible to see not only Palestinians but also Jews as having inherent rights to self-determination.

Israelis appear fully at fault because they have a country and, so far, Palestinians do not. Land itself becomes a vague term in this framing, at times blurring together Gaza, all of the West Bank, and often all of Israel. Here is a selection from a short video broadcasted during the Gaza War in 2014 by *The Washington Post* and published under the title: "The Israeli-Palestinian Conflict, Explained":

> . . . Altogether Israel and the Palestinian Territories are the size of Maryland with a population of 12 million. The UN proposed dividing the area into separate Palestinian and Israeli states but a series of wars would lead to large scale displacements, shifting boundaries, and the Israeli military occupation of the Palestinian territories. Today Israel still occupies the West Bank and tightly controls the flow of people and goods into Gaza . . .[2]

This description may not seem immediately misleading to viewers because it fits so neatly within a familiar framework. The text sounds even-handed with its use of generalized terms such as "shifting boundaries" and "large scale displacements" but it combines disparate historical events and time periods, gives agency only to Israelis, and sets out other inaccuracies we'll discuss that are part of the Struggle Over Land frame.

In its most extreme and increasingly prevalent form, this framing includes the ahistorical implication, or even the direct assertion, that the land in question belonged to Palestinians and the Jews stole it from them. The framing blocks out well-known and well-documented Jewish life in the land of Israel and the Jewish diaspora's attachment to its starting place; then, rather than adding to this history, the Palestinian experience essentially turns into a replacement. *The New York Times* publishes a short multi-media guide for helping students understand the conflict. It begins this way:

The three regions on the map (Israel, Gaza, and the West Bank) were once known as Palestine. Ownership of the land is disputed primarily between two different groups: Israeli Jews and Palestinian Arabs (who are chiefly Muslim, but also include Christians and Druze). After the Arab-Israeli War of 1947–1948, Palestine was divided into the areas you see here. Jewish Israelis, whose ancestors began migrating to the area in the 1880s, say their claim to the land is based on a promise from God, and also for the need for a safe haven from widespread hostility toward the Jewish people (known as anti-Semitism). The Palestinian Arabs say they are the rightful inhabitants of the land because their ancestors have lived there for hundreds of years.[3]

As misleading as is *The Washington Post* statement, this educational guide is even more so and would be especially problematic addressed to young people who may have no prior information about the topic. Like *The Washington Post* passage, this one may not seem deeply flawed because it appears familiar and reasonable. "Rightful inhabitants" sounds a lot less dubious than "a promise from God," and if the area was "once known as Palestine," why wouldn't we assume it belongs to Palestinians? *The Times'* description leaves out the more than 20 percent of Israelis who are Arab Christians, Muslims, and Druze. And although Arabs did live in this area for "hundreds of years," entirely missing from the discourse are the Jews who continued to live there for three millennia, as Khaled Abu Toemeh notes in the article quoted at the start of this chapter.

First Word in the Struggle Over Land Frame

Readers of *The New York Times* student guide might be surprised to learn that the founders of modern Zionism were not religious but secular Jews and, more significantly, that when the modern Jewish state was established,

a country of Palestine—for the first time—could also have been established.[4] Further, the intended audience for the *Times'* student guide would
be unlikely to know that all the way into the 20th century, "Palestine" and
"Palestinian" referred to a geographical area, a district included within the
various conquering empires that ruled from capitals far from Jerusalem
after the Jews lost sovereignty. Among these were the Byzantine Christians
arriving in the 4th century, the Arab Muslims first arriving in the 7th Century, the Crusaders off and on throughout the 11th and 12th centuries, and
the Ottoman Turks for 400 years starting in the 16th century.[5] The word,
Palestine, comes from the 2nd century attempted erasure of Jewish history
by Roman conquerors.

The area was called Judea, which means "land of the Jews," because it
was the country of Jewish sovereignty and the home of the Jews for more
than a thousand years before the Romans renamed it "Syria-Palestina" as
part of their conquest. In both Ottoman and British records the area is still
also identified as Judea and Samaria; and 19th century Western travellers,
including Mark Twain, use these names for the area as well.[6]

The Romans issued a coin that read, "Judaea Capta" (Judea has been captured) and the Arch of Titus that stands near the Colosseum in Rome, Italy,
depicts the Jews' defeat, with the Romans leading away Jewish prisoners as
slaves and carrying off the great menorah from the Temple in Jerusalem.[7]
To mark their victory and to further ridicule the Jews, the Roman emperor
chose to call Judea "Syria-Palestina," including Syria to the north and replacing Judea with the name of an ancient, non-Semitic people from the
Greek, Aegean Sea area, in English, the Philistines, which means invaders.
They had been enemies of the Jews and although they had been extinct by
then for at least 500 years, the Romans knew of them through the Greek
adaptation of the Hebrew *pleshetim,* which appears in the Torah numerous times."[8] The Romans also changed the name of the Jewish capital from
Jerusalem to Areola Capitolus, though it continued to be called Jerusalem.

As we'll discuss in the next chapter, Jews continued to live there throughout the centuries after their years of sovereignty and autonomy, particularly in Jerusalem, Hebron, areas of the Galilee, Acco, and Safed. This recorded history was widely acknowledged until less than a hundred years ago. It would have been inconceivable not to know that the land of Israel was the home of the Jews.

Now such history falls so far outside the framing of Israel that simply including "God" in the discourse, in the way the *Times*' guide writers do, can make historical reality if not fully invisible then easy to dismiss. In the 19th and first half of the 20th century, the people living there were called, and called themselves, Jews, or Arabs, or Turks, or Bedouin, or Druze, or the name of the family or clan to which they belonged. Any of these people might also have called themselves "Palestinian"—as any people living in California might call themselves Californian—but Palestinian was not attached to any ethnic group until less than a hundred years ago. Then, this name was at first most often applied to Jews as they formed the Palestinian Symphony that became the Israeli Philharmonic, the Palestine Post that became the Jerusalem Post, the Anglo-Palestine Company that became Bank Leumi (National Bank) and the Jewish Agency for Palestine that became the Jewish Agency for Israel.[9]

These days it's clear that Palestinian is the name of an Arab people who have shared background and identity. However, the shift from "Arab" to "Palestinian" that started infrequently in the 1920s only began to take hold in the 1960s when Gamel Nasser of Egypt aligned with the USSR to form the Palestinian Liberation Army, although even then Palestinian usually referred to geography rather than to a people. The "liberation of Palestine" was not undertaken for the sake of Palestinians but for pan-Arab/Muslim hegemony in the Middle East.[10]

Yasser Arafat, also born and raised in Egypt, formed Fatah in the late 1950s and became the leader of the PLO in the 1960s.[11] The head of PLO Military operations in 1977 said, "Only for political reasons do we carefully underline our Palestinian identity . . . the existence of a separate Palestinian identity is there for tactical reasons."[12] The term was not adopted by Nasser's or Arafat's organizations for ethnic identification but for the "tactical," expressed purpose of forcibly ejecting Jews from the area.[13]

Changing one's name, whether by an individual or group, can assert one's identity. Inventing and even appropriating history is something else altogether, as Khaled Abu Toemeh notes in "Why Palestinians Can't Make Peace With Israel." Whether purposefully by political leaders or unknowingly by journalists, the history of the words Palestine and Palestinian is suppressed, even manipulated, in ways meant to support an anti-Israel agenda.[14]

Perhaps because Jewish life in the land of Israel is so well known and so well documented—in the religious texts of Christians, Muslims, and Jews, in secular writing, from historical accounts, and in vast archeology—opposition to Israel for some has taken the form of historical invention. It is certainly possible to appreciate the shared identity of Palestinians without creating historical anachronisms that try to denigrate or erase the Jewish past for the purposes of delegitimizing Israel. Most often this invented history simply relabels Jewish experience as "Palestinian," or "Muslim."[15] Perhaps the most fanciful example of these inventions is the renaming of Jesus as a Palestinian rather than a Jew.[16]

False Premise

Of all the frames, this one may the hardest to notice and the most difficult to see beyond because it has become so commonplace. It is based on the simple, simplistic false premise that the conflict is primarily about territory.

A false premise is not so much a fallacy of reasoning as it is an untrue starting point for argument. If a premise is false, it's likely that conclusions from that premise will be false as well, and this means that without the Struggle Over Land frame the conflict narrative falls apart. To see past it calls into question the entire framing of Israel. Outside the Struggle Over

Land frame lie all the indicators that the conflict does not continue because of any particular border dispute but because the Jewish state continues to exist.

The simple premise of territorial struggle requires a complex set of rhetorical moves to maintain. These include taking events out of historical context, ignoring archeological and written evidence, accepting "narrative" as equal to or more significant than historical occurrences (regardless of the multiple ways events may be interpreted), and a willingness to change the meaning of words for political purposes, to drain words of their meaning as Patrick Moynihan observed.

This first false premise leads to a widely accepted vocabulary of redefined and revised key terms, words whose original—and recent—meaning in relation to Israel has all but disappeared. Words such as Zionist, Palestine, Jewish state, colonial, settlement, occupation, West Bank, green line, and right of return have changed meaning. Having examined this process for more than a decade, I'm aware that these rhetorical moves and redefined terms are so widely accepted that stepping outside them—simply offering historical information—has become nearly impossible. In many quarters it is cause for outrage.

Response to the November 2, 2017, one-hundred-year anniversary of the Balfour Declaration offers an instructive case. Much of mainstream media, the mildest source of framing Israel, may have appeared to cover the anniversary evenhandedly but actually did so squarely within the Struggle Over Land frame. As Reuters puts it, "This contested declaration is at the root of the Israeli-Palestinian territorial conflict."[17] *The Herald Scotland* calls Balfour "Britain's Bitter Legacy";[18] the *LA Times* reports, "A Century Later the Balfour Declaration Still Haunts the Middle East."[19] *The Guardian*'s "long view" is headlined, "The contested centenary of Britain's 'calamitous promise,'"[20] and the *UK Daily Mail*, apparently unconcerned about evenhanded appearance, announces "Britain's Legacy of Blood: How a British statesman paved the way for a Jewish state—and the countless deaths that followed after the creation of the state of Israel."[21]

Missing is the possibility that there may be an upside to Jewish autonomy for which the Balfour Declaration was one of several international confirmations including the San Remo Agreement of 1920, the League of Nations resolution of 1922, the Peel Commission recommendation in 1937, and the United Nations Partition Plan of 1947. From the 1920s on through every peace proposal in the 21st century so far, each proposal has recognized self-determination for both Palestinian Arabs and Jews.[22]

Nearly all the coverage in 2017 emphasized the demand by Mahmoud Abbas for an "apology" from England. *The Guardian,* in a news story, sounds like the opinion piece it published by Abbas,[23] and likens the apology demand to "other disputes over historic apologies or redress for wrongs of the past":

> It may be seen alongside recent rows over the Cecil Rhodes statues in Oxford and Cape Town and Confederate memorials in the US, compensation for British mistreatment of Mau Mau rebels in Kenya and French atonement for atrocities in Algeria. But the Israel-Palestine issue is far harder to deal with.[24]

Based on his careful scholarship, Middle East historian Martin Kramer writes, "Those who now cast the Balfour Declaration as an egregious case of imperial self-dealing simply don't know its history (or prefer not to know it).[25] The short statement in 1917, thirty-five yeas after the first large wave of modern Jewish immigration, was "the outcome of a carefully constructed consensus" and an example of "public diplomacy" that included the Allies together: Britain, France, Russia, Italy, and America.

Before it was issued, the US President approved the statement and later on it was supported by China and Japan. Because it had the Allies' international backing, it became part of the League of Nations mandate making it international law. Even more significantly, the declaration supported "self-determination" for Jews, just as self-determination was the principle for establishing many other counties at the time, Lebanon and Syria, for example.[26]

Leaving balanced reporting behind, *The Guardian* treats the suggestion that the Jews could have a modern home in their ancestral homeland as one of many "wrongs of the past" and there appears to be no major difference between *The Guardian*'s view and that expressed by Mahmoud Abbas in his op-ed. Modern Jewish nationalism predated Balfour by forty years or more and Palestinian, as separate from Arab nationalism, had not yet emerged,[27] so the Balfour Declaration could not have identified it specifically. But in no way did Balfour preclude Palestinian rights—quite the opposite:

> His Majesty's Government view with favour the establishment in Palestine of a national home for the Jewish People and will use their best endeavors to facilitate the achievement of this object, it being clearly understood that nothing shall be done which may prejudice the civil and religious rights of existing non-Jewish communities in Palestine or the rights and political status enjoyed by Jews in any other country.[28]

However, initial British support for the Jewish home disappeared so fully that, within a short time, Jewish immigration was severely restricted and in the 1930s was almost completely stopped. By 1939 almost no Jews were allowed to enter from Europe and thereby escape the Holocaust; had this not occurred, millions of lives might have been saved.

No other "colonial" enterprise ever has kept the supposed "colonists" or "settlers" from entering while making other immigration unrestricted; in this case, while Jewish immigration was cut off, there was considerable Arab immigration from the surrounding areas.[29] The British, like the Ottomans before them, controlled immigration because they had sovereignty, and although there was some privately owned land (by Jews, British, Arabs, Turks, and others) most of the land belonged to the ruling governments.

Itamar Marcus, Director of Palestinian Media Watch, notes that because Balfour was only one of many events "contributing to the Jewish people's return to the land of Israel," until the 100-year anniversary there has been no particular attention paid in Israel to the anniversaries of the Balfour declaration. The Palestinian Authority, on the other hand, has focused intently on Balfour. Marcus posits that Balfour is used as a starting point to an anti-Israel narrative in which, rather than having their continued presence in Israel and well-known history acknowledged, Jews are portrayed as having come with no prior connection to the Middle East because of British (or Jewish) imperialism. The Balfour Declaration that was a result of long Jewish history is bizarrely treated as the start of Jewish history.[30]

Arab leaders of the time certainly knew better. Although their positive view was short-lived, figures in the Arab nationalist movement initially saw positive linkage between Jewish and Arab self-determination. Middle East historian Efraim Karsh outlines ways in which "Arabs and Turks Welcomed the Balfour Declaration," because they saw Jewish development of the area as beneficial to themselves, a view codified in the Weizmann-Faisal agreement of 1919.[31] From the Paris Peace Conference, Emir Faisal wrote to Felix Frankfurter, an associate of Chaim Weizmann who would become Israel's first President:

> We feel that the Arabs and Jews are cousins in having suffered similar oppressions at the hands of powers stronger than themselves, and by a happy coincidence have been able to take the first step towards the attainment of their national ideals together.
>
> The Arabs, especially the educated among us, look with the deepest sympathy on the Zionist movement. Our deputation here in Paris is fully acquainted with the proposals submitted yesterday by the Zionist Organisation to the Peace Conference, and we regard them as moderate and proper. We will do our best, in so far as we are concerned, to help them through: we will wish the Jews a most hearty welcome home.[32]

Instead of a "welcome home," most Arab leadership after this time has fought against a Jewish majority country in their midst no matter how small it is. Yet, given the example of present day Israel, there is no reason to think that Jews and Arabs cannot live and work peacefully in countries side by side—as they do now within the one country of the Middle East that is rated by Freedom House as "fully free."[33]

You can see this every day in action in Israel simply by taking a ride on the light rail in Jerusalem, or going shopping at a mall in the North, or visiting any university in the country where you will meet Israeli Arab and Jewish students and faculty. You will see Arabs and Jews enjoying the beaches of Haifa and Tel Aviv, and at Israeli hospitals you'll notice that the doctors and the patients are Arabs and Jews. That there are problems, complaints, and crises within Israel related to the extreme diversity of the country does not diminish this reality.

Disengaging from the Conflict

Looking back on our visits to Israel, I can see that events there in 2005 were my introduction to the Struggle Over Land frame, though at the time I did not see beyond that frame—nor name it—myself. By the time the Intifada seemed to have wound down, like many Americans I felt comfortable enough to return to Israel. When we arrived in Jerusalem that summer, the beautiful city seemed dustier and shabbier than I remembered it. The downtown streets were torn open, a situation that remained to some degree for nearly six years because the municipality was working, with many setbacks, on the new light rail system.

Though bus bombings apparently had stopped by then, I still felt afraid to ride the buses so I rented a car and Jeremy navigated holding a city map. It's true that I also found it scary to drive in Jerusalem and in Israel generally. I think Israelis don't drive quite as fast Italians but still very fast and you hear a very liberal use of car horns. Even more than the speeding, most harrowing for me was slow-moving city traffic where a car might stop and suddenly veer off toward a parking space or roll up a curb to park partly on the sidewalk. Sometimes, a large family pushing a buggy and holding the hands of one or two children with another two or three trailing behind might weave their way through the cars from one side of the street to the other.

Inching our way through Jerusalem traffic we saw cars displaying the orange flags that represented protest against the Gaza "disengagement." The orange color seemed to dominate although everyone I knew favored the plan. In fact, a clear majority of Israelis supported it, with 55 to 60 percent approving.[34] As was the case during the peace talks of 2000, once again Israelis I met were hopeful, this time that rocket fire from Gaza would stop and that dismantling the Jewish neighborhoods there would create a significant step toward peace.

I could not imagine that the disengagement plan would not work. Move the 8,500 Jews living in an area of over a million Palestinians who, it was widely understood, did not want them there—and who required the protection of many soldiers—and the attacks and rockets fired against Israeli civilians would end.

Indeed, what had diminished and nearly stopped the Intifada was also a passive measure: building the security barrier. Though the framing we'll discuss in later chapters mitigates against thinking of the barrier as a passive reaction—the fence intrudes into many Palestinian orchards and towns and many people are inconvenienced by additional check points and construction—a fence or wall does nothing like the violence of firing back. I do still find it unnerving to be talking about rockets and bombs, but that is the reality of the neighborhood. And, in reality, "suicide bombings" decreased by more than 90 percent once the fence was in place.[35] Given the significant difference between a suicidal person and someone wanting to kill as many people as possible, counter-terrorism expert Nancy Hartevelt Kobrin uses the term "suicide terrorism."[36] This small change in language acknowledges the intended victims of the bombers rather than connecting those who commit these murders to victims of suicide.

Nearly 1,000 Israelis were murdered in the years between 2000 and 2005 in attacks on civilians, and thousands more were injured before work on the fence ended.[37] The famous barrier is about 5 percent concrete wall and 95 percent wire fence,[38] though the fencing is rarely photographed or noted. In fact, mainstream coverage often does not treat the barrier as something needed for security[39] nor accurately describe its construction. *The New York Times* cites a "400 mile route of the wall" even though the security fence so effectively stopped terrorists that after 270 miles the rest of the "route" was never built.[40]

Media and political focus on Israel's "wall" contrasts sharply with the lack of attention to other separation structures built around the world. By 2018, there were 77 such barriers world-wide,[41] most taking up no space at all in the press. Even the Jerusalem light rail, which has been gliding along its one line since 2010 in an extremely visible demonstration of Arab and Jewish peaceful co-existence, has received criticism.[42]

Along with seeing the orange flags and bumper stickers that read "uprooting the settlements—victory for terror," several times we suddenly found ourselves at an intersection where tires were burning, this being a favored method of objecting to the government plan in which Jews would evict other Jews from their homes. For this stirred up much of the controversy. Given how few countries of the world have not at some point evicted the Jews,[43] how could the Jewish state force its own citizens to relocate, especially when the government had encouraged them to live there in the first place? Judea and Samaria (West Bank) are at the center of Jewish history but there has also been a Jewish presence in Gaza through the centuries.[44]

When the disengagement actually took place, the IDF, along with the residents of Gush Katif and the four villages in the West Bank (in northern Samaria) that were being moved, accomplished it over a few days without violence, though with quite a lot of crying and shouting.[45] According to a team of researchers from the US and Israel, the uprooted families experienced a greater incidence of posttraumatic stress as a result of the disengagement than other Israelis who had also been subjected to the rocket and mortar attacks taking place during that period (from the start of the Intifada to the date of the disengagement).[46] I know I had no patience for the settlers and their supporters (none of whom I had ever met) who appeared to be getting in the way of a certain peace. If a hawk like Sharon had decided he'd had enough of Jews living in Gaza, surely as someone whose sensibilities aligned with Peace Now, I could not object. As an alternative to meeting rocket fire with an equal response of bombs or tanks, this seemed a rather small price to pay, to remove the ostensible source of conflict: the Jews making their homes in Gaza.

Media did not frame the move as a positive step taken by Israel for peace, nor as a possible "victory for terror," nor even as a debate between these views. Initially, media highlighted the disengagement as an impending, internal Israeli crisis. The heated language of Prime Minister Sharon, whose statement about opponents "inciting civil war" was quoted repeatedly, and the tire-burning protesters provided ample material for the media in this regard.[47]

Yet, here was a major, unprecedented event—moving every Jew out of Gaza unilaterally.[48] Whether it was a bold step toward peace or a travesty of Israel turning on its own people (Sharon had been the country's foremost advocate encouraging Israelis to live in Gaza) this certainly was not a move affecting only Israel. Then, even before the event occurred without the predicted internal Israeli disaster, the storyline reported in the *LA Times*, *The Washington Post*, *The New York Times*, and other press shifted further to claiming that Sharon's plan was actually intended to stop the peace process, that it would simply consolidate Israeli control over the West Bank.[49] In this way, leaving out entirely any possible benefit to Palestinians or that, at the least, the demand for Jews to stop living in Gaza was now being met, the disengagement was made to fit the ongoing Struggle Over Land frame within which the responsibility for conflict lies only with Israel.

The official Israeli government explanation for the plan focused on breaking the "stalemate" that existed after four years of Intifada and the continually failing peace talks:

> Israel is committed to the peace process and aspires to reach an agreed resolution of the conflict on the basis of the principle of two states for two peoples, the State of Israel as the state of the Jewish people and a Palestinian state for the Palestinian people . . . Israel has come to the conclusion that there is currently no reliable Palestinian partner with which it can make progress in a bilateral peace process. Accordingly, it has developed a plan of unilateral disengagement.[50]

Israel would move in a "unilateral" way toward peace and "two states for two peoples" regardless of the impossibility of doing so through negotiations with Palestinian leadership. At Sharm el-Sheikh, Egypt, in February of 2005, "the plan was endorsed by Egypt, Jordan, and the Palestinian Authority,"[51] but these endorsements were not part of any peace plan. The White House also encouraged the disengagement.[52] Knesset.gov lists seven considerations that led to the plan including:

> *i.* The plan will lead to a better security situation, at least in the long term.

> *iv.* The relocation from the Gaza Strip and from Northern Samaria (as delineated on Map) will reduce friction with the Palestinian population, and carries with it the potential for improvement in the Palestinian economy and living conditions.

> v. The hope is that the Palestinians will take advantage of the opportunity created by the disengagement in order to break out of the cycle of violence and to reengage in a process of dialogue.

vi. The process of disengagement will serve to dispel claims regarding Israel's responsibility for the Palestinians in the Gaza Strip.[53]

None of the hoped for goals was realized. When elections were held in Gaza in 2006, Hamas (Islamic Resistance Movement) won and then proceeded to chase out or murder members of Fatah (Conquest by means of Jihad). As of 2019, there has not been another election nor is one expected.

Rocket fire directed at Israeli civilians did not stop but greatly increased. In addition, Hamas dug elaborate, concrete-lined tunnels under Israeli farms and homes from which to conduct terror raids. Since the disengagement, three wars/operations have taken place when Israel responded to Hamas attacks; there have been many Palestinian and Israeli deaths, many injured civilians, and a great deal of infrastructure damage in Gaza. There has been no renouncing of violence on the part of Hamas and certainly no end to "claims regarding Israel's responsibility" for Gaza.

All of these failures may account for the findings of polling research showing that although 55–60 percent of Israelis supported the disengagement when it took place, two years later only 37 percent still supported it with 48 percent deciding it had been a mistake.[54] By 2015, 63 percent said the disengagement was a mistake;[55] and this view has only grown more pronounced as time has gone on.[56]

Conflict Over the Existence of a Jewish Majority Land

If the Jewish settlements in Gaza had been the problem that those of us in favor of the disengagement thought or, perhaps, hoped they were —because then the situation could be solved by Israel alone—at the least, rocket firing into Israel should have decreased after the Jews left. It could have been expected to stop completely. Yet, abandoning the Gaza occupation in 2005 did not end but drastically escalated the number of rockets launched from Gaza toward Israeli population centers. In the five years between 2001 and 2005, Hamas fired 2,535 rockets into Israel; within just the next two years after the disengagement they fired 2,613.[57] Since the time the Israelis left Gaza, the government there has taken some breaks but has never fully stopped firing rockets on Israeli cities or building terror tunnels from which to attack Israeli citizens. Hamas leaders say that their revised Charter is a "renewal" and does not cancel out the original. The 2017 Charter states "Palestine is an Arab Islamic land" holy to Muslims and Christians (but does not include Jews) that extends from the Jordan River to the Mediterranean Sea. "Israel is entirely illegal" and "at the heart" of resistance is "armed resistance."[58] Even when Hamas and Fatah engage in talks about uniting, Hamas is clear that this would not mean giving up any aspect of their armed resistance against Israel.[59] Under the dictatorial rule of Hamas, Palestinians in Gaza who object to these actions have no opportunity to do so and are, themselves, subjected to the use of their schools, hospitals, mosques, and even homes for storing weapons and launching rockets.[60] Close to the Gaza border in the Israeli town of Sderot, 75 percent of the children suffer from posttraumatic stress disorders.[61]

No Israelis are allowed into Gaza and no IDF soldiers are stationed there. The Palestinian government has 100 percent authority over the Gaza Strip. Israel and Egypt both share borders with Gaza, both maintain border crossing controls, and both sometimes restrict or even close their borders due to terrorism.[62] But these are not contested borders. There is no dispute between Gaza and Israel (or Egypt) over sovereignty, although Gaza is still frequently referred to as "occupied" or discussed as essentially occupied.[63]

Almost ten months before Operation Cast Lead in 2008,[64] journalist Yossi Klein Halevy wrote, "Even we Israelis who once wanted nothing more than to leave Gaza forever now realize that we may have no choice but to return, at least until relative quiet is restored to our border." Halevy describes the situation for refugees that we'll discuss in the next chapter:

The rockets, though, are only a symptom of a deeper malaise: the willingness of Palestinian leaders to encourage their own people's suffering for political ends. Despite billions of dollars in foreign aid, successive Palestinian governments have done almost nothing to rehabilitate the nearly 60-year-old refugee camps . . . The U.N. actually considers Palestinians to be permanent refugees, to be protected in squalid but subsidized camps even though they live in their own homeland of Gaza, under their own government.

So long as Gaza refuses to heal itself, Israelis will rightly suspect that the Palestinian goal remains Israel's destruction. Not even a full withdrawal from the West Bank, they fear, will end the war, any more than the pullout from Gaza stopped the rockets. Israel's crime isn't occupying but existing.[65]

Although they are not widely quoted in mainstream press, many other analysts agree with this assessment and in so doing bring to light what is rendered invisible inside the Struggle Over Land frame: the understanding that rather than a conflict over land, it is a conflict over the existence of a Jewish majority land. Islam theorist and reformer Dr. Twafik Hamid commenting on the failure of peace negotiations led by the US in 2011 writes:

Obviously, it's impossible to solve a problem without addressing and treating its true cause. Approaching the Arab-Israeli conflict from the perspective that it is about land, so that giving more land to the Palestinians will solve the problem, is a failed endeavor.

. . . Until US envoys to the Middle East realize that the problem in the eyes of the Palestinians and their supporters is not the borders of Israel but the very existence of the country, all future missions will similarly fail.[66]

Accepting the false premise that the conflict is simply a struggle over borders and land, according to Hamid, keeps even peace negotiators from addressing the deeper problem: the rejection of "the very existence" of Israel.

From a different angle, Bassem Eid, who is the founder and former director of the Palestinian Human Rights Monitoring Group, speaks directly to this problem. In an article republished several times in the Jewish press titled "We Palestinians Hold the Key to a Better Future," he offers his perspective based on his work and lived experience in the West Bank:

> I am a proud Palestinian who grew up in a refugee camp and raised a large family. I want peace and prosperity for my people. I want an end to the misery and the destruction… It is time that we stopped pretending we can destroy Israel or drive the Jews into the sea. It is time that we stopped listening to Muslim radicals or Arab regimes that use us to continue a pointless, destructive, and immoral war with Israel…
>
> Despite what we tell ourselves, Israel is here to stay. What's more, it has a right to exist. It is the nation of the Jews but also a nation for Israeli Arabs who have better lives than Arabs anywhere in Arab countries. We must accept these facts and move on. The antisemitism promoted by Hamas, Fatah, and the BDS movement is not the answer for us Palestinians. The answer is to live in peace and democracy, side by side with Israel.[67]

Advocating for fellow Palestinians to "live in peace and democracy, side by side with Israel" Eid asserts that the first step is to accept reality ("these facts") and the most basic fact that Israel, "has a right to exist." This is not something that needs to be asserted for any other country of the world as only Israel's existence is questioned.

Khaled Abu Toameh, an award-winning journalist who is Israeli, Palestinian, and Muslim, explains where the idea originates that Israel's "existence" is a problem:

In Islam, if land has ever been under Muslim control, like southern Spain, *el-Andalus*, it must belong to Muslims . . . in perpetuity. As the entire Middle East was under the control of the Muslim Ottoman Empire from 1259-1924, many Arabs and Muslims believe that the entire area belongs only to Islam, regardless of who may have lived there before.

Jews, who have lived continuously in Biblical Canaan and Judea for three thousand years, might well wonder how they can be accused of "occupying" their own land . . .

One of the leading clerics, Dr. Ali Daghi, Secretary-General of the International Muslim Scholars, wrote: 'There is a consensus among Muslims, in the past and present, that if an Islamic land is occupied, then its inhabitants must declare jihad until it is liberated from the occupiers.'

Clearly the two-state solution is not the goal of this cleric and his friends. Nor are they interested in "Palestinian rights." Rather Dr. Daghi is concerned about the "right" of Muslims to all the land, including those parts on which Israel exists today.[68]

Palestinian leaders repeatedly have stated their expectation for having "all the land" as Abu Toemeh explains. These views are clear in the language of the Hamas charter[69] and also appear in the PLO Constitution as well as the Fatah Charter.[70] In 1970, Yasser Arafat was quoted in *The Washington Post*:

> The goal of our struggle is the end of Israel, and there can be no compromises or mediations . . . the goal of this violence is the elimination of Zionism from Palestine in all its political, economic and military aspects . . . We don't want peace, we want victory. Peace for us means Israel's destruction and nothing else.[71]

A decade later Arafat was still saying the same thing. The UK *Times* ran an article quoting him: "Peace for us means the destruction of Israel. We are preparing for an all-out war, a war which will last for generations . . ."[72] A decade after that, in 1996, he had not changed. Speaking to Arab diplomats in Stockholm he said:

> We plan to eliminate the State of Israel and establish a Palestinian state. We will make life unbearable for Jews by psychological warfare and population explosion. Jews will not want to live among Arabs. I have no use for Jews. They are and remain Jews. We now need all the help we can get from you in our battle for a united Palestine under Arab rule.[73]

Rather than referring to "Israel's destruction," Arafat's replacement, Mahmoud Abbas, most often uses the words, "ending the occupation." This sounds encouraging because it would allow for two states to live side by side. Yet, like Arafat, it appears that Abbas regards all of Israel as Palestinian. "How long can this occupation of our land last?" he asked, addressing the United Nations Security Council in 2015. "After 67 years, how long?"[74] In 2015, the modern state of Israel had existed for 67 years so Abbas' statement places the beginning of "occupation" at the moment of the establishment of the State of Israel. Indeed, the Palestinian National Security Forces posts photos of Israeli cities such as Haifa and Ashkelon with the label, "occupied Palestine."[75]

Trying to get historical events straight is nearly impossible within the Struggle Over Land frame. A history show on BBC, for example, introduces discussion of the Middle East by calmly announcing that Israel was "carved out of Palestinian land," a statement that is simply false.[76] "Carved" might be applied to the Ottoman Empire whose lands these had been for 400 years until the Ottomans and Germans lost to the Allies in WWI. The subsequent "carving" of these lands in the 1930s and 1940s led to independent Lebanon, Iraq, Syria, Jordan, Israel and, if it had been accepted by the Arab leadership, would have included an independent Arab Palestine as well.

West Bank, Green Line, and Missing History

Instead of supporting the establishment of a new Arab state alongside the new Jewish state, the surrounding countries declared war against Israel and announced their intention to destroy it.[77] The armies of Egypt, Lebanon, Syria, Iraq, and Transjordan attacked the Jewish state, ultimately losing the war that lasted from the first day of Israel's independence, May 14, 1948, to January 1949. Under UN supervision, the defeated nations each signed agreements with Israel to mark the armistice lines of that war. These armistice lines figure prominently in the language about Israel, although they are almost never referred to as 1949 armistice lines and although Jordan, not Israel, occupied land for which it had no legal standing.

The defeated countries insisted that the armistice must not be taken to represent borders nor an agreement of peace nor recognition of Israel. Israel's individual agreements with each county included a stipulation like this one with Egypt: "The armistice demarcation line is not to be construed in any sense as a political or territorial boundary..."[78] The military representatives used a green crayon to draw the armistice lines and before long, the term, "the green line" became the common way of referring to the armistice.

But these words, too, seem to have lost their meaning. Most often "the green line" is defined as "the '67 borders" or occasionally "the pre-'67 borders." Yet, the lines simply marked the location where the fighting stopped. Although the war ended in 1949 with the Arab countries defeated, they accepted only an armistice but not an agreement for peace.[79]

During the war, when Transjordan invaded the Old City as well as other sections of Jerusalem, it also seized the area still called Judea and Samaria, and renamed it "the West Bank." Transjordan, which had been established by the British in 1921 out of 78 percent of the Mandate, had taken its name from its location across the Jordan River. After the war, because the Hashemite king who ruled it now held land on the west side of the river as well as the east side, the country was renamed simply, Jordan, and the new holdings were given the name "West Bank."

So accustomed have we become to the name "West Bank" that its three-millennia Jewish history seems nearly erased. Under Jordanian control, Jews were expelled after centuries of living in these areas. In Jerusalem, 58 synagogues were either badly damaged or fully destroyed;[80] no Jews were allowed to visit the Western Wall or other sites; and large areas of the city, including Hebrew University that had been founded in 1918 and opened in 1925, were made inaccessible to Jews. Also inaccessible was the 2,500-year-old Mount of Olives cemetery, the oldest continually used Jewish cemetery in the world. Thirty-five thousand graves were demolished and a road was intentionally cut through the ancient gravesites leading to a hotel that was built on the grounds.

Christians' access to their holy sites was also restricted and these and other limitations on Arab Christians caused about half the Christian population to emigrate.[81] The years between 1948 and 1967 are the only time in Jerusalem's long history that the city has been divided.

Although no countries except Britain and Pakistan recognized Jordan's take-over during these 19 years, the newly named West Bank was never called "occupied." No one sought to make the West Bank a Palestinian country, and the PLO Charter specifically stated that Arab Palestinians do not claim lands of the Hashemite Kingdom, that is, Jordan and the West Bank, or Gaza which was controlled by Egypt.[82]

Understanding that the conflict is not about land but rather about the existence of a Jewish majority land also explains the lack of outrage and absence of the label "occupation" in response to Egypt's takeover of Gaza and to Jordan's takeover and renaming of Judea and Samaria. It appears that only Jewish control of land is objectionable.

In 1967, Israel again fought a defensive war against attacking armies who had made clear their goals. Gamal Abdel Nasser who led the war said in both 1965 and May of 1967: "Our basic object will be the eradication of Israel."[83]

The defeat of Egypt, Syria, Lebanon, and Jordan occurred in only six days and resulted in Israel pushing back the Arab armies into their own territories and in reuniting Jerusalem. After Israel's victory, again there was no conciliatory response or acceptance of peace. When the Arab League met a few months later in Khartoum, Sudan, it issued its declaration of three no's: "No peace with Israel; No recognition of Israel; No negotiation with Israel."[84]

Negotiation finally did take place with Egypt in 1979 and Israel traded the entire Sinai Peninsula for mutual recognition and peace.[85] Jordan gave up its claims to the West Bank in 1994 and signed a peace treaty with Israel, creating permanent borders between Jordan and Israel. Once the West Bank and Gaza came under Israeli authority, the PLO changed its Charter to demand these areas in a Palestinian state.[86]

The King of Jordan's 19-year-old invention, "West Bank" became the only name for the area used by nearly all the world in the same way that "Green Line" became confused with actual borders; further, West Bank became synonymous with "Palestinian land." Certainly, wars or peaceful times most impact the people living through them, but the forgotten shifts in language have significant influence as well on our ability to remember history and to see present events with clarity.

chapter 7

Double Standard Fallacy:
Frame of Refugees

*Israel is the world's first modern indigenous state: the creation and
declaration of the sovereign nation of Israel marks the first time in history
that an indigenous people has managed to regain control of its ancestral
lands and build a nation state.*[1]

—Ryan Bellerose,
Metis First Nations activist

I confess I had known almost nothing about the diversity of Jews in Israel
before our first trip there in 2000, and it wasn't until I my second sabbatical
semester in fall, 2007 that I began learning about the histories of Middle
Eastern Jews. That year, I was invited by the English department at the
Hebrew University of Jerusalem to teach a weekly seminar for graduate
students and faculty on the teaching of academic writing and I used my
sabbatical to do this. For Jeremy, who was looking forward to being back
in Israel, arrangements were more complicated. Eventually, we found a
distance program through his high school with which he could complete
some of his courses and a Jerusalem public school signed him up to join the
English and physical education classes, the school band with his saxophone,
and to go to an *ulpan* (language school) for teenagers. When we arrived in

Jerusalem just after Rosh Hashana, we met with the high school principal who seemed very stern and imposing as she explained Jeremy's schedule to him, even when she added, commandingly: "The most important thing is that you have fun while you are here!"

It was a period of quiet in terms of rocket firing or terrorist attacks into Israel and maybe for this reason the country had some breathing room for attention to other issues. In any case, by the time school was to start, the high school teachers, as well as university faculty in Jerusalem, had gone on strike. The strike turned out to last nearly the full semester. My seminar wasn't affected because it counted as staff development and though the high school classes were cancelled, the teenager ulpan was still in session. With some last minute rearranging and the good luck of finding an affordable two-bedroom apartment in the central and usually unaffordable Talbieh neighborhood of Jerusalem, we managed what was a more educational semester than any California semester I could remember.

Along with his ulpan and the excursions we took together, Jeremy also found his way to frequent punk rock shows. He had been following several bands that he had learned about on our previous visits and was excited to find that even bands who had the biggest billing and had toured in Europe or America, at Israeli venues, hang out with their friends in the audience before and after their shows. When we got home that winter, Jeremy sent photographs he had taken and an article he wrote on the Israeli punk rock scene to a music magazine that published them under the title, "In the Midst of a War Zone: Punk Rock." Like everything else about Israel, its music, along with other arts, fashion, culinary, educational, and cultural life, stay mostly hidden beyond the country's usual framing.

Likewise hidden are Israeli demographics, though by that time I was well aware that a majority of Jewish Israelis are of Middle Eastern and North African ancestry. With the possible exception of university English Departments (where nevertheless, announcements, administrative work, casual conversations as well as undergraduate lectures are conducted in Hebrew) the Middle Eastern country of Israel is full of Middle Easterners. This was certainly true among the Israelis we knew. The grandparents of our adopted family, the Kimchi's, were from Egypt and Turkey. Ayala's father was born in Morocco. My Hebrew teacher's family was from Tunisia. And Avi, whom we'd met through a university colleague, hailed from an old, Jerusalem family; he seemed to know people everywhere. One time he gave us a ride to Ben Gurion airport and, while we were waiting to board, he kept running into fellow Israelis he knew who happened to be meeting or dropping someone off at the airport. He had grandparents who had been forced to leave everything behind in Iraq as well as family who were already in Israel well before the founding of the modern state.

Perhaps because many more Jewish immigrants of my grandparents' generation came to America from Eastern Europe than from the rest of the world, Americans may tend to think that most Jews in Israel have European ancestry. The false notion that modern Israel was established simply in response to the Holocaust adds to this perception. Of course, long before the Holocaust, European Jews very often were not considered European and were treated as outsiders, confined to ghettos, attacked, or expelled. For example, Jews were expelled from much of Europe between the 12th and 16th centuries, including England, Hungary, France, Germany, Spain and Portugal. They were not allowed to return to England until 1656 or to France until 1789. Between 1516 and 1797 Jews of Venice could live only in the ghetto, locked from early evening, to which they were restricted.[2]

The idea that Jews are only European does feed perfectly into the false premise that they are unconnected to Israel and the Middle East, though it is obvious that Jews have lived in the Middle East longer than they have lived in Europe. Following their periods of sovereignty and autonomy in the land of Israel that totaled around a thousand years, Jews had been brought to Rome as slaves after the Bar Kochba rebellion in the 2nd century. But their first exile had been to Babylonia in 596 BCE. The Iraqi Jewish community is 2,500 years old.

Jewish History and First Nations
vs 21st Century Postcolonial Studies

That Jews are indigenous to the Middle East seems to pose a special problem, in some academic circles, were their history acknowledged and they were recognized as native to Israel. The rights of indigenous peoples are of particular concern in academic settings and perhaps this leads some academics to ignore or to revise the story of Middle Eastern and North African Jews. The complicated categorizing of Jews as white, or as having "become white" by an ability to assimilate as such in the US, leaves out the actual diversity, varieties of self-identification, and historical status of Jews as "other" in European lands.[3]

Academic work on Jewish immigration to America considers these nuances with some care,[4] while such complexity seems to disappear when it comes to Israel. Edward Said had impact not only on rearranging Middle East Studies but also on establishing a "Palestinian narrative" as the one ideologically acceptable storyline about Israel in many fields.[5] These moves have been further reinforced by the degree to which the oppressor/oppressed binary is infused into much of the discourse of the humanities and social sciences, sort of a bad guys/good guys categorizing. In this environment it seems to run counter to academic norms to acknowledge Jews as historically Middle Eastern with roots in Israel.

Instead, Israel becomes defined as a colonial or "settler-colonial" foreign implant with Jewish history and attachment to Israel treated as mythology, whether that history records spiritual or physical connection. Jewish traditions everywhere in the world are steeped in connectedness to Israel. Jerusalem is mentioned hundreds of times in the Jewish religious texts; synagogues all over the world are arranged so that one prays facing the direction of Jerusalem; and the three times a day pattern of Jewish prayer includes three times a day that Jews pray for the return to Zion.[6]

The Jewish calendar maintains this attachment with holidays corresponding to the seasons in Israel and the Passover seder ends with "next year in Jerusalem." I'm familiar with these traditions and, though a secular Jew, I feel their resonance because of cultural and ethnic connections. Not surprisingly, these connections hold no weight against postcolonial theory. Pointing to Jewish (or Christian) tradition mostly may demonstrate that one is out of touch with current intellectual thought.

Harder to explain is how easily the physical presence of Jews has been ignored. Even a glimpse into Jewish history reveals Jews continuing to live in what they continued to call the Land of Israel—usually under very poor conditions—throughout the centuries. In the 4th century, Jews of Beit She'an rebelled against the high taxes put on them by the Byzantine rulers and were massacred. In the 6th century, Jews living in the Golan and Galilee areas built several new synagogues, although Emperor Constantine outlawed Hebrew in favor of Greek or Latin for religious texts. By the 8th century, Jews living in Jerusalem relocated to Tiberius for their safety from both Christians and Muslims. And, in the 11th century, when the Muslim caliphate destroyed the Church of the Holy Sepulchre in Jerusalem, Jews were required to wear bells and a wood block marking them as Jews.

By the end of that century, the Crusaders kept Jews and Muslims out of Jerusalem and Jews were taken as prisoners to Ashkelon; members of the Egyptian Jewish community paid ransoms for them. The end of the Crusades came with Jews and Christians killed in Acco. In the 15th century, fines were placed on Christians and Jews in Jerusalem; the Mamluks who ruled at the time destroyed the Rambam synagogue for late payment of taxes. In 1560, Sultan Suleyman allowed Jews once again to pray at the Western Wall.

In Safed, the first Jewish printing press was established in 1577, although in 1576, the current Sultan deported around 1000 Jews living in Safed to Cyprus. In the 17th century Jews were living in Safed, Jerusalem, Gaza, Hebron, Tiberius, Nazareth, Jaffa, and Acco. In 1740, the Constantinople Administrative Committee for Jews in Eretz Israel opened a hostel in Jaffa for Jewish travellers. By the middle of the 1800s, Jews formed the majority in Jerusalem.[7]

For a number of First Nations activists, like Ryan Bellerose who is quoted in the epigraph to this chapter, modern Israel offers inspiration for native peoples. Bellerose, the Metis founder of Canadians for Accountability, a native rights advocacy group, explains that throughout their diaspora Jews have had a "root culture" and all the other conventional markers of indigeneity to Israel. These include having "become a people" in a the land of Israel; maintaining religious and spiritual ties to that particular land; continuing to have presence there; having a distinct language and distinct customs; and having traditions associated with the land. Not all of these markers are necessary to be considered an indigenous people, nor is there a rule that only one people may be indigenous to a place. Bellerose notes that Jews are indigenous to Judea while Arabs are indigenous to Arabia, which does not diminish either group's rights of long-standing presence.[8] Bellerose argues that not recognizing the Jewish people's birthplace threatens the claims of all indigenous peoples because it makes their status a matter of political whim rather than of historical record; he sees the renewed Jewish country as a model for the rights of other indigenous peoples.[9]

Likewise, American Indian tribal leaders, among them Santos Hawk Blood, a Native American fishing rights activist, Chief Ann Richardson of the Rappahannok Tribe in Virginia, and Kathy Cummings-Dickinson, head of the Lumbee Tribes of North Carolina, have spoken out about the common cause they find with Jews and Israelis. Richardson and Cummings-Dickinson came to Israel in 2009 delivering a message: "We want to encourage Israel and the members of the newly elected Knesset not to give in to those who try to pressure them to give up parts of their homeland."[10] Navaho Nation President Ben Shelly visited Israel in 2012 to meet with agriculture specialists and said at the Knesset, "What I read of you—you are no different than we are. How did you survive while moving forward in technology [and] greenhouses—I am interested in that and in becoming partners."[11]

Aboriginal Australians and Maori people of New Zealand have recognized the indigenous connection of Jews to Israel as well.[12]

Recently the Jerusalem Center for Public Affairs published a comprehensive and clarifying study on this topic by Israel's former Ambassador to Canada, Alan Baker, titled "The Jews: One of the World's Oldest Indigenous Peoples.[13]

Nevertheless, a group of academics who had already signed boycott petitions, condemned Navaho President Shelly's Knesset statement and the intention of the Navaho Nation to partner with Israel.[14] When the Native American and Indigenous Studies Association (NAISA) supported a boycott of Israeli universities, some academics objected. Jay Corwin, a Native American and Alaskan native who teaches at University of Cape Town, in a piece titled "Native American Academics Do Not Endorse the Boycott of Israeli Academics," criticized NAISA directly: "If you know so little about Native American culture that you commit the worst social blunder by speaking out of turn and insulting a country and its academics, who would believe in your supposed expertise?"[15]

Until the case of Israel, colonizers were defined as people arriving, as settlers or conquerors or both, in a country to which they had no historical connection; they were sent by and did their conquering for a home country that expanded its reach in this way. In many cases the conquerors expected anyone living in the "new land" to follow the home country's religion or to give up their own language.

None of this applies to the founding of modern Israel and the terminology of colonialism has gradually been revamped to make Israel into an example of colonization.[16] Prevalent in current academic articles and numerous books, it is a given, an essential premise rather than something open for debate, that Israel is a colonial or settler-colonial country. This work appears not merely in the fields of Palestine Studies, Settler Colonial Studies, and Middle East Studies but also in a wide range of academic journals, among them: *Anthropological Quarterly*; *Journal of Historical Geography*; *International Journal of Applied Psychoanalytic Studies*; *Social and Legal Studies*; *State Crime Journal*; *Theory, Culture and Society*; and *Women's Studies Quarterly*.

Academics who take this position consider Israel to be worse than other settler-colonial countries like the US, Australia, Canada, and New Zealand because, the argument goes, Israel is newer and was established after Western nations, understanding the wrongs of colonialism, had moved on to postcolonial times. That Israel should not exist, that it should be dissolved into a Palestinian state, that there is no justification for a Jewish state, and that Palestinians are indigenous to the area but Jews are not—all are noncontroversial in the work of many academics such as Ilan Pappe, Rashid Khalidi, Joseph Massad, Lorenzo Veracini, and David Lloyd.[17]

The majority of academic publications remain unknown and to varying degrees unintelligible outside academe. That's because academics usually write for each other in the specialized vocabulary of their disciplines and within the established, previous scholarship in their fields. This expected background naturally means that nonacademics cannot simply jump into the conversations taking place in academic journals. Likewise, academic work most often needs substantial rewriting if the author wishes to address a general audience.

On campus, where academic rather than general audience sources are most valued, a student confronted with Israel "apartheid" week or boycott resolutions, who wants to learn about Israel, will find vast academic support for boycott—regardless of how few professors may actually sign on as boycotters. That is, a quick search on an academic database that a student might conduct into "Israel" or "Palestine" in many fields of the humanities and social sciences will turn up overwhelmingly negative views of Israel, views from which boycott of the country will not seem an extraordinary measure, though the writing need not have referred to boycott or direct political action at all.

The register, vocabulary, and audience of academic discourse about Israel differs markedly from that of official government statements by Palestinian leadership, or anti-Israel UN resolutions, or the language of Palestinian Authority textbooks in which Israel is demonized.[18] Yet oftentimes the premises are the same: Israel is a foreign element disrupting the native inhabitants and is uniquely worthy of elimination as a sovereign nation.

Of course, many academics disagree with these positions. And some share their disagreement offering alternatives to the general patterns I'm describing. Along with those professors connected to Scholars for Peace in the Middle East and the Amcha Initiative, a newer organization, the Academic Engagement Network (AEN) speaks out against BDS. Former president of the University of California system Mark Yudof chairs the AEN advisory board. There are also three affiliated groups that specifically define themselves as progressive scholars whose values lead them to oppose boycott and other extreme responses to Israel: The Third Narrative, Scholars for Israel and Palestine, and Alliance for Academic Freedom.[19]

Nevertheless, academic fields chart out the range of their scholarly work by necessarily developing "givens," general frameworks within which most of their discussion takes place; disciplinary scholarship investigates, problematizes, argues, and elaborates from agreed upon starting points. Only with a major paradigm shift in a field do these givens change. And at the moment, the starting points for academic discussion of Israel in many fields do not include the Jewish state's clear right to be.

Fallacy of Double Standards

The well-known fallacy of double standards or special pleading occurs when one makes an exception to accepted, conventional meaning. In daily life, it's a common fallacy because our biases so easily influence our arguments. Though intellectually, perhaps, we may recognize when we make an unfair exception for our cause or for ourselves, we may justify it, as in, "Because I was speeding for a good reason, I should not have to pay the traffic fine." However, a valid exception is not the same as a double standard. If you are speeding to rush someone to the hospital, you may get out of a ticket, but redefining "speeding" to mean "whenever I break the speed limit it doesn't count" sets a double standard.

The fallacy of double standards shows up in several of the frames, especially in the Neighborhood Bully and Cycle of Violence frames. In fact, media watch organizations as well as members of the media themselves note the overall double standards applied to Israel.[20] Likewise on campus, singling out Israel among all the countries of the world for special condemnation and its universities for boycott requires a dramatic double standard. I've identified this fallacy with the frame of Refugees because the double standard here appears so clearly at all three levels of rhetoric—in the mildest form in the media, in the abstract form in the academy, and in the more direct form of political language where a double standard about refugees is enshrined as public policy by the United Nations.

Like the other frames, this one does not begin with the press but has been adopted by it to such a degree that while English speakers have heard a great deal about Palestinian refugees, many of us have heard nothing of the somewhat larger group of Jewish refugees from Middle Eastern lands. The term Jewish refugee seems to refer exclusively to European Jews. Through the frame of Refugees, nearly a million Jews from Middle Eastern and North African communities that had existed for centuries, people who were persecuted, forced to leave their homes and their belongings and lost all their assets during about a twenty-five-year period between the 1950s and 1970s, are rendered invisible as refugees.

The Refugee frame also makes invisible the unique double standards by which Palestinians are defined as refugees and treated differently from any other refugees in the world. Of course, media do not have breaking news to report about the Jewish refugees because, like most of the world's refugees, they quickly settled into the areas to which they moved. In fact, the only people who remain refugees indefinitely are Palestinian. Even thousands of Palestinians living in Gaza and in West Bank cities fully under Palestinian authority are still considered refugees. The press, as we will see, generally does not appear to notice these double standards—the world's refugees on the one hand and Palestinian refugees on the other—standards that do not merely add to the negative framing of Israel but cause enormous hardship for Palestinians.

Who is a Refugee?

> . . . a refugee is someone who "owing to a well-founded fear of being persecuted for reasons of race, religion, nationality, membership of a particular social group or political opinion, is outside the country of his nationality, and is unable to, or owing to such fear, is unwilling to avail himself of the protection of that country."[21]

The definition by the United Nations High Commission for Refugees (UNHCR), in place since 1951 and used worldwide, focuses on people forced to leave their home country because they are being persecuted. Refugees are not people who move for economic reasons or who are displaced or displace themselves temporarily during wars or disasters. They are not immigrants who move for jobs and other opportunities or for a temporary respite. A refugee is someone who must leave because of being the target of persecution, regardless of what else is happening more generally in the home country. Everyday use of the word "refugee" sometimes includes people who leave home countries that are at war or that experience natural disaster. UNHCR has been asked by advocates and, in turn, has asked governments to expand the definition of refugees from people targeted for persecution to those fleeing conflict, natural disaster, or climate change.[22] Although UNHCR's 2019 webpage lists escaping "conflict" in its explanation of refugees, it keeps separate the categories of "migrant" and "refugee"[23] to make clear that refugees cannot return to their home countries because of persecution they would face. UNHCR and resettlement organizations have helped millions of refugees to settle into more hospitable locations since the start of these programs in 1951.

Creating a unique definition of refugee, manipulating the usual meanings of the word, identifies an entire approach to Palestinian refugees that differs markedly from the United Nation's work with all the refugees of the world. First, in no other case are the children of refugees—and grandchildren, and great-grand children—also considered refugees. No other people inherit refugee status.

This unique definition means that the number of Palestinian refugees grows every year even though, by the standards applied to the rest of the world, there have been no new Palestinian refugees since 1948.[24] The UN's 2017 report states that in 1950 there were around 750,000 Palestinian refugees and now there are five million, less than one third of whom live in refugee housing.[25]

Second, while the definition of refugees as people who are outside their "country of habitual residence due to a fear of persecution" holds for the rest of the world, Palestinian refugees are defined as anyone who had lost "means of livelihood and place of residence" between 1947 and 1949 "from the territory that had been under the British Mandate for Palestine regardless of nationality.[26] Whereas the rest of the world's refugees had "habitual residence" in a home country and then had to leave because of being targeted, a Palestinian refugee is anyone who had lost work and a place to live that had been theirs for even as little as two years. "Habitual residence" and "country of nationality" in this case are irrelevant.

Trying to account for this unique definition does suggest that the large number of new Arab residents who came into pre-state Israel from the surrounding areas were counted as Palestinian refugees when they moved again though they had come recently from Egypt, Syria, Lebanon, and elsewhere. Because the British had placed severe restrictions on Jewish immigration and no restrictions on Arab immigration, new Arab immigrants were not registered as such. Once someone is classified as a "Palestinian refugee," these anomalies naturally disappear from public record.[27]

Most significant to the present lives of Palestinians, these invented distinctions between Palestinian and all other refugees are so acute that the UN has two refugee agencies, one for Palestinians and one for the rest of the world. The two operate with dramatically different agendas. While the United Nations High Commission for Refugees (UNHCR) helps settle the world's refugees into their new homes, the United Nations Relief and Works Agency (UNRWA) focuses on providing education and social services for Palestinians but does not include settlement into their places of residence as a goal.

The imbalance in support and funding for each agency is stunning. In 2017, tens of millions people throughout the world were served by UNHCR with a budget of 7.7 billion dollars and a staff of 11,000. In contrast, a staff of 30,000 served the five million people considered by the UN to be Palestinian refugees.[28]

Services to refugees are funded at the rate of 246 dollars per person for Palestinians and only 58 dollars per person for refugees worldwide.[29] Nearly all UNWRA staff are local Palestinians. In 2007, fewer than one hundred UNWRA staff were international UN workers whereas, for all other refugees in the world, UNHCR and United Nations International Children's Fund (UNICF) make clear a distinction between who needs refugee aid and who works for the UN.[30]

Rather than integrating refugees and, in this case, all of their descendants, into the areas where they are living, UNRWA maintains refugee "camps," whole neighborhoods in Syria, Jordan, Lebanon, the West Bank, and Gaza. Unlike UNHCR's goals to help the world's refugees settle into their lives within a few years, the goals of UNWRA seem to be to create an ever-growing population of refugees who remain refugees indefinitely.

Impact of Defining "Refugee" Uniquely for Palestinians

From inside the Struggle Over Land frame, the conflict appears territorial, resulting from the absence of a Palestinian state; conflict that results from not accepting a Jewish state lies outside the framing. From inside the Refugee frame, it appears that only Israel can make it possible for Palestinians to stop being refugees.

Outside this frame lie the history and experiences of all the other refugees of the world, the actions of anyone other than Israelis and Jews, and even the possibility that living in a Palestinian state next to Israel would solve the "refugee problem." Mainstream media framing, most often implicit rather than direct, may be especially subtle in the Refugee frame where most of the coverage takes place within human-interest stories.

These often quite moving accounts, usually accompanied by evocative photos, illustrate current hardships and past memories. Unlike academic work that labels Israelis as colonizers, or the direct incitement against Israelis by Arab leaders, human-interest stories in the media focus on the lives of individuals, recording their memories, concerns, and difficulties.

For example, the Associated Press runs "Plight of Palestinian Refugees Now Spans Five Generations," looking at the struggles of an extended family living in Jordan for 50 years without being given citizenship. No direct information explains why they are not citizens, though the writer does mention that Arab countries grant citizenship to families only through the father. In this family, the great-grand father, who is the focus of the story, lived in Egyptian Gaza from the time he was six or seven-years-old and "was born in a Bedouin camp" in the Negev. The great-grandmother is Egyptian.

According to the writer, the family is among thousands "uprooted… from historic Palestine, the land between the Jordan River and the Mediterranean Sea."[31] Perhaps, as this is a human-interest story, the phrasing is simply poetic. Perhaps the writer does not intend to echo "from the River to the Sea," the most popular slogan of anti-Israel demonstrations. The great-grandfather looks around at the home he has built for his large family in Amman and says, "We don't belong here." The article suggests that the family belongs somewhere between the river and the sea, though not in Gaza, where the elders of the family lived, and also not east of the river in Jordan where they have been for fifty years.[32] We readers do feel sympathy for the travails of this family and the apparent impossibility of resolution to their problems.

Similarly, *Yahoo News* runs an AFP story headlined "Palestinian refugees' dreams of returning home fade." In a short space, the writer drops in on refugees in Amman, Bethlehem, Nablus, and Ramallah, starting with one man, who "fifty years ago left the ancient West Bank city of Jericho, running to dodge the crossfire of Jordanian and Israeli soldiers."

The lack of context in the article embodied in the phrase "*ancient* West Bank city" is typical of this framing. Jericho is ancient but "West Bank" is a modern invention. Reasons for the crossfire are not included, that Jordan, having overtaken the area for nineteen years and renamed it the "West Bank," joined four other countries trying a second time to destroy Israel.

Suddenly leaving a Jordanian-controlled city in a crossfire for Jordan's capital 25 miles away indeed would create trauma; yet why would it create generations of refugees? Furthermore, why are Palestinians who live in areas fully under Palestinian control and that are off-limits to Israelis, like the West Bank cities mentioned in the article, still refugees waiting to go somewhere else? We gain sympathy for the people in these stories but learn nothing about what keeps them refugees.[33]

In fact, Jordan is the only Arab country that has allowed Palestinians to become citizens. None of the other 21 Arab countries accepts Arab Palestinians as citizens. The great-grandfather in the Associated Press story doesn't qualify for citizenship apparently because he does qualify as Palestinian and therefore the whole family remains refugees.

"UNWRA followed the lead of the Arab states," write Asaf Romirowsky and Alexander H. Joffe in *Religion, Politics, and the Origins of Palestinian Relief*:

> These states had prevented Palestinian resettlement in their own countries . . . By giving up on resettlement and repatriation and accepting the roles of providing refugee housing, education, and health, and more

recently as a legal protector and advocate, UNWRA has, in reality, per-petuated the refugee problem.[34]

The Arab League adopted Resolution 1457 that reads, "Arab states will reject the giving of citizenship to applicants of Palestinian origin in order to pre-vent their integration into the host countries."[35] All Arab countries except Jordan have held to this decision, codified in 1959, regardless of the harm it causes to Palestinian people and regardless of the contradiction it is to the way all the world's refugees are treated. In fact, it is the opposite of any other refugee "program" in the world, all of which seek to settle refugees as soon as possible. Yet, Arab countries have prevented rather than welcomed Arab Palestinians as citizens.

Jordanian Prime Minister Abdullah Ensour said in 2015 that there are more than two million Palestinians in his country with temporary citizen-ship.[36] Although there is no official count, it is estimated that between one-half to two-thirds of Jordan's population is Palestinian. Jordan accepted over 600,000 Syrian refugees of the conflict there, but since 2013 has not allowed Palestinians living in Syria to enter, not even some who hold Jor-danian passports.[37]

In Lebanon, Palestinians' situation is far worse than in Jordan. They face inadequate housing conditions, a lack of jobs, and restrictions barring them from many professions or from owning property, according to Human Rights Watch.[38] UNWRA's 2016 report cites 36 different professions closed to Palestinians in fields as diverse as medicine, farming and fishing, and transportation. The report also cites their own UNWRA housing as over-crowded and in disrepair.[39] Lebanon released its first ever census of Pales-tinians in December 2017 revealing about 174,000 Palestinian people living in the country rather than the 450,000 that UNWRA had been reporting.[40]

Israeli journalist, Ben-Dror Yamini, who writes for the Hebrew daily *Maariv*, has published detailed articles explaining the unique status of Palestinian refugees and analyzing the "Arab Apartheid" against them. He points out that during the same years that Palestinians became refugees "over 52 million people" in the world experienced such displacement. Resettlement took place all over the world, populations exchanged, most often "where they joined a population with similar background."

> The Arab states, alone, behaved inversely from the rest of the world. They trampled the refugees, even though they were members of their religion and members of the Arab nation. They instituted an apartheid regime, for all intents and purposes.

Yamini describes the harsh treatment of Palestinians by fellow Arabs, most of which has been ignored by media. He cites, for example, the expulsion of 450,000 Palestinians from Kuwait in 1991, some of whom had lived there since the 1930s, that "was barely mentioned in the media" and is the topic of "close to zero academic studies." He refers to the laws in Libya "that make Palestinians' lives impossible" and observes the "hypocrisy" of passing such laws while at the same time sending a "humanitarian aid boat to Gaza."[41]

Journalist Khalid Abu Toameh, who, like Yemini, has been reporting on these issues for decades, writes:

> Jordan and the rest of the Arab world are not interested in helping solve the problem of the Palestinian refugees. Jordan, Lebanon and Syria—the three Arab countries where most of the refugees are living—are strongly opposed to any solution that would see Palestinians resettled within their borders.
>
> That is why these countries and most of the Arab world continue to discriminate against the Palestinians and subject them to Apartheid laws and regulations.[42]

In an earlier article, Abu Toameh also notes the lack of attention to how Arab countries treat Palestinians: "What is disturbing about the Apartheid laws in Lebanon and the mistreatment of Palestinians by Arab countries is the silence of the international community and media."[43]

Even the Palestinian Authority itself cannot be counted on to help Palestinians. Trying to escape the Syrian civil war, a group of Palestinians asked to relocate to the West Bank but were turned down by Mahmud Abbas. Israel, whose government agreed for them to come, asked that the refugees specify that they were coming to live in the Palestinian controlled West Bank areas rather than in Israel. "So we rejected that and said it's better that they die in Syria than give up their right of return," Abbas said.[44]

Abbas's shocking response arises from an idea of "right of return" that seems to be another shift of language, in this case, designed neither to help Palestinians nor to lead to a Palestinian state alongside the Jewish state. Rather, as Abbas demonstrated, it expresses a gross unconcern of Palestinian leaders for the lives of Palestinian people. In this, it is unlike Israel's law of return, with which the phrase seems to have become confused. First, there is no "right" mentioned in the UN resolution usually cited as the source for the "right of return" demand and second, there is no precedent for such a right in international law.[45]

Israel's law of return, in contrast, is a piece of immigration policy that fast-tracks Jewish immigration to Israel; it's designed to help Jews around the world escape persecution and for Jews to have the opportunity to live in the Jewish state. Indeed, most first-generation Jews in Israel came as refugees from countries where it had become impossible for Jews to live. For these refugees, most often Israel was the only country in the world that would quickly take them in or take them in at all.

The "right of return" to which Abbas refers is the idea that Palestinians have rights to specific places where they or their ancestors lived before 1948. However, according to legal scholars, UN resolution 194, which is used to support this claim, "does not grant refugees the right to return to Israeli territory."[46] Nor is this a right available to any of the world's refugees. Ben-Dror Yamini explains: "In fact there is no such right...It does not exist;

nor has it been recognized or implemented on the political level virtually anywhere in the world, and certainly not as a tool to destroy an existing nation-state."[47] In his response to the people wanting to leave Syria, Abbas demonstrated that helping fellow Palestinians is not the goal of a Palestinian "right of return."

Yamini refers to "a tool to destroy a nation-state" because if millions of people currently designated by the UN as Palestinian refugees had a "right" to live in Israel rather than in their own Palestinian state, there would simply be two Palestinian majority states and no Jewish majority state. The leaders of BDS actually envision such a situation[48] and Arab countries refuse citizenship to Palestinians, keeping them "from integration" where they are living in order to keep alive this goal rather than to encourage building a Palestinian state.[49]

The UNWRA school curriculum conforms to the most radical version of that agenda. An in-depth study of grades 1–4 finds:

> The curriculum teaches students to be martyrs, demonizes and denies the existence of Israel and focuses on a 'return' to an exclusively Palestinian homeland . . . The vision of an Arab Palestine includes the entirety of what is now Israel, defined as the '1948 Occupied Territories.' . . . Struggle against Israel and its disappearance are the main themes. Martyrdom, demonization, and 'return' are educational keys. Children are expendable.

Research into the UNWRA school curriculum concludes that there is "urgent" need for reform.[50] At the same time, billions have been given by the US and EU in support of Palestinian people but much of this funding has wound up in the bank accounts of Fatah and Hamas officials and in actually supporting terrorism. This clearly occurred after the 2014 Gaza war when Hamas focused on rebuilding terror tunnels into Israel, preparing for more attacks against Israeli citizens, rather than building public infrastructure or housing for Palestinians.[51]

Refugees from War

Nor can we attribute the commitment of Arab countries to defining "refugee" uniquely for Palestinians to any particular differences between the ways Palestinians and other people have become refugees. Along with tens of millions of people during the last century, in the midst of a war thousands of Palestinians were displaced.

Widely acclaimed historian of that war Professor Benny Morris has written many histories including *1948, The First Arab-Israeli War* and *The Making of Palestinian Refugees, Revisited*, a new edition to his earlier research.[52] Morris is a "revisionist" historian credited with contradicting previous work that emphasized positive aspects of Israel's eventual success against five invading Arab armies who aimed, as Morris describes it, "at a minimum, to abort the emergence of a Jewish state or to destroy it at inception."[53] Praised for his even-handedness, Morris does not hesitate to examine the excesses of war on both sides, which he describes in detail, concluding, "Like most wars involving built-up areas, the 1948 War resulted in the killing, and occasional massacre, of civilians":[54]

The immediate trigger of the 1948 War was the November 1947 UN partition resolution. The Zionist movement, except for its fringes, accepted the proposal. Most lamented the imperative of giving up the historic heartland of Judaism, Judea and Samaria (West Bank) . . . The Palestinian Arabs, along with the rest of the Arab world, said a flat "no" as they had in 1937, when the Peel Commission had earlier proposed a two-state solution. The Arabs refused to accept a Jewish state in any part of Palestine. And, consistently with that 'no' the Palestinian Arabs, in November-December 1947, and the Arab states in May 1948, launched hostilities to scupper the resolution's implementation.[55]

Based on thousands of pieces of documentation he details the complexities of the war that caused people to flee, concluding definitively: "The war created the Palestinian refugee problem." He reports that the first to leave were wealthy Palestinian Arabs who had the resources to relocate, and notes that this lowered the morale of others who did not have such resources yet followed suit by leaving, nonetheless. Given the widespread expectation that they were leaving only until the Jews' inevitable defeat, it makes sense that people wanted to escape the surrounding dangers.

Furthermore, they could relocate to nearby countries, an option unavailable to the Jews. Also significant was the far greater cohesion among the Israelis than the Palestinian Arabs, who at the time had more sense of community within their own villages and towns than "as a people." Morris records a few specific battles during which people were persuaded to leave by Israeli propaganda and for their own safety. However, he emphasizes, ". . . expulsion was never adopted by the Zionist movement . . . at any stage of the movement's evolution—not even in the 1948 War."[56]

In a recent article on this topic in *Haaretz*, Morris writes, "For the most part, historians distort history not by means of gross falsehoods but rather by ignoring important documents and important facts," as does a book by Adel Manna that occasioned Morris's article. Indeed, Manna explains in the preface to his book that he chose "not to adopt the stance of an impartial historian who in his writing sets aside his personal and ideological preferences." The result, argues Benny Morris, is not "historiography" of Palestinian refugees, but story, "a narrative" in which "conflict between two national movements, each with legitimate claims did not happen; and, in fact, there was hardly even a war: There was just an uprooting and nothing else."[57]

Mainstream media seem to be much influenced by the narrative perspective Morris describes. While ignoring the double standards that create unending generations of Palestinian refugees, often the press also ignores or distorts the war that caused the displacement. In addition to work by historians like Benny Morris, there are easily accessible news reports and videos of Palestinians describing how they fled based on fear of what might happen during the war or because they were encouraged to leave by Arab leaders (though some were also encouraged to stay). Nevertheless, media frequently obscure the war with terms like "uprooting" or "expulsion."[58]

Often the language, as in a NBC photo piece titled "Ghostly Exodus: Palestinians Reenact 1948 'Catastrophe,'" includes the formulation "fled or were expelled."[59] This phrasing could suggest that both occurred or perhaps that no one is sure what happened. But in the context of "catastrophe," in Arabic "*nakba*," the word used by many to mark Israel's Independence Day, it hardly matters. NBC's report suggests that Arabs of the time were only passive victims. A photo caption cites "the war that *led* to the founding of Israel"(emphasis added)[60] which certainly mischaracterizes and reverses history since the war was an attempt to destroy Israel *because* it had been founded.

Reuters uses the same language as NBC and offers a definition: "the nakba (catastrophe), when the creation of Israel caused many to lose their homes and become refugees." The video soundtrack embedded in that article reports on "the war that led to the founding of Israel."[61] The images evoked by this language, images of violence and displacement perpetrated on Palestinians, frame Israel as illegitimate rather than as a new country under attack after having been legally founded though diplomacy and the building of civil institutions necessary for statehood.

BBC goes far beyond the other media I have cited and follows a strictly "narrative" telling in which it becomes doubtful that a war actually took place. (The war lasted more than a year and cost thousands of lives.) Using a photograph of tents from the 1940s to illustrate an article about present-day Palestinians, the story describes people made refugees "in the course of Israel's creation" that "Palestinian historians and some Israelis call a clear case of ethnic cleansing perpetrated by the Haganah—later the IDF—and armed Jewish gangs."[62] Here, in an example of the framing of the World's Worst (chapter 10), Israel has become not only illegitimate but evil.

Although BBC takes the most unsupportable stance, none of this coverage mentions the 160,000 Arab Palestinians who did not leave, and the many others who came back into the country even though they could not do so legally, who then became citizens of Israel after the war ended.[63] Unlike in Arab countries, Arab Israelis, who make up more than 20 percent of Israel's population—1.8 million people as of 2019—have exactly the same rights as other Israeli citizens.

Tellingly, the BCC article I've just quoted is headlined "Obstacles to Arab-Israeli peace: Palestinian Refugees,"[64] for it has been a political role and an exploitation of Palestinians to make their refugee status serve as an "obstacle" in the way of peace. Such a headline is unthinkable in reference to Jewish refugees from the Middle East and North Africa both because they did not remain refugees and because their experience has been ignored.

The Forgotten Refugees

Focus on Palestinian refugees by the UN, the press, and academics need not have blocked out acknowledging the Jewish refugees from Muslim lands, for many populations shifted during the twentieth century and some historians have called this one of the population exchanges that were common in the past century.[65] At the same time, lack of attention to Jewish refugees from the Middle East and North Africa can be seen as more of the norm than is the intense focus that has framed Palestinian refugees. Like Mizrahi Jews, most of the world's refugees have integrated into their new environments and raised second, third and fourth generations who are citizens of the countries in which they live.

In contrast to Palestinian refugees, Jewish refuges were not fleeing their homes in the Middle East and North Africa during a time of war but because they were targeted for persecution by their governments. The experiences of these communities are told in a number of books and films depicting the "forgotten" refugees. In fact, "forgotten" is the most frequent descriptor used by these writers and filmmakers.[66]

Several organizations work to advocate for the "forgotten millions"[67] and to preserve their history. These include Jews Indigenous to the Middle East and North Africa (JIMENA), Justice for Jews from Arab Countries (JJAC), and Association of Jews from the Middle East and North Africa, (Harif). The website *Point of No Return* calls itself a "one-stop blog on Jews from Arab and Muslim countries and the Middle East's forgotten Jewish Refugees."[68] Lyn Julius has written a book that includes much of the research published on *Point of No Return*.[69] For many years no efforts were made, even by Jewish and Israeli groups, to insist that Jewish refugees be recognized, and that "final status" negotiations about refugees in Israeli-Palestinian peace talks include attention not only to Palestinians but also to the Jews who were displaced.[70]

"Forgotten" is an accurate term. For Western media did report on the situation facing the Jews of the Middle East while it was happening. As Jews were being stripped of their citizenship, having their bank accounts frozen and their properties confiscated by Arab and Muslim governments, these actions were known in the West, at least to the extent that major newspapers like *The New York Times* were following the story. On May 16, 1948, a *Times* headline read, "Jews in Grave Danger in All Moslem Lands." The *Times* reported on the "wrath facing nine hundred thousand Jews in Asia and North Africa"; the violence against Jews "openly admitted in the press, which accuses Jews of poisoning wells, etc."; and a ruling proposed by the Political Committee of the Arab League that Jews would no longer be citizens in their countries but would be considered citizens of "the Jewish state of Palestine."[71] Years later, *The New York Times*, too, has become forgetful, and of its own data base. For example, in a story it ran under the headline "Are Jews Who Fled Arab Lands Refugees, Too?" it treats its own past news account now as merely the "clashes of narrative."[72]

Along with media coverage, Arab officials had very publically made clear their violent intentions against Jewish citizens. Addressing the UN General Assembly before the partition plan vote, Egyptian delegate Heykal Pasha said:

> If the United Nations decides to partition Palestine, it may be responsible for the massacre of a large number of Jews . . . If a Jewish State were established, nobody could prevent disorders. Riots would break out in Palestine, would spread through all the Arab states, and might lead to a war between two races."[73]

That is, including a modern Jewish state in a part of the Mandate that since its inception had planned for Jewish self-rule, should be expected to wreak havoc on Jewish citizens in "all the Arab states." The current prevalence of anti-Israel rhetoric may desensitize us to just how outrageous these plans were, that Jewish citizens of Syria or Libya or Egypt should be punished, and even murdered, because spokespersons for "all the Arab states" disapproved of a new Jewish state at the same time that the first Palestinian state would also have been established.

As varied as were the Jewish communities among the countries of the Middle East and North Africa, the situation for Jews throughout this large area did indeed become life-threatening. Whether in Yemen, where many Jews lived in impoverished communities, or in Egypt, where many Jews were professionals and financially secure, or in the ancient and flourishing Jewish community of Iraq, within about twenty-five years nearly a million Jews fled their homes.[74] Most settled in Israel, though more than 200,000 moved to France, Canada, and the US, a statistic that, in itself, mitigates against the claim that Jews left primarily because of Zionist influence.[75] On the contrary, the role of Israel regarding these refugees was to fulfill its mission as the world's one Jewish state and to provide safe refuge for endangered Jews.

As Nathan Weinstock, author of *A Very Long Presence, How the Arab World Lost Its Jews*, explains, the Jews were "deeply connected to Arab culture . . . The great mass of Jews left only under duress. They were expelled. They were subjected to such enormous pressure, they had no choice but to leave."[76] Between 1948 and 1972 besides riots in Arab countries driving Jews away, official government policy criminalized Jewish life. Jews were stripped of their citizenship in all Arab counties except Lebanon and Tunisia. Their property was confiscated and their assets frozen throughout the Arab world (except Morocco). Jews were not allowed to work in certain fields or were fired from the jobs they held in Egypt, Lebanon, Morocco, Syria, Yemen, and Iraq. The Jews of Iraq were allowed a single suitcase and were told they could never return. Almost the entire community settled in Israel.[77]

The new state was unprepared to absorb hundreds of thousands of people fleeing countries of the Middle East, regardless of its accomplishment in doing so. Though Israel provides the only automatic citizenship in the world for Jews, for many Mizrahi refugees their abrupt departure after generations in other countries and their absorption into Israel were grueling experiences.

Although there is a Hebrew word for refugee (*palit)*, this word is not used for Jewish refuges arriving in Israel. Whether refugees or immigrants, they are called *olim,* from the verb *la'alot,* to go up, and becoming an Israeli citizen is *aliyah.* This is a Biblical term that denotes "going up" to the land of Israel, not because of a particular terrain but in a spiritual sense. The same word is used for "going up" to read Torah in a communal service. This semantic anomaly reflects the emphasis Israel places on the Jewish people's homecoming rather than on their traumatic losses and it points to a pattern built into the language that also may help obscure the refugee status of these immigrants.

Whether or not they were called "refugees" in Hebrew or in any other language, Jews who had lived in the Middle East for centuries were made refugees as a result of persecution against them by the governments of their countries and by targeted violence that endangered their lives. These actions started well before the founding of modern Israel, as did the threats by Arab leaders and the boycott by Arab countries, realities that counter the claim that these measures were retaliation for the displacement of Palestinians.

Within the lexicon of terms created to describe the destruction and persecution of Jews (genocide, holocaust, ghetto) is the Russian term pogrom, the Eastern European and Russian rampages perpetrated by members of the majority population and ignored by or instigated by authorities, though sometimes also stopped by them.[78] Days and nights of rioting against unarmed Jewish citizenry—including killings, rapes, beatings, and the destruction of synagogues, Jewish homes and businesses—also occurred throughout the Middle East and North Africa. The 1934 pogrom in Thrace, Turkey led 15,000 Jews to flee, some to Mandatory Palestine and some to other parts of Turkey.[79] During the two days of the Bagdad Farhud in June of 1941, around 150 Iraqi Jews were murdered, 600 were injured, and an untold number of girls and women were raped.[80] Around 1,500 Jewish homes and businesses were looted. The bloody violence of the Constantine pogrom of August 3–5, 1934, one of several incidents against Jews of Algeria at around the same time, is hard even to read about.[81] Horrifying, too, is the pogrom of April 17, 1912 in Fez, Morocco. Though a random review like this may erroneously suggest that violence against Jews in the Middle East and North Africa was rare, or confined to the 20th century, this is not the case; in the city of Fez, alone, there were major pogroms in 1033, 1276, 1494, and in 1790.[82]

What we now refer to as "Arab lands" or the "Muslim world" outside of Arabia are places that Arab Muslims once conquered. Jews were living in these areas long before the start of Islam, from 1,200 years before Islam in the case of Iraq and Syria to 1,600 years before Islam in Israel.[83] Within a few decades (1950s to 1970s) the Jewish population of Muslim majority countries dropped from over one million to a few thousand. Whole Jewish communities disappeared, for instance, in Syria, Libya, Iraq, and Algeria and now 99 percent of Mizrahi Jews live in Israel or Western countries.[84]

On the one hand, because of Israel the Middle Eastern Jews had somewhere to go when their countries set out to punish them. On the other, the Jews were only building a single, small state in Israel, and one that was always intended to include a minority population with equal rights, as enshrined in the 1948 Israeli Declaration of Independence:

> We appeal—in the very midst of the onslaught launched against us now for months—to the Arab inhabitants of the State of Israel to preserve peace and participate in the upbuilding of the State on the basis of full and equal citizenship and due representation in all its provisional and permanent institutions.

> We extend our hand to all neighbouring states and their peoples in an offer of peace and good neighbourliness, and appeal to them to establish bonds of cooperation and mutual help with the sovereign Jewish people settled in its own land. The State of Israel is prepared to do its share in a common effort for the advancement of the entire Middle East.[85]

Why should there have been any negative impact at all on Jewish citizens outside of Israel?

From an American or Western perspective, it may be easier to understand conflict that comes from opposing nationalisms or from border disputes than that which comes from traditions with which we are not familiar. Though the modern countries of the Muslim world are diverse in their history and in the histories of their minority populations, it is also true that a tradition of Muslim rule holds that Christians and Jews have "protected" rather than equal status to Muslims. This means that although non-Muslims may become successful and even prominent, non-Muslim groups can also be subject to restrictions and, depending on the leadership at the time, to sanctioned persecutions and violence against them. The extreme reaction of various Muslim majority countries against their Jewish citizens corresponds to traditional Islam's laws (*Sharia*) prescribing the acceptable status for non-Muslims. Enforcing these laws includes a special tax levied on non-Muslim communities each year that affirms their acknowledgement of the primacy of Islam, that allows them not to convert to Islam, and that guarantees their "protection" or safety. According to Sheikh Muhammed Abu Zahra of al-Azhar University, the Jews, as a protected class (*dhimmi*), with their sympathy for Israel had "betrayed their covenant and broken their pledges" and, therefore, had lost their protected status. Where these laws were not enforced at that time, in Iran under the last Shah and in Turkey under Ataturk, this persecution of Jews did not occur.[86]

To the degree that there is advocacy for the forgotten Jewish refugees, it is primarily for recognition of their history and secondarily for some compensation for the enormous losses they suffered. Of course, there is no advocacy for return to these countries. For the purging of ancient Jewish communities from Arab and Muslim countries left no possibility that Jewish communal life could be revived there at some future time.

Naturally, the double standard Refugee framing has had the greatest impact on refugees themselves, both Palestinian and Jewish. It has exerted great influence as well on how Israel is perceived. Were the Refugee frame to include the Jews forced to flee their homes throughout the Middle East for the safety of Israel or Western countries, were it to include their long history in Syria, Iraq, Libya, or Egypt, the notion that Jews came to Israel only from Europe would be exposed as falsehood.

There is another and an urgent reason for bringing the history of the Jewish refugees to light: history is now repeating itself. Just as the Jewish population in Muslim majority countries across the Middle East and North Africa has almost entirely disappeared—from more than a million people to only a few thousand now—similarly the Christian population is being decimated.

Saturday People, Sunday People

At the time of the forgotten Jewish exodus there was a saying attributed to Islamic groups: "First the Saturday people, then the Sunday people." This "ominous phrase" is included in a 1976 analysis by renowned Middle East scholar Bernard Lewis in his discussion of "resurgent Islam," currently called "Islamic extremism." He poses what he calls "the basic question: Is a resurgent Islam prepared to tolerate a non-Islamic enclave, whether Jewish in Israel or Christian in Lebanon, in the heart of the Islamic world?"[87] Lewis's "basic question" has in no way lost relevance through the decades. In those countries lacking religious freedom and where the Jewish communities have vanished, the Christian population and other non-Muslims such as the Yazidhi are disappearing.

A report by Aid to Churches in Need notes that "an eradication of Christians and other minorities, was—and still is—the specific stated objective of extremist groups at work in Iraq, Syria and . . . Egypt." Suicide bombings and other violence have caused Syria's Christian population to "drop by two-thirds in five years."[88] The Christian Broadcasting Network produced a video reporting on "the mass exodus . . . when Jews were forced to leave Muslim lands" and on the current attempt to "do the same to Christians."[89]

Raymond Ibrahim, who chronicles the treatment of Christians in Muslim majority countries, writes of a "Christian exodus from the Islamic World."[90] He reports that 100,000 Copts fled after the "Arab Spring" and that thousands of Christian Ethiopians "were forced to flee their homes" when there were riots against them. Northern Nigerian Christians "are fleeing by the thousands" because their churches are being bombed and they are being attacked. He cites a 2011 US Commission on Freedom of Religion report suggesting that soon "Christians might disappear altogether from Iraq, Afghanistan, and Egypt."[91]

In her research-based, personal account, *Saturday People, Sunday People, Israel through the eyes of a Christian sojourner*, Lela Gilbert records some of the current atrocities taking place against Christians. Islamic groups like Boko Haram in Nigeria and ISIS in Syria have murdered hundreds of Christians and she writes of the diminishing population of Christians in the Middle Eastern countries where almost no Jews remain. She calls Christians and Jews "natural allies in a dangerous world":[92]

> . . . it cannot be overlooked that the bloodshed suffered by Jews at the hands of so-called Christians is a matter of historical record; it is no wonder that bitter mistrust continues to this day. Yet whether we live in Israel or are scattered among the nations of the world, to radical Islamists we Jews and Christians look astonishingly alike . . . [93]

So far, little specific help has been offered to Christians and others who are being persecuted. Western governments have not prioritized helping targeted Christians. And Muslims who speak out against the Islamists can find themselves marginalized in the West or treated as if they are the extremists.[94] "I've worked for years on books about both Christianity and Islam." writes Lela Gilbert. "Israel is the only place in the Middle East where Christians, Muslims, and Jews live more or less side-by-side, shop in the same stores, eat in the same cafes, and share the same streets and sidewalks."[95]

It is also the only Middle Eastern country where the Christian population is not shrinking but growing.[96] Israeli Christians, like American Jews, make up just over 2 percent of their county's population (2.10 percent Christians in Israel[97]; 2.20 percent Jews in America).[98] But in countries that respect diversity and individual freedoms, a small community can flourish. Father Gabrial Nadaff, who is a Greek Orthodox priest in Nazareth, says Israel's Christian community is thriving, and Israel is "the one safe place" for Christians in the Middle East[99]:

> Today, there is just one country in the Middle East where Christians live in peace and security. In Israel, they have freedom of speech and religion, they can exercise their faith freely, and they have democratic rights . . .[100]

Aid to Churches in Need titles their report on the status of Christians in the Middle East, "Persecuted and Forgotten," and Raymond Ibrahim contrasts the way media seem to ignore the Christians' situation while at the same time constantly focusing on Israel. He labels this "mainstream media's great shame that those who slaughter, behead, crucify, and displace people for no other reason than because they are Christian rarely if ever get media coverage." And yet, he observes that media give enormous space "to demonizing Israel for trying to defend itself."[101] This picture of Israel shows up especially in the next frame where Israel is established as the Neighborhood Bully.

chapter 8

Bandwagon Fallacy:
Frame of the Neighborhood Bully

Well, the neighborhood bully, he's just one man
His enemies say he's on their land
They got him outnumbered about a million to one
He got no place to escape to, no place to run
He's the neighborhood bully

—Bob Dylan

It's worth revisiting Bob Dylan's lyrics to "Neighborhood Bully" in which he offers a stinging and sarcastic critique of what is said about Israel. For if there is a frame that most effortlessly and frequently positions Israel as the only party at fault, it is the Neighborhood Bully frame. The song's eleven stanzas (the first is quoted above) touch on many features of the frame.[1] Not only is Israel seen as responsible for the long impasse with its enemies, but viewed as the neighborhood bully, the country is "not supposed to fight back" no matter what happens.[2] Within this framing, Israeli response to attacks on its citizens necessarily appears excessively forceful. Its defense spending on bomb shelters and intelligence appears to give Israel an unfair advantage as measured by the media's literal scorecard of fatalities.[3]

To be framed as a bully is to be identified by one's very nature as the aggressor. Whereas other contested parts of the world are called "disputed," suggesting a two-sided, as yet unresolved situation such as "disputed Western Sahara," here instead, only the term "occupation" appears, less as a descriptor than as an accusation against Israel.[4] While, for example, the travel tourism website run by the government of Cyprus emphasizes the Turkish occupation, world-wide we simply do not hear of "occupied" Cyprus.[5]

Dylan has been ridiculed for this song by some of the most vocal supporters of Boycott Divestment and Sanction (BDS). Railing against the impossibility of getting him to cancel his 2011 performance in Israel, the *Mondoweiss* website published "No Surprise Bob Dylan is Visiting the 'Neighborhood Bully,'" describing the song as "a bitter and indignant defense of Israel's actions, an exercise in Zionist mythology, eternal victimization, and bogus 'right to self-defense' *hasbara*."[6] Yet, in *The Dylan Albums*, an analysis of Bob Dylan's work, Anthony Vareisa writes:

> The song is perfectly in line with Dylan's life-long affinity for the underdog . . . It touches on the condescending attitude of most nations toward Israel (...'Well, he's surrounded by pacifists who just want peace/they lay in wait for the bully to fall asleep') and castigates those who subscribe to racial stereotypes about Israel as a state 'that just likes to cause war.'[7]

Indeed, I have found that who is seen as the underdog and who is seen as the bully form the heart of animus toward Israel in many academic and progressive circles. "Neighborhood Bully" makes perfect sense to the Bob Dylan expert, who sees the song as a natural commentary from the Bard of championing the underdog. For the anti-Israel website, it indicates that the folk-rock legend's ". . . civil and human rights bonafides have faded over time—to the point of non-existence." The writer goes so far as to say that by performing in Israel ". . .Dylan is solidifying his reputation as one who— when it counted most—didn't stand for morality and humanity."[8]

A growing number of academics report that voicing positive views of Israel or negative views of BDS quickly discredits all of their progressive credentials. Where one stands on Israel serves as a litmus test, an identifier of political acceptability.[9] Deciding that Bob Dylan doesn't "stand for morality and humanity" because his touring schedule includes Israel shows up the absurdity. At the same time, anti-Israelism mainstreamed on many campuses has become so disruptive to the lives of young and even well established scholars that support, long called for by pro-Israel students, now appears as an issue for faculty.

Andrew Pessin, a full professor of philosophy at Connecticut College, experienced "a witch hunt" against him as the college's "only pro-Israel professor" when a comment he had made on his private Facebook page criticizing Hamas' actions during the Gaza war was nine months later called out by a student activist as something that made her "feel unsafe."[10] Although Pessin immediately reiterated that he was being misinterpreted since he was (clearly) only criticizing the actions of Hamas terrorists and not "a whole people," as was the accusation, the campus as a whole rushed to condemn Professor Pessin, who until then was known simply as a well-respected scholar and well-liked teacher. In an interview with *The Times of Israel* he said:

> The one-sentence version is a Connecticut College student affiliated with Students for Justice in Palestine basically went through all of my writings about Israel, everything on Facebook and the *Huffington Post*, until she could find one thing she could twist out of context to look racist against Palestinians to ignite a whole campus storm in the name of defending racism."[11]

In retrospect, the experiences I recounted in the first chapters of this book were simply an early indication of what appears now as a far more prevalent and more extreme tilt against Israel and its supporters on many US and UK campuses. Andrew Pessin and co-editor Doren S. Ben-Atar have published a book of essays prompted by scholars' and students' experiences of *Anti-Zionism on Campus*.[12]

Rooting for the Underdog

Some identify the Lebanon war in 1982 as the point at which Israel stopped being viewed as David and turned into Goliath. ("Neighborhood Bully" was recorded in 1983.) But most people place the turning point earlier, in the years after Israel's startling and decisive victory in 1967 over armies from Egypt (United Arab Republic), Jordan, Syria, Iraq, Morocco, Libya, Saudi Arabia, and Tunisia, whose leaders had repeatedly announced their purpose: "the eradication of Israel," as President Gamal Nasser of Egypt declared.

Nasser had closed the Straits of Tiran blocking Israel's access to the Gulf of Aqaba and had expelled the UN peacekeeping forces that had been there since the 1956 Suez Canal Crisis. President of Iraq Abdel Ramen Arar said: "Our goal is clear—to wipe Israel off the map." Syrian General Mustafa Tlas announced, "the UAR and Syria can destroy Israel in four days at most."[13] Chairman of the newly formed Palestinian Liberation Organization Amed Shukairy said at the time, "The Jews of Palestine will have to leave ... but it is my impression that none of them will survive."[14]

The US press, public, and members of the 1960s anti-war movement expressed clear support for Israel, for defending Israel from the threatening onslaught against it, and even called upon the US government to help. Public intellectuals including Ralph Ellison, Hannah Arendt, Milton Friedman, Lionel Trilling and Robert Penn Warren took out an ad in *The Washington Post* that read: "The Issue can be stated with simplicity. Whether to let Israel perish, or to ensure its survival and to secure legality, morality, and peace in the area." 3,700 academics signed a declaration that was published in the *New York Times*, "calling on the US government to break the blockade of Aqaba." *Time Magazine* ran stories supportive of the Israelis.

Joshua Muravchik, author of *Making David into Goliath, How the World Turned Against Israel*, writes: "Israel was above all a cause championed by liberals." These included civil rights and union leaders as well as political organizations such as Americans for Democratic Action led at the time by

John Kenneth Galbraith. Galbraith, along with other Israel supporters like Democratic Senators Eugene McCarthy and George McGovern, were vocal opponents of the Vietnam War.

> McGovern, who would capture the Democratic presidential nomination as a peace candidate in 1972, said on the conclusion of the fighting that he hoped Israel 'did not give up a foot of ground' until the Arabs made peace.

Support for Israel was strong in the UK and Europe as well, and included renowned writers and artists such as Jean-Paul Sartre, Simone de Beauvoir, and Pablo Picasso.[15]

But then, Israel actually won the war. In six days its territory expanded into the Sinai as well as into areas that had been held by Jordan, where Jews had been living before the 1948 war. While the initial reaction was celebration of Israel's accomplishment, the vastly outnumbered underdog began to be seen as the stronger party. Most of Muravchik's exhaustively researched book examines how this complete rhetorical reversal occurred. The fact that Israel had demonstrated its ability to defend itself against great odds, while initially viewed as inspiring, in itself worked to change its underdog status.

However, the change was also the result of a concerted effort by Arab and Palestinian leaders to change perception. With the support of the Soviet Union, the pan-Arab agenda to get rid of Israel became reframed as a Palestinian movement for liberation like that of other "colonized people," while using the attention-getting tactics of terrorism backed up by Arab oil embargos and pricing manipulation.[16] The murder of eleven Israeli athletes and coaches at the 1972 Olympics and airplane hijackings from 1968 through the 1970s may have made the "Palestinian cause" the most well known in the world.

Abu Daoud, who wrote a book outlining his role as "mastermind" of the Olympics murders considered them a success: "Before Munich we were simply terrorists; after Munich, at least people started asking, who are these terrorists? What do they want? Before Munich, nobody had the slightest idea about Palestine."[17] Similarly, the head of the PFLP (Popular Front for the Liberation of Palestine), George Habash reflected on the public relations value of their terrorism: "To kill a Jew far from the battlefield is worth more than killing 100 in battle."[18]

In 2016, on Palestinian television, Nabeel Shaath, the first Foreign Minister of the Palestinian Authority, expressed his frustration with US involvement in Israeli-Palestinian negotiations: "The US has never been a reliable, honest broker. Never. " Directing his remarks to countries who might be involved in further peace talks, he said:

> Do we have to hijack your planes and destroy your airports again to make
> you care about our cause? Are you waiting for us to cut off your oil sup-
> ply? You always wait for things to reach boiling point and explode, caus-
> ing you harm, before you intervene to end the crimes and violations.[19]

The 1967 Declaration of the defeated Arab countries asserting "no recognition of Israel, no negotiation with Israel, no peace with Israel" also included statements of their intention to use oil pricing to influence the West to support Arab interests.[20] Joshua Muravchic explains:

> If terrorism succeeded in placing the cause of Arab Palestine on the
> world's agenda, a second, less dramatic form of intimidation also helped
> to tip the balance of international support from Israel to the Arabs. It in-
> volved no bloodshed, but rather the lifeblood of the global economy: oil.[21]

By the time of the first Intifada (1987-1993), which Yasser Arafat explicitly promoted as David versus Goliath, the rhetoric had fully shifted. The *New York Times* quotes Arafat using this language in his address to the Arab League in 1988, "The Palestinian people need your help to continue; it's David and Goliath all over again." The *Times* notes "Israel's attempts to control the continuing Palestinian protests have been criticized not only by Arab countries but also by such friends as the United States and Britain."[22]

The first Intifada included nonviolent protest against the Israeli government and lethal, "increasingly anarchic" violence toward Israeli citizens and soldiers as well as toward other Palestinians. Hundreds of Palestinians were murdered for being "collaborators" with Israel.[23] There is no question that by then television and press coverage had taken up the storyline of a reversed David and Goliath; media have been presenting images of a youthful, defenseless Palestinian underdog versus a callous, Israeli military giant since at least the 1980s.

Jumping on the Bandwagon Fallacy

When it must be true because everyone says so, or when peer pressure to conform replaces logic, we encounter the bandwagon fallacy. I identify the Neighborhood Bully framing with the bandwagon fallacy because of the way media and world discussion moved completely and seamlessly from one extreme to another. Before 1967, the Israelis were underdogs; soon after, they had catepulted to the opposite extreme as a giant of aggression. This picture of Israel, disseminated widely and uncritically, sets up a simple dichotomy: Israel is the oppressor, always the bully in any conflict, and the other side, no matter who makes up that side, appears as victim.

One might argue for either Israelis or Palestinians to claim the status of underdog. In spite of UN recognition, embassies in many countries, self-rule in Gaza and in all the Palestinian population centers of the West Bank, as well as NGOs working for it around the world, the Palestinian state does not yet exist. Palestinian areas do not have the infrastructure or GNP of their powerhouse neighbor nor do Fatah and Hamas have the unity of even the contentious, around 40 Israeli political parties (half of which usually earn enough votes to serve in the Knesset). The Palestinian Authority receives vast financial support from foreign governments, but Israeli jobs are far more lucrative for Palestinians than anything the not-yet-state of Palestine provides. Except for financial help and supplies of weaponry, the Arab world leaves Palestinians mostly to fend for themselves on a front line against the Jewish state that some of these countries would like to see disappear. In fact, since the Arab defeat in the 1967 war, the underdog image has been actively promoted by Palestinian leaders and by international supporters. Perhaps the most influential anti-Israel academic of all time, Edward Said, chose to publicize photos of himself throwing rocks at Israeli soldiers.[24]

In dramatic contrast, Israel and its advocates promote images of the country's strength: economically, technologically, and militarily. Yet, it is a tiny nation that takes up less than 1 percent of the Middle East and is surrounded by well-armed enemies, some of whose leaders are committed to its annihilation. It ought to have no trouble being seen as the underdog. Though Israel is able to buy weapons from the US and elsewhere, the fact that no army has ever come to fight alongside it demonstrates that it is alone to defend itself against constant attacks on its civilian population. Given that Jews have been persecuted and kicked out of countries around the world, and number only 14 million world-wide, the existence of a single Jewish majority state, when many of the world's 50 Muslim states are hostile to it, adds to the underdog status. Nevertheless, the Biblical story of David and Goliath is well-established as one of the most effective rhetorical weapons against the only country whose flag displays the Star of David.

Determining who really is the underdog remains excluded beyond the framing; for as with any frame, we are talking about perception. This frame creates the perception of Israel as the Neighborhood Bully with the reversed roles of David and Goliath as its most frequently recurring metaphor. The metaphor gains power in the hands of leaders like Arafat and anti-Israel academics like Said from the inversion: Jews are expected to be like David yet here they are acting like Goliath. Jews with power, with their own army for the first time since the Macabees; Jews with the eighth strongest military in the world, may still seem confusing or unsettling, even for some Jews. As Ruth Wisse writes in her eloquent analysis of the complexities of *Jews and Power*, "Once damned for their lack of power, Jews would now be accused of becoming too strong."[25]

Moreover, the winning side is not always wrong; stronger is not necessarily less deserving, nor is bigger necessarily "badder." In fact, some rhetoricians have referred to this mistake in logic as the David and Goliath fallacy, a fallacy of attributing positive intentions and qualities to whichever side appears weaker or smaller.[26] Terrorists, for example, are usually a tiny minority of any population and with this illogic will be valued over their large population of targets. We like rooting for the underdog, and we also want to see the underdog win. Yet, if our underdogs win too much, we have to locate more ways to keep them as underdogs or we will find ourselves rooting for the big, bad, constant winner. This attraction to the underdog occurs in many areas of Western life: in sports events, in political contests, and in all things countercultural. Once our underdog interest is adopted by the mainstream, we either enjoy our successes, or we seek out new ways to go against the norm. It is on this ledge that advertising as well as advocacy try to balance. If Israel is seen as defending itself against the giants of the Muslim and Arab world who are committed to its destruction, surely it is David fighting Goliath. But if the framing features individual Palestinians facing off with stones against one of the most powerful armies in the world, David and Goliath reverses.

Isolating the conflict as Israeli-Palestinian rather than Israeli-Arab supports this reversal. Israel is not in active conflict with the 22 Arab countries that surround it, though sometimes it is in conflict with one or another of these countries, for instance, with Hezbollah in Lebanon. And the Palestinians get much of their support from the non-Arab, Muslim country of Iran. But replacing "Arab" with "Palestinian" does obscure Israel's physical reality; in fact it is surrounded. There are no road trips possible for Israelis to any neighboring countries. 16 Muslim countries do not allow holders of Israeli passports even to enter.[27]

I believe the map of the Middle East, with its tiny distances between Israel and hostile countries disturbed me much more than it does Israelis who are used to this reality. At this point the term "Arab-Israeli" conflict has been replaced by Israeli-Palestinian and the view of Palestinians as underdog is assumed in campus discourse as well as in much of media imagery. That Israeli spokespersons long have highlighted the country's strengths and resilience also mitigates against seeing Israel as the underdog. In the immediate aftermath of a terror attack, Israelis, including public officials, make a well-pubicized point of going to the site of the attack and continuing on as usual.[28]

The Neighborhood Bully Frame Up Close

Within this frame, however, Israel is more than simply Goliath, for Goliath operates only out of brute strength. In contrast, even as Goliath, Israel retains David-like qualities of intelligence and cunning. The Jewish Goliath does not blindly wield power but does something far worse, intentionally using "excessive" or "disproportionate" force. This is no unthinking bully but rather one who is a bully on purpose.

Increasingly, even before the Israeli government responds to terror attacks, even at the moment of condemning terrorism, Western leaders call upon Israel to "exercise restraint," suggesting that the Jewish nation's preferred response would be an unrestrained one.[29] Further, as we'll discuss in the next chapter on the Cycle of Violence frame, often when a new terror attack in Israel takes place or when other violence against Israelis occurs, "all sides" are told to "lower the tensions." This familiar comment following terrorism against Israelis would likely be considered quite heartless a way of talking to leaders of other countries whose citizens have just been murdered. When three teenagers: Eyal Yifrach, Naftali Fraenkel, and Gilad Shaar were kidnapped at a bus stop, immediately the US state department and the UN called for Israeli "restraint" while the IDF searched for the boys who were later found to have been brutally killed by their Hamas captors.[30]

Though I had no name for it at the time, I first directly encountered the Neighborhood Bully frame when we returned home from our third trip to Israel. Of the five trips we took during Jeremy's childhood and teen years, this was the shortest, made shorter by my plan to stay in other places in the country for a week after a six-week rental in Jerusalem. One day, we drove from Jerusalem up to Haifa, a ride of about an hour and a half. We toured the lush Baha'i Gardens, took Haifa's mini, one-line subway, the Carmelit, on its eight-minute ride from the top of the three-level city to the downtown stop and back again, and ate in a Chinese restaurant where the fortune cookies had passages from Proverbs. Back in Jerusalem late that night, the phone woke me up—a friend from the University calling to see if we were all right. "Don't you know they started bombing the North?" she asked.

"They" were Hezbollah (Party of Allah), the terrorist paramilitary organization that had taken control of southern Lebanon when the Israelis left in 2000. Led by Sheik Hassan Nasrallah, Hezbollah has never stopped amassing arms, and in far greater quantities than in 2006, for the purpose of attacking Israeli citizens. As with Hamas (Islamic Resistance Movement), there is no mystery about Hezbollah's goals. Reiterating this passage from the official Hamas Charter: "the land of Palestine is an Islamic waqf (trust) consecrated for further generations until Judgment Day. There is no solution for the Palestinian question except through jihad," Mahmoud al-Zahar, a Hamas spokesman in Gaza, said: "We do not recognize the Israeli enemy, nor his right to be our neighbor, nor to stay (on the land), nor his ownership of any inch of land." Leading Hezbollah, Hassan Nasrallah summed up the same position: "There is no solution to the conflict in this region except with the disappearance of Israel."[31]

On July 12, 2006, Hezbollah began firing rockets at Israeli civilians and crossed the border into Israel from Lebanon kidnapping and killing two soldiers as well as killing another three soldiers who attempted to rescue them.

The IDF responded, attempting to take out rocket launchers and weaponry with targeted bombing from the air. A few days later, Jeremy and I went to the Ben Yehuda pedestrian walkway in downtown Jerusalem where there are usually crowds of tourists. It was deserted.

That summer, about a third of all Israelis were displaced as Hezbollah fired around 4,000 rockets into cities in the northern part of Israel. During the 34-day war, the Israelis' aerial response changed direction, in something actually called "Operation Change of Direction," and they sent in ground troops. The results of the Second Lebanon War (which wasn't named this until about a year later) were inconclusive in terms of winning or losing. Israel's border with Lebanon remained relatively quiet and in the years since the war there has been a more positive reassessment. At the time, many Israelis felt that the war had been mismanaged.[32] When the ceasefire went into place on August 14, 2006, and then officially a few days later, Hezbollah claimed victory.

We had been back in California for about ten days by then having cancelled the last part of our planned trip. Most people we knew in Israel were hosting friends or relatives from the north and others were donating money to house families in hotels in the south and center of the country, out of the range of the rockets. In the north, kids on summer vacation from school, as well as their parents, were stuck much of the time in bomb shelters. It was scary.

Jeremy, at fifteen, was not the least bit scared, and in fact no rockets were reaching Jerusalem. My friends and family assumed that I came home early because we were unsafe, and because it made me feel guilty as a parent possibly endangering my son. Yes, I did feel guilty but at the same time, I think I would have left immediately if Jeremy had not been there to provide a continual reality check. In Jerusalem, we were out of rocket range and for this reason people were relocating to the capital city. During later confrontations, the Gaza War in 2014 for instance, all of Israel has been exposed to rocket fire. In any case, we were tourists taking up space needed for displaced families. And unlike the Israelis, we had somewhere else to go.

I remember arriving at JFK airport and seeing Anderson Cooper on the TV monitors reporting for CNN from the Israel-Lebanon border. I bought a copy of *Time Magazine* with its cover story on the war (it features a gray-tone cover photo of a single figure walking amid what looks like total devastation) and I remember reading through the photo essay as we flew to San Francisco, searching for some mention of the impact of Hezbollah's attack on Israel—on Israelis. There was one photo from Israel spread across two pages and the rest left Israelis, except as military analyists or soldiers, out of the story.[33]

Back home I watched the broadcasts on ABC, NBC, and CBS and read the news reports with a sick feeling. Whatever would be the outcome of the war, beaming in to American homes on the major networks were Israeli troops unrelentingly and for no particular reason destroying Lebanon. That every rocket from Lebanon targeted civilians, that the Israeli infrastructure of safe rooms and bomb shelters and the effort of private citizens to provide housing were what kept vast carnage from occurring in Israel, remained almost invisible.

Researcher Tamara Liebes found that both Israeli and American television reports (Israel during the first Intifada and US during the Gulf War) tended to focus on their own country's losses and even to block out the other side. At the same time, she found that while US television reporting on the Intifada did not block out either side and was therefore more balanced than when they were reporting on the American Gulf War, broadcasts did "clearly forground Palestinains and not Israelis," framing Palestinians as the weaker side struggling against the Israeli Goliath. In-depth reporting such as a newscaster going into families' homes with them, showcased Palestinians and not Israelis. News reports usually started with the number of Palestinian casualties.[34] During some Israeli conflicts, that Israelis had fewer casualties has been counted essentially as an unfair advantage, with television news displaying a running scorecard of the number of fatalities on each side, the lower death count for Israel supporting the storyline of Israel as the overbearing aggressor. This scorecard tallying for each side, often with accompaning graphics to empasize the differences, does not appear in US media for wars in other countries.[35]

Asymmetrical Media Coverage

A study of media coverage of the Second Lebanon War by Harvard scholars Marvin Kalb and Carol Saivitz, found that rather than offering objective reports, media actually became "fiery advocates," taking their information and photo opportunities from Hezbollah who tightly controlled what the press was allowed to see and--under threat—to say.[36] The researchers describe Israel as "victimized by its own freedoms," its culture of free speech and a free press actually working against it.

In this "asymmetrical conflict" between Israel's open society and the closed society ruled by Hezbollah, the narrative that Hezbollah presented in which Israel was the aggressor whose actions were "disproportionate" was followed by the press with only a few exceptions. Kalb and Saivitz note that after the first week, there was almost no mention of Hezbollah's initiation of the war and the focus was intensely on Lebanese civilians or Israeli military, a pattern that I've observed as well, for instance, in the coverage of the Palestinian terror wave against Israelis in the fall of 2015.[37] Kalb and Saivitz write, "Throughout the war, the rarest picture of all was that of a Hezbollah gorilla. It was as if the war on the Hezbollah side was being fought by ghosts." As a representative example, they describe a Hezbollah-led press tour:

> The point was to again use the media as a weapon in the propaganda war for public approval, and the media did not mind being used, though they were forced to pay a price. Foreign correspondents were warned, on entry to the tour, that they could not wander off on their own or ask

questions of any of the residents. They could only take pictures of sites approved by their Hezbollah minders. Violations, they were told, would be treated harshly. Cameras would be confiscated, film or tape destroyed, and offending reporters would never again be allowed access to Hezbollah officials or Hezbollah-controlled areas.

So far as we know, of all the reporters taken on this guided tour, reminiscent of the Soviet era, only CNN's Anderson Cooper described the rigid ground rules for what they were—an attempt to create and control a story.

And Hezbollah succeeded. All of the other reporters followed the Hezbollah script: Israel, in a cruel, heartless display of power, bombed innocent civilians. Casualties were high. Devastation was everywhere. So spoke the Hezbollah spokesman; so wrote many in the foreign press corps. At one point, apparently on cue, a Hezbollah minder signaled for ambulances to rev up their engines, set off their sirens and drive noisily down the street. The scene was orchestrated, designed to provide a photo op, and reporters went along for the ride.

Reporters stayed on the Israeli side of the border where they would be protected, and broadcasted Israel's impact on Lebanon. Or they stayed in the "rest of Beirut," that is, in the major part of the city that was undamaged and unmentioned in media reports, taking only brief, Hezbollah-controlled forays to sites the terrorist group wanted them to see and, in any case, knowing full well what was safe for them to report. They cited unnamed "sources" that were in fact Hezbollah itself and used casualty figures given to them by Lebanon, at times including the Israeli accounting as a possibly unsubstantiated "claim." Even years later, Lebanon makes no distinction between civilian and combatant casualties.[38] That reports on the Second Lebanon War, and on the Gaza conflict eight years later, treated Hezbollah and Hamas as reliable sources means that the public's overall sense of what took place during these conflicts likely remains distorted.[39]

The well-established Neighborhood Bully framing ensured that the storyline about the Second Lebanon war, a war that could not be described as arising from border disputes or occupation or settlements, differed not at all from the storyline of armed conflicts with Palestinians in Gaza or the West Bank. Even when Israelis deal with individual terrorists who commit knifings, car rammings, bombings, or shootings, strange contortions of language show up in mainstream press that seem to conflate terrorists with victims or that may obscure who committed an act of terror.

After Aryeh Kupinsky, Rabbi Avraham Shmuel Goldberg, Rabbi Kalma Levine, and Rabbi Moshe Twersky were hacked and shot to death while at prayer in the Har Nof neighborhood of Jerusalem, BBC's headline almost seemed to blame a building: "Jerusalem synagogue attack kills four Israelis." CNN broadcasted: "4 Israelis, 2 Palestinians dead in Jerusalem," making it impossible to know that the two Palestinians were shot by police before they killed even more people. CNN issued an apology after complaints about that particular headline.[40] They had also initially reported that the attack was on a mosque and before that had run their breaking news television report with "Israeli Police Shot . . . Killed two Palestinians."[41]

Keeping inside this framing causes media to invert victims and perpetrators or to equate them. Often this is accomplished by implying that Israelis are overreacting. The "knife intifada" in 2015–2016 was reported in such a way that one would need to read carefully through to the end of an article to understand that people were killed during the act of trying to kill others, or that the Israelis were responding to Palestinians who were shooting at them or trying to stab them. Though BBC's headline puts in quotes, "after attacking Israelis," we find out in the article that the Israeli soldiers were responding in one of the cases to someone firing a rifle at them and in another to two people firing machine guns.[42] Sometimes, the story provides no details and merely leaves the reader with doubt that there was any need for response since the attacks were simply "alleged."[43] On MSNBC while a photo is being broadcast plainly showing American viewers a knife-wielding terrorist, the commentator reporting from Jerusalem tells the audience, "Israel claims there was a knife but there's no evidence of this."[44]

It is hard to make sense of such headlines and reporting as they obscure rather than enhance our access to the news. That there are many, many instances of this kind of journalism can be understood, however, as resulting from the expectations for a particular framing. Journalist Matti Friedman published a powerful essay in *Tablet Magazine* in August, 2014, followed a few months later by an even more detailed piece in *The Atlantic* titled "What the Media Gets Wrong About Israel" that observes the framing of Israel from his lived experience as an Associated Press reporter. At AP he experienced the spotlight fallacy as well as the frame of the World's Worst;[45] the *Tablet* essay is titled "An Insider's Guide to the Most Important Story on Earth." He writes, "The cumulative effect has been to create a grossly oversimplified story—a kind of modern morality play in which the Jews of Israel are displayed more than any other people on earth as examples of moral failure."

Most directly, Friedman describes the mechanisms through which Israel has come to be presented as the Neighborhood Bully. In this case, once the bandwagon fallacy gets rolling, it is hard to go one's own way. The purported traits of the Israeli bully: willful use of excessive force, lack of restraint and, at the most extreme, disregard for civilians' lives are not conclusions drawn from observable evidence but they are the features of a required storyline. A shift from objective reporting to activism, what Friedman describes more gently as "helping," along with a specific political and social environment support the negative framing:

> Journalistic decisions are made by people who exist in a particular social milieu, one which, like most social groups, involves a certain uniformity of attitude, behavior, and even dress . . . In these circles, in my experience, a distaste for Israel has come to be something between an acceptable prejudice and a prerequisite for entry . . .

The bandwagon effect of such "uniformity" is further enforced by editors' demands for keeping to the "oversimplified story" of Israel as the aggressor. As with any framing, this involves promoting as well as suppressing some news items rather than others. Friedman identifies a number of stories that should have made headlines but that were rejected by the AP bureau because they didn't fit the framing of Israel as the bully.[46] The most obviously newsworthy example has to be Israel's 2009 peace offer. Journalist Mark Lavie had the "confirmed on the record" information about the peace offer but the story was "banned." According to Lavie, "AP suppressed a world-changing story for no acceptable reason...It fit a pattern, described by Matti [Friedman], of accepting the Palestinian narrative as truth and branding the Israelis as oppressors."[47]

Middle East media analyst and former reporter Tom Gross identifies the same "pattern" in BBC coverage that Lavie and Friedman describe from their Associated Press experiences. Again we see how distorted news frames are built not merely from what is included but from what is left out. During the Second Lebanon War, Gross wrote:

It is not just that the supposed crimes of Israel are completely overplayed, but the fact that this is a two-sided war (started, of course, by Hizbullah) is all but obscured. As a result, in spite of hundreds of hours of broadcast by dozens of BBC reporters and studio anchors, you wouldn't really know that hundreds of thousands of Israelis have been living in bomb shelters for weeks now, tired, afraid, but resilient; that a grandmother and her seven-year-old grandson were killed by a Katyusha during a Friday night Sabbath dinner; that several other Israeli children have died. You wouldn't have any real understanding of what it is like to have over 2,000 Iranian and Syrian rockets rain down indiscriminately on towns, villages and farms across one third of your country, aimed at killing civilians. You wouldn't really appreciate that Hizbullah, far from being some ragtag militia is in effect a division in the Iranian revolutionary guards and that it has a global terror reach, having already killed 114 people in Argentina . . .[48]

The Bandwagon Goes Off the Rails

Many things can go wrong when members of the media believe they are "helping" by keeping to a familiar, though misleading, storyline, while others simply follow these established patterns and those who are prepared to offer different perspectives are discouraged, even prevented, from doing so. With so much competition for stories and photos within a single, narrow frame, perhaps it's inevitable for the public not only to miss out on significant news but sometimes to see or hear "news" that hasn't actually happened.

Delivering the image of Israel as the always aggressive bully, at times requires knowing complicity with a made-up story as Matti Friedman observed:

> Cameramen waiting outside Shifa Hospital in Gaza City would film the arrival of civilian casualties and then, at a signal from an official, turn off their cameras when wounded and dead fighters came in, helping Hamas maintain the illusion that only civilians were dying.[49]

At other times it requires a willingness to accept, as true, accusations of Israeli brutality without need for evidence. Such was the case when a "massacre" was declared by the Palestinian Authority to have taken place in Jenin. After an especially devastating month during the second Intifada in which Hamas, Islamic Jihad, and al-Asqa Martyrs Brigade conducted 13 different terrorist attacks on Israeli civilians that included murdering 30 people and wounding 140 at a hotel Passover seder in Natanya and another 16 deaths in a restaurant in Haifa, Israeli ground troups were sent to Jenin because about a third of the terrorists had come from there.[50] The terrorist goups in Jenin had booby trapped the houses in the area prior to the hand-to-hand combat that ensued between the IDF and them and afterwards the Palestinian Authority announced that a massacre had taken place.[51]

Without any corroborating evidence, the claim of a "Jenin massacre" spread lightning fast around the world and news sites stated that hundreds or five hundred or maybe more Palestinians had been murdered, or that total devastation had been perpetrated on the people of Jenin by the IDF. The British media in particular issued dozens of articles supporting this claim, with gruesome verbiage about dead bodies piling up; the US press mostly did not join in. The UN began investigations and held emergency meetings.[52] Once the boobytraps were removed and observers could come in, the accurate IDF report was confirmed by the UN, Amnesty International and others, and was duly noted in the press: 39 Palestinian fighters, 14 civilians, and 23 IDF soldiers had been killed.[53]

If Israel were really the brutal bully it is made out to be, why would it be necessary to invent these stories? And an even more disturbing question: why would educated, rational people be willing to assume the worst about the Jewish state to the extent that they feel no need for observable evidence before using a term such as "massacre"?

Although focus on language helps us see how this comes about more readily than why it happens, it's clear that the Neighborhod Bully framing is promoted by the majority view, even "groupthink," that can take place in media as it did in the British press about Jenin, and as it does routinely at the UN where Israel is singled out more than any other country for condemnation. This pattern leads to the final, Worst in the World framing where accusations against the state of Israel pick up images and libels that have hounded Jews for most of their history, refashioned to fit current times. But before we examine this last frame, there is one more frame, one that can easily be overlooked because it gains its rhetorical power from appearing even-handed.

chapter 9

Faulty Analogy:
Frame of the Cycle of Violence

The Arab world is almost one thousand times larger than Israel, so the existence of Israel was never a threat to the Arab world, but it was a great opportunity to allow corrupt Arab leaders to keep their peoples distracted. This is the tragedy of the Arab nations, and they need to deal with it themselves—and we Palestinians are tired of paying the price for it.

Despite the Arabs' betrayal of the Palestinians, today's situation is in our hands. We cannot expect our situation to improve while terrorism continues and while Palestinian youth are taught to believe that killing Jews—even Jewish children—is honorable. It is not honorable, and such hate will never benefit the Palestinians.[1]

—Bassem Eid,
founder Palestinian Human Rights Monitoring Group

Thirteen-year-old Kobi, and his friend, Yossi, went hiking in the rocky hills around their neighborhood. When the boys didn't return home by evening, their parents called the police and a search party went out. The next day, the dead, bloodied bodies of the two boys were found in a cave; they had been bludgeoned to death with large rocks. Islamic Jihad claimed responsibility.

It was May of 2001 and the second intifada had been raging for eight months. Offering no evidence to warrant its headline, *The Guardian* published: "Israel vows revenge after boys are stoned to death." The headline emphasizes imagined Israeli violence and imagined "vows" rather than the murders that actually happened. The URL for this article, indicating an earlier version, accused as wildly: "Israel cries for vengeance."

> The Israeli-Palestinian conflict entered a new and bloody phase yesterday when the bodies of two teenage Jewish settlers were found bludgeoned to death in a cave on the West Bank.
>
> The brutal and callous nature of their deaths shocked an Israel that has almost become conditioned to violence. Their attackers, who bound them and possibly stoned them to death, dipped their fingers in their blood and smeared it on the cave walls.
>
> The murdered teenagers, Kobi Mandel [sic], 14, a US citizen, and Yossi Ishran, also 14, who was born in Israel, had skipped school on Tuesday to go hiking. The Israeli Prime Minister, Ariel Sharon, said he was revolted, adding ominously that their deaths marked a new escalation in the conflict.[2]

This article, like many others, reveals in nearly every line the agenda promoted by its reporting. *The Guardian* seems intent on implicating Israelis in a news piece on the murder of two Israeli middle-schoolers by Palestinian terrorists. Toby and Yossi are labeled "teenage Jewish settlers," surely an inappropriate descriptor for 7th graders, and strangely pejorative. "Settler," one of the many redefined words of Israel's framing, no longer refers to Israelis who settle—entirely legally—in areas of the West Bank designated by the 1993 Oslo accords as fully under Israeli control, as the Palestinian areas are fully under Palestinian control, but appears now to mean "interloper," or "troublemaker," even "colonizer." As we have seen, some academics apply the term "settler-colonial" ever more loosely until it encompasses all of Israel, helping to create the Neighborhood Bully and Refugee framing. Here, we learn from *The Guardian* that Israel "has almost become conditioned to violence," yet the writer does not discuss this violence: the on-going intifada whose only method is the intentional targeting of Israeli civilians. Nor does the article offer evidence that Israelis have "almost become conditioned" to it. The story implies, less subtly as it progresses, that Israelis can be held responsible for violence against them and also that they engage in an equal and revengeful violence.

Like most of the reports I read on the murders, this one identifies Kobi as a year older than he was and includes a qualifying doubt: "*possibly* stoned to death." ABC News accomplishes this doubt by giving the news within a quote: "The bodies of two Israeli teenagers killed in what Israeli police called a 'stoning to death' incident were found in a cave in the West Bank today, the latest in a bloody cycle of violence that has engulfed the region."[3] That this is part of a "cycle of violence" is simply asserted. *The Guardian* writer identifies Kobi as "a US citizen," rather than a dual-citizen in contrast to Yossi who "was born in Israel," perhaps encouraging readers to question Kobi's Israeli residence. Then, justifying the "revenge" accusation of the headline, the words of the Prime Minister are editorialized with "ominously."

"Escalation" in Sharon's statement, which otherwise would be seen as a comment on the escalating nature of violence against Israelis, now can be read to indicate something "ominous" forthcoming from Israel. To make sure we read it this way, writer Ewen MacAskill asserts "Palestinians on the West Bank were last night braced for retaliation by Israeli forces and revenge attacks by Jewish settlers."[4] In real life, Israeli police interrogated suspects, and "Jewish settlers" railed against their own government for not protecting them from terrorism. That same day there had been a demonstration in Jerusalem calling for better security. But *The Guardian* has a framework in which to fit Kobi's and Yossi's murders:

> The already hard-pressed Palestinians were on the receiving end of three Israeli army raids in Gaza yesterday. In one of them a three-month old baby, Reema Ahmed, was hit by a bullet in the Rafah refugee camp. Her condition was described as stable.

The funerals of the murdered boys were held last night. Pictures of the shy, smiling youngsters were handed round the mourners, adding to the festering desire for vengeance.[5]

This is the Cycle of Violence framing. For every violent action from one side, there must be violence from the other side. On the one hand, the cycle is endless. On the other, the cycle starts only as a result of Israeli action. Media reasonably might have reported on the murders of Kobi and Yossi within the context of the ongoing intifada, the terror war whose agenda was precisely this, the killing of civilian Israeli Jews. Instead, most often media told the story in the context of Israeli response to the intifada: that there were "raids in Gaza," that Palestinians were "hard-pressed," and most tenuously, that a baby in Gaza was accidentally injured. Luckily, Reema Ahmed was in "stable condition" that same day; the Palestinian hospital reported that she was injured by a piece of tank shrapnel. However, the IDF patrols who were "attacked with hand grenades" thrown at them by Palestinian fighters in the area of the Ahmed's house were using "light weapons," not tank guns, that day.[6] Media include baby Reema in their stories as if to create balance, or even a sense of equivalence between actions on each side. *The Washington Post* makes this intention explicit with commentary from Yasser Arafat and Saeb Ereket: "Today a small baby was exposed to the same crime," and "killing civilians is a crime, whether on the Palestinian or the Israeli side."[7]

For the Cycle of Violence framing to hold up, we must see these events as the same: an unintended injury that may or may not have occurred during a cross-fire between armed combatants and the Palestinian government promoted and honored murder of Israeli civilians.[8] Connections can always be made, of course: the concern of parents for their children, the human costs of wars, the need for peace, and more. Yet here, the press tries to connect the murders near the Israeli town of Tekoa with the Gaza incident and imagined Israeli bad character. We can assume that the location of Tekoa "over the green line" appears to give media greater license for this kind of reporting. However, the Cycle of Violence framing that suggests balance while at the same time holds Israel most to blame, shows up regardless of where the incidents occur.[9]

The Guardian describes these murders as "brutal and callus," yet applies terms of condemnation only to Israelis. "Conditioned to violence," "ominous," "retaliation," "revenge," "festering," and "vengeance" implicate Israelis as perpetuators, and ultimately, initiators of the cycle of violence.[10] That Kobi's mourners look at photographs becomes—with no supporting evidence—an indication of revengefulness. Astoundingly, at the end of the article we are given *"the"* reason why there is no peace. This is not presented as a quoted opinion of an authority or political analyst but simply is stated as fact: "The continued expansion of Jewish settlements on the West Bank and Gaza is the main obstacle to any deal."[11] At the least, in an article about the deliberate murder of Israeli children by Palestinian terrorists, additional "main" obstacles to peace might have been mentioned.

Five years after Kobi's death, I met his mother, Sherri Mandell, at a Hebrew course event in Jerusalem. Sherri spoke to the group in Hebrew and afterwards I had the chance to talk with her privately in English. It turned out that she had taught in the writing programs at Penn State and University of Maryland before she and her husband, Seth, who is a rabbi, had moved to Israel. She was warm and engaging. At that time she had published one book, *The Blessing of a Broken Heart* and since then has published another, *The Road to Resilience: From Chaos to Recovery.*[12] With Sherri Mandell's books and with the foundation they started, the Mandell's have turned their grief into positive as opposed to "revengeful" action, creating support for children and adults who have lost loved ones to terror. The Kobi Mandell Foundation runs summer camps and therapy groups, raising funds for these projects through "Comedy for Koby," performances by professional comics in the US and Israel, as Koby loved jokes.[13] Likewise, other major Israeli organizations such as One Family that provides ongoing support for victims of terror, and United Hatzalah that includes 4,000 doctors, medics, and first responders who volunteer during emergencies in Israel and internationally, were developed by Israeli survivors of terror who have chosen to dedicate themselves to helping others.[14]

Where's the Cycle?

Like the Jewish David that transformed after 1967 into Goliath in the language of framing Israel, the conflict since then has been routinely called a cycle of violence. The wording is so familiar and repeated so often that we may not notice how much distortion and inaccuracy is required to make the claim seem credible. This framing with its catchy phrase establishes itself even if we only scan the headlines: "The Problem of Gaza: An Endless Cycle of Violence" (*Time Magazine*); "Killings in Jerusalem Raise Fears of New Cycle of Violence (*The Economist*); "In Israel, Resignation to the Cycle of Violence" (*The Washington Post*).[15]

We may have a hard time remembering that cycle of violence is only a metaphor. It presents events as if analogous to a cycle, evoking the image of a wheel on which violence keeps firing round and round because each party reacts to the other. Though the image is cyclical, writers and speakers use the saying "tit-for-tat" interchangeably with cycle of violence, emphasizing that each side participates, back and forth, in equal measure.[16] Yet, it's a faulty analogy and, empirically, an inaccurate description of the conflict.

All of the framing of Israel distorts and mislabels. The overarching Conflict frame leaves out everything else about Israel and forces the conflict to center stage. The other frames misrepresent, by now perhaps we can't help but say, lie about the conflict, beginning with the false premise that it's a struggle over land rather than a struggle over the existence of a Jewish state of any size. Likewise, the Refugee frame hides the unique definitions of Palestinian refugees and makes invisible the Jewish refugees of the Middle

East and North Africa. Certainly, by the time we reach the Neighborhood Bully frame, if not before, any Israeli action has become suspect.

Although cycle of violence is a metaphor, in this framing it's used as a transparent descriptor, as simply another name for the conflict. Since rhetorical framing need not rely on factual evidence, it doesn't weaken the power of the frame that, actually, there is no cycle.

Author Micah Halpern notes the "calculus," rather than a "tit-for-tat" reaction, with which Israel determines whether or not to respond to attacks. Then, if the IDF does respond, they calculate how they will target fighters and commanders, or destroy control centers, while going "to great lengths not to injure innocents."[17] They may respond more forcefully if civilians have been harmed and may react in more limited ways to Fatah-connected than Hamas attacks because Fatah leaders at times are willing to negotiate while Hamas rules out negotiation.[18]

These careful calculations lead former Commander of the British Forces in Afghanistan Richard Kemp to describe the Israel Defense Forces as having done "more to safeguard the rights of civilians in a combat zone than any army in the history of warfare."[19] As Halpern explains:

> The objective of Hamas rockets is to wound, kill and frighten as many Israelis as possible. The objective of Israel's measured response is to target the specific forces who fired those rockets in a bid to protect its civilians. The difference is not just military—it is a moral response against an extremist and ideological agenda.[20]

Unlike underdog status, which may be primarily a matter of interpretation, whether or not there is a cycle of violence can be empirically examined. If a cycle exists, we would expect to find violence by one side causing violence by the other side and vise versa. Yet, academics who have studied the conflict using statistical analyses reach a firm conclusion:

Despite the popular perception that Palestinians and Israelis are engaged in "tit-for-tat" violence, there is no evidence to support that notion. Rather, the Israelis react in a predictable and statistically significant way to Palestinian violence against them, while Palestinian actions appear not to be related to Israeli violence . . .[21]

Language was not the focus of research by David A. Jaeger and M. Danielle Paserman; they wanted to know whether a cycle of violence really occurs. Analyzing fatalities data collected by the NGO B'tselem between 2000 and 2005, they found that the IDF did react to Palestinian attacks. However, Palestinians connected to Hamas, Islamic Jihad, Al-Asqa Martyrs Brigade (the military part of Fatah), and smaller groups did not react to IDF action and instead attacked Israelis in no predictable pattern.

These differences fit with the differing goals of each side. Jaeger and Paserman note that Palestinian paramilitary forces are "decentralized," making coordinated actions difficult, and significantly, that their goals would not be served by a tit-for-tat response:

. . . it is probably optimal for the Palestinians to randomize the timing of their response if they wish to increase the likelihood of inflicting costs on Israel. The effectiveness of terror attacks in disrupting day-to-day Israeli life is, almost by definition, greater if these attacks are unpredictable.[22]

By contrast, the Israeli Defense Forces are a centralized national military responsible for protecting the country, so violence against people in Israel does cause the IDF to respond predictably. Many attacks into Israeli territory occur without any Israeli counterresponse as the IDF assesses each situation. The researchers also "find no evidence of a short-term net deterrent effect of Israeli actions."[23]

Other studies by researchers from Harvard, New York University, University of California San Diego, and Hebrew University, use a kind of statistical analysis that differs from previous research. Their results even more dramatically refute claims of a cycle of violence. In fact, using italics they call their findings *"Not* a Cycle of Violence: An Episodic Analysis of the Gaza-Israel Conflict."[24]

Using United Nations security reports from 2007 to 2014, a period of time during which there were "over 16,000 Palestinian projectile launches" and "over 8,000 Israeli airstrikes, the researchers examined episodes of conflict between Israel and Gaza." Their results are statistically overwhelming. The violence is not "cyclically related: 91 percent of violent episodes are initiated by Gaza militant attacks and 84 percent of violent episodes end with a Gaza militant attack."[25]

The expressed goals of Hamas and of Israel align with these findings. Hamas and other jihadist groups advocate for a Middle East without Israel and without Jews, so initiating violence and only temporarily stopping it match their purposes: to make life unlivable for Israelis. These groups advocate killing Jews inside and outside of Israel. One need only look at the founding covenant of Hamas, its current governmental agenda,[26] to see that, as *The Atlantic* editor-in-chief Jeffrey Goldberg writes, the Hamas Covenant is "a frank and open call for genocide, embedded in one of the most anti-Semitic documents you'll ever read."[27] On Palestinian television, co-founder of Hamas Mahmoud Al-Zahar speaks clearly: "There is no place for you Jews among us, and you have no future among the nations of the world. You are headed for annihilation."[28]

In stark contrast, Israel's founding declaration sets goals to be "based on freedom, justice and peace" and to "guarantee freedom of religion, conscience, language, education and culture; it will safeguard the Holy Places of all religions . . ."[29] The IDF's "Mission and Ethics" statement includes as "Basic Values": "To defend the existence of the state of Israel, its independence, and the security of the citizens and residents of the state" and "...to protect human dignity. Every human being is of value regardless of his or her origin, religion, nationality, gender, status or position." Their operational

"Basic Points" include: "Combating terrorism"; "Very low casualty rate"; and "Desire to avoid war by [using] political means and a credible deterrent posture."[30] Goals, of course, do not always match results, but the current framing of Israel seems to require ignoring what Hamas and Israel actually strive for and what they publish as their official guidelines.

In line with their goals, Israel initiated violence only 9 percent of the time during the seven years of the "*Not* a Cycle" study. The vast majority of the time, a violent episode both started and ended with attacks on Israelis. Yet media obscure and even invert this pattern.

Cycles of Faulty Analogy

These statistical studies document what would already be visible to anyone watching or reading mainstream news, if media did not go to such lengths to maintain the Cycle of Violence framing. Lacking actual tit-for-tat responses and with only a small percentage of instances in which Israelis start an episode of violence,[31] the press seems to wait for Israeli action before news coverage begins. *Honest Reporting* calls this "It all started when Israel fired back."[32]

For example, after 35 rockets had been fired from Gaza into Israeli cities where they hit a school in Ashdod, injured many Israelis, and killed Moshe Ami, a father of four who lived in Ashkelon, Israel responded by targeting a Hamas training camp. The BBC reported, "Militants Killed in Israeli Air Strikes on Gaza."[33] Journalist Melanie Phillips critiques this coverage:

No mention of the Palestinian rocket attack on Ashdod last Wednesday. No mention of the 35 rocket attacks on Israel during the past day, nor the Israeli killed in Ashkelon. Instead, the BBC has given the false impression on its website that the Israelis initiated the attacks—and the only casualties it reported were Palestinian.[34]

When Israel does respond immediately to direct threats such as Iranian military aircraft coming into its airspace, reports tend to make Israeli action the start and focus of the episode. After the Israeli Air Force intercepted an armed Iranian drone that flew into Israel from Syria, misleading headlines like this one appeared: "Israel Launches Air Strikes Deep into Syria" leaving out mention of the Iranian drone to which Israel was responding.[35]

Yet when Israel delays response to a large amount of aggression against it and finally does start a military operation, the media "cycle" most often begins with Israel. During Israel's three-week counter-offensive, Operation Cast Lead, media focused on that three-week period, decontextualized from what had preceded it: more than 10,000 rockets fired into Israel from Gaza. *The New York Times*' very visually compelling report "The Toll in Gaza Day by Day" starts on the first day of Cast Lead without referring to the previous years of rocket fire,[36] the nearly 1,000 Israelis who had been injured during that time, or the 1,500 Israeli homes that had been damaged.[37]

The Cycle of Violence framing, however, does not depend merely on starting the cycle with Israeli action but on blurring the whole category of "violence" so that everyday distinctions no longer apply.

> . . . the picture is not clear. Every 'provocation' is seemingly preceded by another, a long progression of people on both sides making choices that have, taken as a whole, kept Israel and Gaza on a seemingly circular path of violence and recrimination.[38]

This perspective is attractive because it allows us to feel we are being even-handed and unbiased. It may be especially compelling for media since it seems to demonstrate balanced reporting.

But the above analysis from *The Washington Post* expects us to equate "provocation" with the "choices on both sides" that have kept the cycle going. To do so, not only must we accept that no one can tell how a particular, violent altercation started, we must also accept that no significant differences exist among kinds of violence or kinds of provocations. In rhetoric this is called a faulty analogy.

A faulty analogy is the mistake of arguing that because two things are the same or similar in one way, they are necessarily the same in other ways. In daily life we make distinctions about violence. We recognize that a fatal car accident and an intentional "car ramming" murder are unalike even though both cases result in violent deaths and people in mourning. We are able to see that the fighting of armed combatants is distinct from a violent attack on a civilian although people may be harmed with weapons in both cases. We don't equate someone whose job it is to protect a community building with someone who breaks into the building although the guard as well as the attacker may use violence. Common sense and our legal systems rely on these distinctions, and when a situation seems unclear, we examine the evidence, including the intentions for the violence. But framing Israel within the Cycle of Violence requires that such distinctions no longer hold; an illusion of evenhandedness overrides them.

In fact, the Cycle framing is not even-handed. To make the conflict into a story that follows a "circular path of violence and recrimination," self-defense needs to seem as provocative as the intentional killing of civilians.[39] Referring to the wave of Palestinian stabbings of Israelis in 2015 as "The Cycle of Violence in Israel," a *New York Times* staff editorial argues that "in the heat of stabbings, shootings, roadblocks, and checkpoints" breaking the cycle will be hard to achieve.[40] But roadblocks and checkpoints are not established in the heat the moment; they are routine measures intended to prevent violence. Nor in other settings is someone who tries to stop civilian deaths by shooting at a terrorist mid-stabbing spree considered part of a cycle of violence.

The saying, "one man's terrorist is another man's freedom fighter," likewise sounds balanced and unbiased. However, it confuses the method of fighting with the label of "freedom fighter."[41] Although no single, internationally agreed upon definition of terrorism exists, there are clear consistencies according to academics who have been compiling and examining scholarly definitions of terrorism since the 1970s. Nearly all definitions include "violence and force" and "political." Other frequent terms are "threats," "fears," "intentional" and "directed at non-combatants." These scholars, as well as US and UK government agencies, consider attacks on civilians for political goals to be terrorism.[42]

Terrorism is a complex subject but book length studies also include starting point definitions:

> Terrorism simply means deliberately and violently targeting civilians for political purposes . . . if the primary tactic of an organization is to target civilians, it deserves to be called a terrorist organization, regardless of the political context in which it operates or the legitimacy of the goals it seeks to achieve.[43]

It is quite possible to be a terrorist, that is, someone who targets civilians "in order to achieve political aims" and also be considered a freedom fighter. At the same time, freedom fighters can be those who use negotiation and peaceful means. As Professor Boaz Ganor, Director of the International Institute for Counter-Terrorism in Israel writes:

> The claim that a freedom fighter cannot be involved in terrorism, murder and indiscriminate killing is, of course, groundless. A terrorist organization can also be a movement of national liberation, and the concepts of "terrorist" and "freedom fighter" are not mutually contradictory.[44]

When media avoid the word terrorism for attacks on Israelis, yet use the term for similar attacks elsewhere, the effect on viewers and readers is significant. The words "militants," "shooters," "gunmen," or even using only the name of the particular, recognized terror group instead of the pejorative word "terrorist" help maintain the balanced façade of the Cycle of Violence.[45] A terrorist clearly poses a threat to innocent people, so we expect defensive response, including firing back. Less clear may be the need to defend against a "militant" or a member of a group whose acronym means nothing to us.

After complaints that BBC does not report that terrorists attack Israelis though they do report that terrorists attack people in other countries, the BBC wrote: ". . . to use the term, 'terror attack' or similar terms might be seen as taking sides. There are those who might consider the actions of the Israeli government to be considered as terrorist acts."[46] This is a fascinating admission. BBC's sense of fairness extends to Hamas and Islamic Jihad but not to Israelis.

Although out of synch with many terrorism scholars and with the UK and US government definitions,[47] BBC's view does align, for instance, with a Marxist perspective in which Western countries are the world's biggest terrorists because they use their huge power in the exploitive services of capitalism. It corresponds, as well, with the worldview popularized by Edward Said in which the West projects its own violence onto Arabs.[48] Looking through this perspective one may be unable to see citizens of Israel as victims of terror. Within such theories, everyday distinctions like the ones I described, and the widely accepted definition of terrorism as the violent targeting of civilians for a political agenda, can be labeled simplistic or culturally insensitive. Regardless of philosophical discussion of the meanings of terrorism, BBC and other mainstream news bureaus most often do not find themselves unable to identify terrorism when it takes place in countries other than Israel.[49]

How to Keep the Cycle Turning

One of the worst aspects of the Cycle framing is its dehumanizing caricature of Israelis and Palestinians. The cycle seems to dominate as if the participants have no control over their actions. It assumes that Hamas and the other terror groups are fighting Israel on behalf of Palestinians rather than in their own dictatorial interests. Israeli self-defense must be seen as excessive or there would be no way to "balance" self-defense with intentional murders of civilians and children. And, excusing terror as just part of a seemingly inevitable cycle discredits Palestinians who focus on leading their lives and have no interest in participating in violence.

Palestinian human rights advocate Bassem Eid, whose words begin this chapter, clarifies how far removed from the lived experiences of Palestinians are those who claim to support Palestinians by boycotting Israel and by treating settlements as the problem.

Outside Israel and the Palestinian territories, much of the world sees us through the lenses of the Boycott, Divest, Sanction ("BDS") movement—which Palestinians largely do not support. Since the Palestinian-controlled economy is so weak, many Palestinians are employed by Israeli firms—the only source of good jobs for Palestinians. The BDS movement, however, is not interested in hearing the Palestinians' pleas because they would rather see Palestinians live in poverty than relent in their pursuit against Israel . . .

The BDS movement and other anti-Israel activities use Israeli settlements in the West Bank to demonize Israel, but they do not seem to understand that the building of settlements benefits Palestinians. The settlements are a great source of well-paying jobs . . . Jews residing in the West Bank is not a problem. Why should it be? Muslims live all over the world, so why should there be areas where Jews are not allowed? That would be apartheid.[50]

Furthermore, it is not as if the governments that support and incite terrorism do so to make a good life for their own citizens. Eid points to the lack of freedom and democracy under both the dictatorship of Hamas and the "corrupt" and "weak" leadership of the Palestinian authority:

If so-called pro-Palestinian activists truly want to help the Palestinians, then they should demand freedom, human rights, democracy, and justice for the Palestinians. They should demand that the incitement of Palestinians stop. They should assist Israel in creating jobs in the West Bank for Palestinians. They should assist Palestinians in developing an economy while ensuring that the money is not used to enrich the terrorists' rule or to augment the terrorists' arsenal. They should encourage Palestinians to live in peace with Jews. If and when these things happen, a permanent solution will be found. Until then it is waste of time to even talk about it.[51]

So far, the talk continues, unabated. Rather than amplifying the voices of those like Bassem Eid, who address the everyday concerns of Palestinians who want good jobs and a good quality of life, we get intense media focus on conflict and the increasingly hard to sustain Cycle of Violence framing.

This distorted framing has even expanded so that events consisting entirely of attacks on Israelis and attempts to stop attacks while they're in progress create a cycle. For example, CNN published "West Bank's cycle of violence," a video embedded in an article that begins, "After a period of relative calm, the Israeli-Palestinian conflict has reignited, leaving five people dead and several others injured in 48 hours."[52] Of the "five people dead," four were in the process of attacking Israelis, three by stabbing their victims and one by intentionally ramming his car into Israeli drivers. The fifth was a suspect shot while Israel police were trying to apprehend him. All the injured were Israeli. The story is illustrated by the "cycle of violence" video of Palestinians hurling rocks at Israeli soldiers in Hebron. The reporter in the video tells us, "Jewish soldiers stationed around the settlement in the heart of the Old City battle it out with boys and young men" in a "low intensity struggle with no end in sight."[53]

Over the time that I have been analyzing the Cycle of Violence framing, it has become so fully an acceptable way of talking about the conflict that a tit-for-tat response from Israel is no longer necessary. Any defense—stopping further disaster by apprehending or shooting at a perpetrator in mid-killing spree—creates a "cycle." In fact, the deaths of the attackers are emphasized as the most significant part of the story.

The New York Times published "Anger in a Palestinian Town Feeds Cycle of Violence," a human-interest story about "young people" who stab Israelis. The piece uses "Mr." before a named terrorist but no such formality before the name of a victim. The article explains that Palestinians in the town of Sa'ar "embrace the young dead as martyrs to the cause of Palestinian resistance" and reports on "young Palestinians killed from Sa'ar . . . with a long history of resistance to Israel." An accompanying photo caption reads, "Sa'ar is *heralded* as a hotbed of the latest wave of stabbings."[54] This "cycle" consisted of "young Palestinians" who were killed or arrested while trying or succeeding to kill Israelis.

A few of the victims are named but without the empathy afforded the terrorists. The *Times* explains the "cyclical violence":

> . . . for example, Dafne Meyer, an Israeli mother of six was stabbed to death in her home in a settlement just south of Hebron (a 15 year-old Palestinian boy was arrested) and Israeli soldiers killed a Palestinian who attempted a stabbing near Nablas and arrested a Palestinian woman they said had approached a checkpoint with a knife.[55]

Daphne Meir's 16-year-old killer said Daphne fought back but "I stabbed her until I could no longer pull the knife out of her body . . . I would have continued stabbing her and if I saw another Jew I would stab and murder him."[56] The *Times'* story of a "cycle of violence" is actually the story of murders followed by arrests or attempts to stop murders in progress.

Like the Neighborhood Bully framing, the Cycle of Violence frame suggests that, for Israelis, no defensive response is allowable, even one whose "violence" does not consist of shooting back but of passive measures attempting to thwart further attacks from occurring: putting up entrances through which cars and pedestrians must be checked; creating check-points on highways; or building the famous security fence to place a barrier re-routing traffic and pedestrians to central entry points into Israeli cities.

More and more frequently, the Cycle of Violence framing portrays Israel as at fault for the whole cycle: both for its own actions and for actions against its citizens. Although the "tit-for-tat" framing remains, there doesn't seem to be any comment or action on the part of Israel that does not contribute to the cycle. The Cycle of Violence frame no longer consists of "it all started when Israel fired back." No firing is needed for Israel to have initiated the cycle.

Some news sites have made explicit their decision to endorse this fallacy, though, of course not by calling it a fallacy. Here, for instance, a *Los Angeles Times* staff editorial laments the "tit-for-tat mentality" of a "continuing cycle of violence." The editorial begins, "One of the most depressing characteristics of the Palestinian-Israeli relationship is the self-destructive tit-for-tat mentality that often seems designed to keep the conflict alive rather than to end it."

> We're currently witnessing the cycle in real time. On Saturday, five members of an Israeli family living in the West Bank settlement of Itamar, near the Palestinian city of Nablus, were killed, including an 11-year-old boy, a 4-year-old boy and an infant girl, presumably by Palestinian militants. In response to this brutal tragedy, the Israeli government announced that it would build 500 more houses in existing settlements in the West Bank . . . Which is worse—stabbing children to death or building new houses in West Bank settlements? The answer is obvious. But that's not the point. The point is that no matter how abhorrent the murders are, it serves no purpose to aggravate the provocation that led to them in the first place.[57]

This is remarkable. According to the writer, the Fogel family's house caused their murder. The terrorists, who were connected to the PFLP (Peoples

Front for the Liberation of Palestine) are not so much responsible as "provoked." This "cycle" does not start with the murders but with the provocation of houses in the neighborhood of Itamar. The editorial notes that there is no question but that murder and announcing plans to build houses in Israeli neighborhoods are not comparable actions and yet, "that's not the point." The writer equates them anyway, claiming that houses in neighborhoods legally under full Israeli control have provoked the murders.

There was enough criticism from readers of this editorial that the *LA Times* responded the following week, doubling down on its claims and reiterating that they didn't mean to equalize murders with talk of building houses. "But as for the idea that a cycle exists," the editors write, "one only has to read this week's news."[58] This, of course, is the problem. For the news is packaged in the Cycle of Violence frame.

The editors conclude: "To deny that there's a cycle of violence seems pointless."[59] As evidence they link to *The Guardian*'s coverage that week of a terror attack in Jerusalem that injured 39 people and killed a UK citizen, Mary Jean Gardner, a Christian Bible translator who was studying at Hebrew University. Hodaya Aslan, who was 14 at the time, died of her injuries in 2017. *The Guardian* headline reads: "Israel Warns of Aggressive Response to Jerusalem Blast."[60]

Keeping Score

American and UK media report on the casualties of many conflicts but I have not found cases other than those conflicts involving Israel where media use a running scorecard, almost like a tally during sporting events, to count up casualties on each side. Israel's fewer losses then become evidence that the Jewish state overreacts or uses "excessive" force. As a CNN report asks, "Why are the death tolls lopsided?"[61]

Although we can learn from media sources how many people are killed in other conflicts, this information does not usually appear in a tally sheet as a kind of gruesome competition. CNN's explanation of the ongoing conflict between India and Pakistan over Kashmir includes a timeline of the conflict since 1947 and reports, "violence has killed over 47,000 people," but adds no further demographics.[62] The same year that *The New York Times* computed the "Daily Toll" between Gaza and Israel,[63] they reported on the 191,000 people killed in Syria between 2011 and 2014 without adding up how many were killed on the sides of that war.[64] Media did not create a balance sheet of American and allied forces versus Afghan civilian casualties.[65] There would have been public outcry if they had since American soldiers were not targeting Afghan civilians but were fighting the Taliban and al-Qaeda militias.

Yet, we put up with wildly misleading reporting about Israelis as they fight Hamas and Islamic Jihad militias within civilian areas. Although CNN's headline cites a "Hamas-Israel War," only the IDF appear to be combatants; there's no discussion of Palestinian combatants. That the targets of Hamas rockets are only civilians is not mentioned. The article appears to treat Israeli focus on protecting the residents of Israel as an unfair advantage. And when the IDF warns Gazan civilians to leave before they strike a building where Hamas has set up rocket launchers, CNN describes Israel's warnings, phone calls, texts, "roof knocks," and leaflets *not* as measures taken to prevent civilian casualties but as "a measure of just how powerful Israel is in this battle."[66]

The BBC acknowledges, ". . . it is hard to say with certainty at this stage how many of the dead in Gaza were civilians and how many were fighters." Their solution to this problem is to create a bar graph contrasting the deaths of all Palestinians with those of Israeli soldiers. In another bar graph, BBC has one category for Palestinian civilians and one called "Other" that includes Palestinian police, unnamed fighters, and those who may have been participating in fighting. As a result, these graphs don't include the category "Palestinian fighters" at all.[67]

The purpose of the scorecards seems to be to highlight that the casualties are "lopsided,"[68] that, uniquely among the conflicts of the world, the numbers on each side of this conflict should be evenly balanced. With little or no media concern for identifying armed Palestinian fighters among the casualties nor for noting that the Hamas *targets* are civilians,[69] the brightly colored graphics may lead us to accept the word, "lopsided," as appropriate, as if some major problem would be solved if only there were more dead Israelis.

Atheist philosopher and neuroscientist Sam Harris remarks that he has been questioned many times about why he does not speak against Israel, as some of his readers and podcast followers assume he might. His answer, the conclusion to which I've quoted below, articulates why the Cycle of Violence framing so misrepresents Israel and the conflict. Harris disapproves of religions including Judaism, but his focus is on the "hugely consequential moral difference between Israel and its enemies."

> What would the Israelis do if they could do what they want? They would live in peace with their neighbors, if they had neighbors who would live in peace with them. They would simply continue to build out their high tech sector and thrive . . .
>
> What do groups like ISIS and al-Qaeda and Hamas want? They want to impose their religious views on the rest of humanity. They want to stifle every freedom that decent, educated, secular people care about. This is not a trivial difference. And yet judging from the level of condemnation that Israel now receives, you would think the difference ran the other way.
>
> This kind of confusion puts all of us in danger. This is the great story of our time. For the rest of our lives, and the lives of our children, we are going to be confronted by people who don't want to live peacefully in a secular, pluralistic world, because they are desperate to get to Paradise, and they are willing to destroy the very possibility of human happiness along the way. The truth is, we are all living in Israel. It's just that some of us haven't realized it yet.[70]

chapter 10

Poisoning the Well:
Frame of the World's Worst

. . . the hatred of Israel expressed in our streets, on our campuses, in our
newspapers, on our radios and televisions, and now in our theatres.
A discriminatory, over-and-above hatred, inexplicable in its hysteria
and virulence whatever justification is adduced for it; an unreasoning,
deranged and as far as I can see irreversible revulsion that is poisoning
everything we are supposed to believe in here—the free exchange of
opinions, the clear-headedness of thinkers and teachers, the fine tracery of
social interdependence we call community relations, modernity of outlook,
tolerance, truth . . .
But I am not allowed to ascribe any of this to anti-Semitism. It is, I am
assured, 'criticism' of Israel, pure and simple.

—Howard Jacobson
British novelist,
winner of the Booker Prize for *The Finkler Question*

A woman walking past us on San Francisco's Montgomery Street stops to
yell at me standing inches away. "What's the difference, this side and the
other side?!" She points across the street. And before I can speak she answers herself: "There's no difference! Right? Right?"

We're standing in the rain near the Israeli Consulate and the woman is shouting amid the chorus of shouts from the other side of the street. Here on the quiet side we are the counterprotest, maybe thirty of us to their hundred and fifty or more. They're pushing against the police barriers, yelling, "Viva, viva, intifada!" and "From the river to the sea, Palestine will be free!" We just stand there holding signs that read "Hamas: stop using Gaza as a launching pad" and "We stand for Israel; we stand for peace," our American and Israeli flags unprotected from the rain. The increasingly angry crowd across the street continues screaming, many of the screamers presenting the backs of their hands to us with their middle fingers extended.

Surely the woman who has chosen me to question sees or at least hears some differences. "What?" she yells, "What's it about?"

And although I have talked about this for years—I'm even writing a book on this very topic, which means I've struggled through thousands of words about the situation—the moment seems to demand the fewest possible words and I blurt out: "We think Israel should live; they want to kill us."

"Ha! You don't want to kill them?"

"No, no way!" I answer just as the crowd across the street roars, "Zionist scum, your time has come!"[2]

I had joined new friends I'd made in the Bay Area who organize counter-protests, like this one where anti-Israel locals gathered across the street from the Israeli Consulate. My friends, leaders of the San Francisco Voice For Israel/Stand With Us groups, who had far more stamina and plain nerve than I, went frequently to hold signs at the Berkeley campus or in San Francisco representing the larger group of Americans who disagree that "from the river to the sea" is the scope of Palestine.[3] I find it frightening to be faced with the shouting, the threatening verbal assault. I'm also not happy with what I said to the woman questioning me. Maybe no one was thinking murder while shouting the usual slogans. Perhaps the protesters did not take their catchphrases literally. I certainly hadn't when I first noticed bumper stickers in Berkeley that read "Israel Out of Palestine!" Maybe they viewed their protest as a kind of sport, cheering on their team. Although cheering on an intifada is a clear call for killing civilians, given the Neighborhood Bully and Cycle of Violence framing, the protesters likely saw any Israeli response to attacks on its citizens as unacceptable.

The shouting unnerves me because I do hear these words literally and feel their power to inspire or, at least, support terror bombings and attacks on people sitting in cafes or standing at bus stops or walking down the street. I only hope that the protesters themselves did not actually believe what they were shouting. Of course, on that day we were lucky. At other events the shouts have included, "Hamas! Hamas! Jews to the gas!"[4] I can't think of multiple ways to interpret that one.

The ability to consider all of Israel as Palestine, to erase any legitimacy for Israel, rests at least in part on a manipulation of language: what might have been political or policy discussion instead becomes mere accusation. One skips past a hundred years of internationally sanctioned legal decisions, including legal agreements between the Israelis and Palestinians, ignores Jewish and Arab history, and reaches the current discourse in which protesters shout outside the Israeli Consulate or academics calmly claim that—in accordance with the maps used in Palestinian schools, media, and government—there is no Jewish state.[5] Or at least, there shouldn't be.

To American ears, perhaps "Jewish state" sounds undemocratic. But many, many democratic countries, including England, Iceland, Costa Rica, and Finland, have a state religion. Israel, however, does not have a state religion but uniquely defines itself as "the nation state of the Jewish people." As is the norm for other democracies, in Israel, the majority religion's holidays are often also national holidays, while at the same time, minority religions have full freedoms and their own religious authorities. The designation "nation state of the Jewish people" acknowledges that Israel is not a religious state but a democratic Jewish country. Interconnected in the word "Jewish" is religion and at the same time all the qualities of peoplehood; the comparison to First Nations people is instructive. Jews likewise have unique and ancient traditions, customs, foods, rituals, religious practice, ancestral lines, a world creation story, religious objects, as well as genetic markers, a separate language, and a specific land. The majority of Jews in both Israel and the US define themselves as culturally or ethnically rather than religiously Jewish.[6]

"From the river to the sea" had been familiar to me for at least a decade before I accepted its literal meaning, before I began acknowledging the enormous difference between advocating for the establishment of an independent, Palestinian state and advocating for a Palestinian state in place of Israel. The latter, with support out on the street in San Francisco, aligns against "two states for two peoples" between the Jordan River and the Mediterranean Sea. This anti-Israel alignment and its accompanying language give the Jewish state a uniquely negative position in the world.

Character Attack

Renowned legal scholar Alan Dershowitz describes the status of Israel as "the Jew among the nations." Professor Dershowitz doesn't need to explain his wording, for "Jew" across much of the world has never stopped being a pejorative word.

> No nation in the history of the world that has faced comparable threats to its survival—both external and internal—has ever made greater efforts at—and has ever come closer to—achieving the high norms of the rule of law. Yet no civilized nation in the history of the world—including totalitarian and authoritarian regimes—has ever been as repeatedly, unfairly, and hypocritically condemned and criticized by the international community as Israel has been over the years.[7]
>
> Privately admired for its pioneering spirit, intelligence, aggressiveness and tenacity, the state of Israel has been publically condemned as racist, militant, xenophobic, uncompromising, authoritarian, and stiff-necked.[8]

Dershowitz has returned to this assessment many times and has pointed out that the familiar tropes of anti-Semitism are now visited upon the Jewish State.[9] These extreme accusations are not about actual Israeli actions or policies but more accurately can be described as character attacks. These also include turning Israel's positive contributions into signs of wrongdoing:

> The core of classic anti-Semitism is that everything the Jews do is wrong and everything that is wrong is done by Jews . . . For the anti-Semite both capitalism and communism are Jewish plots . . . the Jews are both too docile having allowed themselves to be led to the slaughter like sheep and too militant having won too many wars against the Arabs . . . When Israel sent help to tsunami and hurricane victims, the Jewish state was accused of merely trying to garner positive publicity calculated to offset its mistreatment of Palestinians. When Israeli medical teams save the lives of Palestinian children, they must be up to no good . . .[10]

I identify this perspective as The Frame of the World's Worst. The rhetorical move it suggests is a form of character attack (*ad hominem*) called "poisoning the well." In argument this is a preemptive trap that discredits you so that you have no real opportunity to be heard. What you have to say is made irrelevant by charges that are already laid out against you.

Although the frame of the World's Worst is the culmination of the other framing, it may be the first perspective some university students encounter about Israel. A student may arrive on campus never having thought about Israel and knowing nothing in particular about the country only to be presented with Israel as the worst place in the world, the one country deserving boycott. Supporters of Israel can find themselves in the position of arguing against a caricature, a most evil place, because the language of poisoning the well is necessarily negative and hyperbolic, in this case made up of the wild range of accusations that leads Professor Dershowitz to use the phrase, "Jew among the nations."

Perhaps this last and most extreme framing is inevitable. For all the other frames to some degree are infected by the possibilities of this one, beginning with the Spotlight on Conflict that focuses relentlessly on Israel showing it in the worst light, to the excesses of the Neighborhood Bully and Cycle of Violence framing. In retrospect, it was the language of this framing that set me onto my long journey tracking public rhetoric about Israel. For this is the frame within which it's unremarkable to equate Israeli Jews with Nazis and a multicultural democracy with apartheid South Africa.

Examples of the World's Worst frame abound in anti-Israel discourse from the Middle East and are prevalent in the language of boycott activism. Western mainstream media, too, spread slanders that otherwise would be recognized as conspiracy theory or more likely would be seen as lies. It is the bizarre perspective within which *The Independent* builds an article out of accusations that Israel has cut off water supplies affecting Palestinians during Ramadan.[11] The article does include an Israeli statement about the actual culprit: a broken main pipe already repaired.[12] Inside this framing where claims of Israeli misdeeds are believed without any need for verification, the *Daily Mail* publishes the charge that southern Israel's dams have been opened intentionally to flood homes in Gaza. In reality, there are no dams in southern Israel to open; rainstorms caused the flooding.[13]

At the UN, Israel is framed as the world's worst country. It is the only country singled out by the World Health Organization for condemnation and, in 2017, the only country in the world condemned as a violator of women's rights! From 2012 through 2015, the UN General Assembly passed 97 resolutions against countries, of which 85 were against Israel. In 2018, the General Assembly condemned Israel 21 times and Hamas not at all. Between 2006 and 2016 more than half of the Human Rights Council's 137 resolutions were leveled against Israel,[14] the same country recognized by the United Nations as the world's leading first responder of emergency humanitarian medical aid.[15]

In academe, 40,000 collaborations took place between researchers at

American and Israeli universities from 2006 to 2016, a 45 percent increase from the previous decade. Medicine was the top field in which Israelis and Americans collaborated, followed by many of the sciences, mathematics, and computer science.[16] This ever-growing, scientific collaboration stands in marked contrast to the actions of other academics who single out Israeli universities for boycott, apparently willing to threaten university support for their colleagues' research.[17] Fortunately, hundreds of university administrators have made clear their opposition to academic boycott of Israel.[18]

Spy-Fish, Mossad Dolphins, and Other Evils

Inside the frame of the World's Worst, condemnation of one country of the world—for its very existence—becomes normalized. The exclusion of one nation from the family of nations becomes a reasonable possibility while the annihilationist rhetoric that faces Zionism, and no other nationalism, becomes uncontroversial. Tellingly, as Alan Dershowitz and others observe, the traditional libels against Jews are updated for use against the world's only Jewish state.

Criticizing Israeli policies, identifying internal and external problems facing the country, or pointing out Israel's limitations fall *outside* this framing. No actual Israeli policy is under scrutiny within the frame of the World's Worst. No actual issues are up for debate. It is a frame that focuses our attention on what has not happened, on mere accusation. As such, it may be the most important framing of Israel to notice. Melanie Philips describes it when she writes in *The World Turned Upside Down*:

> Israel stands proxy for a rational and moral outlook because, of all the causes in the world, it alone has been singled out for systematic demonization built on fabrication, distortion and misrepresentation. If people stand truth and logic on their heads over Israel, it is very likely that they will do so elsewhere . . .[19]

There is a genre of this framing that is actually comical. Here, the Israeli army or government or most often, Mossad, is accused of sending birds as spies, or sending animals to cause problems in various places. It isn't hard for most media to see these claims as nonsense:

> This just in: Saudi Arabia has arrested a bird on charges of spying for Israel. According to the newspaper *Al Weeam*, the alleged spy is a vulture . . . discovered to have a leg bracelet and a transmitter marked 'Tel Aviv University' . . . Some might be tempted to believe Israel's story, which is that the bird was part of a scientific study tracking the movement of vultures in the region. But not the Saudi press . . . The vulture, said *Al Weeam*, was most likely part of 'a Zionist plot.' (*The Washington Post*)[20]

Or this, one of my favorites:

> Sudanese authorities say they have captured an Israeli spy in the town of Kereinek, but Israeli authorities have cast doubt on the claim, noting that the alleged Mossad agent is covered in feathers and weighs less than thirty pounds. (ABC News)[21]

Jordan-based, independent news outlet *Al Bawaba News* published "You'd be surprised by how many animals are arrested for being Israeli spies." The article lists a number of animals "arrested for espionage" including "probably the most bizarre of the alleged spying incidents," what was at first identified as a "Zionist spy duck."[22]

Other accusations are quickly noticed as "wacky conspiracy theories" as *Newsweek* calls this "gem" from Egypt's Governor of South Sinai: "What's being said about the Mossad throwing the deadly shark into the sea to hit Egyptian tourism is not out of the question. But it needs time to confirm."[23]

Hamas claimed it captured an Israeli spy dolphin fully equipped with a camera and a device with arrows, according to the Palestinian newspaper,

Al Quds.[24] A number of news sites reported by quoting *Al Quds* and using photos of the friendly looking dolphins "purportedly conducting 'a spying mission.'" Media connected this claim to others about Israeli spy birds, making clear that this story likewise was laughable.[25]

There is, however, a rather thin line these funny allegations straddle between what is quickly dismissed and what is taken seriously. It "would be laughable if it weren't so dangerous" an Israeli official remarked when asked about another wacky, animal claim. This one has been reported many times in the Palestinian press: that Jews raise thousands of wild boars and then release them to destroy Palestinian crops. "Every night they [the Israelis] release wild pigs against us. Why are they doing this to us?"

Raising pigs, at least for religious Jews, would be impossible and in any case the claim is obviously ridiculous. But the real story is that Palestinian President Mamoud Abbas is the source of the above quote. The Israeli official said Abbas's "remarks were dangerous because 'they fit into a consistent and ongoing pattern of incitement.'"[26]

The Problem of Libels and Hoaxes

When Israel is framed as the worst place in the world, complex and tedious issues, investigations, or discussions are no match for outrageous charges of wrongdoing. The hyperbolic language with which the Jewish state by its very existence is presumed guilty preempts rational discourse. Indeed, that is the purpose of "poisoning the well."

This rhetorical strategy actually gets its name from the way Jews in the Middle Ages were accused of *literally* poisoning wells and causing the Black Plague. These accusations led to the slaughter of thousands of Jews and the destruction of Jewish communities in Europe in the 14th century. It is one of the "blood libels" in which Jews were accused of murdering non-Jews, particularly children.[27]

These libels can reappear in current times, in some cases couched in academic language,[28] in others, as political attack. In 2016, Mahmoud Abbas charged Israelis with plotting to poison Palestinian drinking water. He received a standing ovation for a speech to the European parliament during which he said that Israeli rabbis had called on their government to poison Palestinian water. In its report on the speech, Reuters clearly does not take Abbas's claims seriously and writes that his statement "appeared to be an invocation of a widely debunked media report that recalled a medieval anti-Semitic libel."[29]

However, if the accusations had mounted, especially since the President of the Palestinian Authority had made the charge, obvious falsehoods might have built into a full-blown hoax like the famous fake story in 1983 when Israelis were accused of poisoning Palestinian school girls. It was a complete hoax that anyone had been poisoned (medical staff and scientists found no evidence whatsoever of any poisoning) yet European media reported the claims as if they were true.[30]

Abbas apologized for his accusation—he had named a council of rabbis that doesn't exist, for one thing—and the Western press had not taken the story seriously. What has not received attention in the Western press is that Abbas has never recanted the claims of his doctoral dissertation titled, *The Other Side: the Secret Relationship Between Nazism and Zionism*; in fact, he has reasserted that rather than trying to get Jews out of Nazi Germany, Zionists were Nazi collaborators. He also denies that six million Jews were murdered and accuses Jews of exaggerating, for their own political purposes, his (completely unfounded) estimation that there were no more than one million murders.[31] Somehow, Abbas continues to be called a moderate.

Some accusations inside the frame of the World's Worst are not so deadly but are equally untrue. The claim that somewhere there are "Jewish only roads" should be impossible to assert since no one would be able to find such a road. It should be obvious that all roads in Israel are open to everyone living in and visiting Israel. In the West Bank, there are many places where

Israelis are not allowed. You see signs that warn Israelis not to enter Area A where nearly all the Palestinian towns are located. Some Palestinian roads in the West Bank are off limits to Israelis and some roads that connect Israeli neighborhoods are off-limits to Palestinians. Journalist Michael J. Totten, who has reported for years from the Middle East, writes that these roads are:

> *not just for Jews. Israeli Arabs can drive on them*, and so can non-Jewish foreigners, including Arab and Muslim foreigners. Palestinians were once able to drive on them but have not been allowed to do so since the second intifada, when suicide bombers used them to penetrate Tel Aviv and Jerusalem in order to massacre people.[32]

The slander of "Jewish only roads" poisons the well so that discussion of Israel becomes focused on problems that do not exist. The shift of language here, substituting "Jewish" for "Israeli" has spread this falsehood widely.[33]

What I have found most shocking as I continued to research has been how readily wild claims about Israelis become acceptable. Even play-acting an injury can show up as news. Over many years, Professor Richard Landes has compiled examples of for-the-cameras performances that find their way into mainstream news.[34] Filmmaker Pierre Rehov has documented how reports from Gaza and the Palestinian Authority, places that lack of freedom of the press, distort views of Israel worldwide.[35]

Well known is the story that an IDF soldier or soldiers shot for 45 minutes at a 12-year-old boy while he and his father crouched behind a barrel. Within a few hours, this charge of Israeli brutality was cemented and has not been undone. In spite of detailed evidence that the claim was unfounded, and in spite of later investigations clarifying that the position of the lookout station where the IDF soldiers were standing made it impossible for any of the soldiers there to have shot at Mohammed al Dura,[36] the incident is used to demonstrate the evils of the IDF. Many people devoted years of time to countering the accusation: Richard Landes, Pierre Rehov, writer, Nidre Poller, and especially, Philippe Karsenty, founder of the French media watch group Media-Ratings.[37] But within the framing of Israel as the World's Worst, impossible and improbable evil behavior on Israel's part can seem believable.

Where is Israel-Palestine?

Primarily in academic circles, a linguistic invention has created a place called "Palestine-Israel" or "Israel-Palestine," sometimes written with a slash and sometimes with a hyphen. This imagined place appears in course syllabi and scholarship in Middle East Studies, literary study, sociology, international studies, and many other fields, and it is also a term used by activist organizations that define themselves as anti-Zionist.[38]

While for some, it may simply be a shorthand way of talking about the whole area of Israel, Gaza, and the West Bank, it may also be the label of choice for academics and activists who regard Israel—with its synonym, "the Jewish State"—as not fully legitimate. "Israel-Palestine" can replace the actual Israel, the Palestinian Territories and Gaza with an imagined or theoretical entity, one for which the term "Jewish state" does not apply. "Palestine-Israel" can be seen as an even stronger attack on Israel's character than the insult term for Israel still used by some Middle Eastern spokespersons and sometimes by Westerners: "the Zionist entity."

Of course "Zionist" in this expression does not mean the liberatory movement of the Jewish people, and the country referred to is a place too despicable even to recognize as a country. It is only an "entity" undeserving of the dignity of a name. There is no mistaking the insult intended by this label.

However, as innocuous as "Israel-Palestine" sounds, it may be more problematic than the slur "Zionist entity." For the hyphenated name leaves no room even to speak of "Israel" apart from "Palestine." Nor does it identify the Palestinian controlled areas as in any way distinct from the state of Israel. It names an imagined country in which Gaza, the Palestinian territories, and Israel are completely merged. No "entity" in this formulation can be called the "Jewish State" and differences between Israel and the Palestinian-controlled areas may more easily be blamed on the government of Israel.

This term facilitates the most popular current slander against Israel that shows up in demonstrations and in seminar rooms in the guise of simple, uncontroversial description. If there is no real state of Israel but instead something called Israel-Palestine, then "apartheid" describes differences between people's lives in the Palestinian controlled areas and the democratic state of Israel--regardless of whether or not these differences are anything like apartheid South Africa.

In fact, since all Israeli citizens are subject to the same laws and enjoy the same freedoms, the distinction between Israel and the PA may have to be blurred to get away with the "apartheid" slander at all. It is a two-pronged strategy; first, confuse whether we are talking about the state of Israel or about the PA and/or Gaza, and second, dismiss as irrelevant the equal rights of all Israeli citizens.

During his years as Vice-Consul in San Francisco, Israeli diplomat Ishmael Khaldi says he found "this assault [of] alleged Israeli apartheid" incomprehensible. The first Bedouin Israeli to serve in Israel's Foreign Ministry writes:

> They say Israel is an apartheid state. My response is: Never. Jews and Arabs use the same buses, clinics, government offices, universities, theaters, restaurants, soccer fields, and beaches. All Israeli citizens, regardless of religion or ethnic origins, are equal before the law, the same laws that accord full political, civil, and human rights to its entire population, including its more than one million Arab citizens, some of whom serve in the Israeli parliament. Israel is the only country in the world to have sought out and brought to its shores, entirely on its own initiative, tens

of thousands of Black Africans for purposes other than slavery, granting them full citizenship.[39]

Israelis cannot freely enter Palestinian towns in the West Bank but this is not called "apartheid." Mahmoud Abbas has made clear that a Palestinian state will not allow any Israelis to live there[40] yet no one has suggested that Abbas wants an apartheid country. The fact that the Palestinian Authority government in the West Bank serves the Palestinian population, while the Israeli communities there are subject to the Israeli government, becomes an example of "apartheid" rather than an example (or problem) of the legal requirements of the Oslo Accords that created civil Palestinian and Israeli controls there. The security fence between parts of the West Bank and Israel is said to have no other purpose than to be an "apartheid wall" rather than to accomplish its intended function of reducing terrorism. The dozens of security or border fences worldwide are not labeled "apartheid."[41]

When seen through the frame of the World's Worst, Israel's democracy itself becomes "Zionist propaganda." One can keep repeating the list of obvious freedoms in Israel—freedom of speech and the press, and assembly and religion, the legal protections against discrimination for citizens of all ethnicities, religions, and sexual orientations—but this has no impact against the charge of "apartheid."

Nor are disparities in income levels or the difficulties individuals and groups face in Israel at all comparable to the racial oppression under apartheid South Africa. It is a powerful word to use, but people who actually lived under apartheid and have been to Israel completely disagree with this accusation. Member of the South African Parliament Kenneth Meshoe, for example, writes:

> There is a widespread allegation, really, a slander, that Israel is an apartheid state. That notion is simply wrong. It is inaccurate and it is malicious. Its only purpose is to demonize, isolate, and delegitimize Israel's

existence. And because it is so inaccurate it betrays the memory of those who suffered through a real apartheid.[42]

Member of the African Congress, Tshediso Mangope, like many other people, found that the stories he had been told, the mischaracterizations of Israel that led him to actually advocate against the country, turned out to be untrue. And learning that he had been misled changed his whole perspective:

> It appears to me that those who compare the State of Israel to apartheid South Africa do not understand the fundamentals of apartheid nor have they experienced it . . . after actually visiting Israel, my views on BDS have changed drastically. I am no longer involved in the BDS movement and don't believe it to be a legitimate cause.
>
> For me, learning about the history of the region and trying to separate the truth from lies was a life-altering moment.[43]

Epilogue

I'm sitting by the Yarkon in Tel Aviv. The little river runs into the sea a twenty-minute walk from here along the park. Behind me are picnic tables where a large Jewish Israeli family is just finishing up a child's birthday party. They're playing Mizrahi music and their kids are running back and forth from the tables to the edge of the river. Next to them a large Arab Israeli family is unloading massive amounts of food out of coolers onto a table. Their kids are running back and forth from the tables to the edge of the river. On the next bench near me a religious family, mom and dad in long sleeves and hats, are sitting with four children; the oldest appears to be about seven. The children now are running around the benches and the oldest picks up the baby as she runs.

On the river, rowers glide by in kayaks. Along the pathway, joggers in tank tops and shorts and many people on bicycles keep coming by. The sun sparkles on the water.

I had wanted to tell you about the river, about the people in Israel, about the peace that is here, the exuberance, craziness, the regular life. Instead, we've been inside the frames.

The material I've sorted through, read and reread, and tried to account for has often felt toxic. For the frames package Israel in falsehood.

Nevertheless, I find it helps to notice: here's a newscast grounded in a false premise of struggle over land, and there, a speaker shouting wild claims of the world's worst. Here's a human-interest story that treats one side as a bully and there again is the familiar faulty analogy of the cycle of violence.

It helps to notice and even share what you notice. This can lead to dialogue. And identifying the frames: to leaving them behind.

Notes

Chapter 1 Berkeley to Jerusalem and Back

1   "Indeed Israel can be a dangerous place . . ." Israel@Heart. My Israel Competition. YouTube, uploaded January 7, 2008. https://www.youtube.com/watch?v=K4-l8XfpkCo

2   "Israel to rebrand itself in the world," *Israel Today*, September 12, 2006. http://www.israeltoday.co.il/default.aspx?tabid=178&nid=9460

3   "The Business Climate in Israel," Israel Ministry of Foreign Affairs. http://mfa.gov.il/MFA/InnovativeIsrael/DoingBusiness/Pages/Business_climate_Israel.aspx

4   Dan Senor and Saul Singer, *Start-Up Nation: The Story of Israel's Economic Miracle* (New York: Twelve, 2009) 11.

5   "My name is Israel," exhibition, *Israel 24C.* http://www.israel21c.org/exhibition/my-name-is-israel/

6   "Israelis Are Happier Than Americans, Survey Finds," *The Times of Israel*, March 16, 2016. http://www.timesofisrael.com/israelis-happier-than-americans-germans-study/; "Israel in top 5 happiest countries in the world," *Israel 21C,* June 9, 2015. http://www.israel21c.org/israel-in-top-5-happiest-countries-in-the-world/

7   "Diplomat's bid to rebrand Israel," *The Jewish Chronicle*, June 17, 2010. https://www.thejc.com/news/israel/diplomat-s-bid-to-re-brand-israel-1.16279

8   Eli Avraham, "Public Diplomacy, crisis communication strategies, and man-

aging national branding: the case of Israel." *International Communication Conference Papers*, 2009.

9   "The Best Destinations for Expat Families," *InterNations*, 2016. https://www.internations.org/expat-insider/2016/family-life-index

10 Eytan Gilboa, "Public Diplomacy: the missing component in Israel's foreign policy. *Israel Affairs*, vol. 12, no. 4, 2006, 721.

11 Essential reading outlining this process is Stephanie Gutmann, *The Other War: Israelis, Palestinians and the Struggle for Media Supremacy* (San Francisco: Encounter Books, 2005) and Ben-Dror Yamini, *Industry of Lies: Media, Academia, and the Israeli-Arab Conflict* (New York: ISGAP, 2017).

12 Yaacov Lozowick, *Right to Exist: A Moral Defense of Israel's Wars* (New York: Doubleday, 2003); Alan Dershowitz, *The Case for Israel*, (Hoboken: Wiley, 2004); Haim Harari, *View from the Eye of the Storm: Terror and Reason in the Middle East* (New York: HarperCollins, 2005); Michael G. Bard, *Myths and Facts: A Guide to the Arab-Israeli Conflict* (Chevy Chase, MD: AICE, 2011); Barry Rubin, *Israel: An Introduction* (New Haven: Yale University Press, 2012); Michael Curtis, *Should Israel Exist? A Sovereign Nation Under Attack by the International Community* (Noble, OK: Balfour Books, 2012); Daniel Gordis, *Israel: A Concise History of a Nation Reborn* (New York: HarperCollins, 2016); David Brog, *Reclaiming Israel's History: Roots, Rights, and the Struggle for Peace* (Washington, D.C.: Regnery, 2017). The English translation of "Ministry of Hasbara" is "Ministry of Information."

13 The two newspapers available at the time were *Haaretz* and *The Jerusalem Post*.

14 For clarity, I usually choose the most widely used terms although almost every place name and event involving Israel has multiple names, and although the most widely used terms (many of which are examined in later chapters) are not necessarily the most accurate or neutral.

15 Susan Fiske and Shelly T. Taylor, *Social Cognition* (New York: McGraw-Hill, 1991).

16 Several studies report on these problems, including: *Amcha Initiative: Protecting Jewish Students*. https://amchainitiative.org; Richard L. Cravatts,

Genocidal Liberalism: The University's Jihad Against Israel and Jews (Sherman Oaks, CA: Freedom Center, 2012) 149–182; Dan Feferman, "US College Campus and Israel De-Legitimization—In Perspective," The Jewish People Policy Institute, 2015; Harold Brackman, "Anti-Semitism on Campus: A Clear and Present Danger," The Simon Wiesenthal Center, 2015. A number of organizations help students to respond to anti-Israel discourse including: StandWithUs Campus. http://www.standwithus.com/campus; Christians United For Israel on Campus. https://www.cufioncampus.org/; Scholars for Peace in the Middle East. http://spme.org/; The David Project. https://www.davidproject.org/; Blue Star. http://www.bluestarpr.com/; Students Supporting Israel. http://www.ssimovement.org/

17   Kenneth L. Marcus, "Anti-Zionism as Racism: Campus Anti-Semitism and the Civil Rights Act of 1964," *William and Mary Bill of Rights Journal*, vol. 15, issue 2, 2007; Lesley Klaff, "Anti-Zionist Expression on the UK Campus: Free Speech or Hate Speech?" *Jerusalem Center for Public Affairs*, November 14, 2010. http://jcpa.org/article/anti-zionist-expression-on-the-uk-campus-free-speech-or-hate-speech/; Tammi Rossman-Benjamin, "Jewish students need more protection on California campuses," *Sacramento Bee*, April 9, 2015. http://www.sacbee.com/opinion/op-ed/soapbox/article17974802.html

Chapter 2 War and PC

1   One of the most famous lines of poetry by Spanish Jewish philosopher and poet, Yehuda Halevy, 1075–1175. He advocated for Jews to return to Israel and died just after arriving in Jerusalem. Daniel Frank and Oliver Leaman, *History of Jewish Philosophy* (London: Routledge, 2005) 155.

2   An example from this time period: "Two weeks ago the Israeli Army bulldozed trees, claiming they had served as cover for Palestinians sniping at the highway . . ." in "Another Casualty of War: Trees." *Christian Science Monitor*, December 8, 2000. http://www.csmonitor.com/2000/1208/p1s2.html

3   Mordechai I. Twersky, "Ten Years Later, mothers of Hebrew U. bombing victims look back," *Haaretz*, July 27, 2012. http://www.haaretz.com/israel-news/

ten-years-later-mothers-of-hebrew-u-bombing-victims-look-back-1.453950

4   The word "diaspora" originates in the Hebrew Bible, Deuteronomy 28:12, translated into Greek and then into English as "You shall be in dispersion in all the kingdoms of the earth." It refers to "the body of Jews living outside the Land of Israel; the countries and places inhabited by these regarded collectively; the dispersion of the Jewish people beyond the Land of Israel." *Oxford English Dictionary* online, Oxford University Press, December, 2016. https://en.oxforddictionaries.com/definition/diaspora

5   The term genocide "appears to have first been used by Raphael Lemkin, in 'Axis Rule in Occupied Europe,' 1944, in reference to Nazi extermination of Jews, literally 'killing a tribe,' from Greek, genos, 'race, kind.'" http://www. etymonline.com/index.php?allowed_in_frame=0&search=genocide

6   The Jewish ghetto of Venice, Italy established in 1516 and lasted almost 300 years. The term seems to have originated with this ghetto, the sections of cities to which Jews were restricted starting in the Middle Ages until the 19th century Enlightenment in Europe. In the 20th century, the Nazis set up over a thousand ghettos in Europe.

7   "The Holocaust was the systematic, state-sponsored murder of six million Jews by Nazi Germany and its collaborators. Nazi ideology cast the world as a racial struggle and the singular focus on the total destruction of every single Jewish person was at its racist core. Millions of other innocent civilians were persecuted and murdered by the Nazis, but the elimination of Jews was central to Nazi policy. As Elie Weisel said, 'Not all victims were Jews, but all Jews were victims.'" "Museum statement on international Holocaust Remembrance Day," The United States Holocaust Museum, January 30, 2017. https://www.ushmm.org/information/press/press-releases/museum-statement-on-international-holocaust-remembrance-day

8   Elie Weisel, "Some Questions That Remain Open," in Asher Cohen, Yoav Gelber, and Charlotte Wardi, eds., *Comprehending the Holocaust* (Frankfort: Peter Lang, 1988) 13 quoted in Manfred Gerstenfeld, "Holocaust Trivialization," *Jerusalem Center for Public Affairs*, 68, April 9, 2008.

9   From 1099 to 1291 the Christian Crusaders controlled the area that is now Israel, a part of southern Lebanon, and a part of western Jordan, calling the whole area the Kingdom of Jerusalem.

10   As historian Gil Troy writes, " . . . championing Palestinian rights to self-determination fits into a Zionist framework, which respects national rights to self-determination." Gil Troy, "Yes You Can Be Pro-Palestinian and Pro-Zionist," *Scholars for Peace in the Middle East*, June 22, 2010. http://. org/spme-research/analysis/gil-troy-yes-you-can-be-pro-palestinian-and-pro-zionist/8327/

11   Judea Pearl, "Formula Could Combat Campus Racism," *Jewish Journal*, June 9, 2005. http://www.jewishjournal.com/opinion/article/formula_could_combat_campus_racism_20050610

12   Judea and Ruth Pearl, "Right of Reply: Daniel Pearl's Last Words," *The Jerusalem Post*, May 14, 2008. http://www.jpost.com/Opinion/Op-Ed-Contributors/Right-of-Reply-Daniel-Pearls-last-words

13   A landmark study analyzing the impact of ideology on an academic discipline of major significance to perceptions of Israel is: Martin Kramer, *Ivory Towers on Sand: The Failure of Middle Eastern Studies in America* (Washington, D.C.: The Washington Institute for Near East Policy, 2001).

14   Lea Speyer, "UCLA Student President Leaves Law School Over BDS Harassment; Blasts College for Capitulation to Anti-Israel Movement," *Algemeiner*, September 1, 2016. https://www.algemeiner.com/2016/0;9/01/former-ucla-student-president-milan-chatterjee-university-administration-has-set-dangerous-precedent-by-capitulating-to-bds-movement-interview/; Jew Hatred on Campus. http://archive.jewhatredoncampus.org/; Mellissa Apter, "Top Intellectuals Mobilize Against Anti-Israel Activity on Campus," *The Times of Israel*, December 23, 2015. http://www.timesofisrael.com/top-intellectuals-mobilize-against-anti-israel-activity-on-campus/?fb_comment_id=976890875712420_977001275701380#f45de4ea6ab73; "Israeli Apartheid Week: A Year-by-Year Report," ADL, 2012. https://www.adl.org/sites/default/files/documents/assets/pdf/israel-international/Israeli-Apart-

heid-Week-Year-by-Year-Report.pdf; Elhanan Miller, "It's Anti-Apartheid week in the U.K.!," *Tablet*, March 1, 2016. http://www.tabletmag.com/jewish-news-and-politics/198027/its-anti-apartheid-week-in-the-uk; Tyler Kingkade, "UCLA's Student Council Tries to Hide Video of its Members Questioning a Jewish Student," *Huffington Post*, March 6, 2015. https://www.huffingtonpost.com/2015/03/06/ucla-jewish-student-video_n_6817918.html; Shoshana Kranish, "McGill Students Claim Forced Out of Student Govt. Due to Antisemitism," *The Jerusalem Post*, October 29, 2017. http://www.jpost.com/Diaspora/McGill-students-claim-forced-out-of-student-govt-due-to-antisemitism-508717.

15   Colin Powell, "Statement on World Conference Against Racism, US State Department," Washington, D.C., September 3, 2001, quoted in Elihai Braun, "United Nations: World Conference Against Racism," *Jewish Virtual Library*, 2001. http://www.jewishvirtuallibrary.org/durban-i-un-conference-against-racism-2001

16   Jed Babbin and Herbert London, *The BDS War Against Israel, the Orwellian Campaign to Destroy Israel through the Boycott, Divestment, and Sanction Movement* (New York: London Center for Policy Research, 2014) 18.

17   Ruth Wisse, "Harvard's Latest Assault on Israel, Promoting the Jewish State's destruction at a school dedicated to 'democratic governance,'" *The Wall Street Journal*, February 28, 2012. http://online.wsj.com/article/SB10001424052970203960804577244932732348366.html,

18   "Funders," *NGO Monitor*. http://www.ngomonitor.org/articles.php?cat_id=3

19   "Boycott Monitor," AMCHA Initiative. http://www.amchainitiative.org/#

20   Cary Nelson and Gabriel Noah Brahm, *The Case Against Academic Boycotts of Israel* (New York: MLA Members for Scholars Rights, distributed, Wayne State University Press, 2014).

21   The evolution of this phenomenon is examined in Gary A. Tobin, Aryeh Kaufmann Weinberg, and Jenna Ferrer, *The Uncivil University, Intolerance on College Campuses* (Landham, MD: Lexington Books, 2009).

22   A significant critique by scholars in Middle East studies, peace studies,

anthropology, Israel studies, and other fields, of the "deleterious impact" of one of the most influential academic theories is: Philip Carl Salzman and Donna Robinson Divin, eds., *Post-Colonial Theory and the Arab-Israeli Conflict* (New York: Routledge, 2008).

23   In fact, there is ample evidence that the majority of these terrorists are more educated and middle class than the general population. See, for example: Claude Berrebi, "Evidence About the Link Between Education, Poverty, and Terrorism among Palestinians," *Peace Economics, Peace Science and Public Policy* (vol. 13, issue 1, article 2) 2008. Abdelaziz Testas, "Determinants of Terrorism in the Muslim World: An empirical cross-sectional analysis," *Terrorism and Political Violence* 2, no. 16, 2010: 253–273. Alan B. Krueger and Jitka Maleckova, "Education, Poverty and Terrorism: Is There a Causal Connection?," *Journal of Economic Perspectives* 4, no. 17, 2003, 119–144.

24   see Judea Pearl, "Our New Marranos," *The Jewish Journal*, March 18, 2009, and Gil Troy, *Why I Am a Zionist: Jewish Identity and the Challenges of Today* (Montreal: Bronfman Jewish Education Centre, 2002).

Chapter 3 Why Citing the Facts Has So Little Impact

1   From "Mission Statement," Scholars for Peace in the Middle East. http://spme.org/mission-statement.

2   Michael G. Bard and Jeff Dawson, *Israel and the Campus: The Real Story*, (Chevy Chase, MD: AICE, 2012) 37.

3   This concept comes from philosopher, Richard Rorty; linguist, John Swales; and in composition and rhetoric, from Kenneth A. Bruffee, "Collaborative Learning and the Conversation of Mankind," *College English*, vol. 44, no. 7, November, 1984, 635–652.

4   Sheryl I. Fontaine and Cherryl Smith, *Writing Your Way Through College: A Student's Guide* (Portsmouth, NH: Heinemann, 2008) 10–18.

5   "Kooky" is one of Rorty's words describing abnormal discourse.

6   The theorizing of Jacques Derrida, Michel Foucault, and Jacques Lyotard, for example.

7 The pale of settlement marked the areas in Russia where Jews were allowed to live.

8 Even academic ideas can be redirected in this way. Thomas Kuhn, *The Structure of Scientific Revolutions* (University of Chicago, 1962), became one of the most influential texts in the social sciences and humanities although its premise that major scientific breakthroughs are dependent on their acknowledgement by the scientific community was intended (as even the title suggests) only to describe work in the sciences. Nevertheless, Kuhn's term, "paradigm shift" is equated with the move from modernist to postmodernist views that underlie work in the humanities and social sciences.

9 Two major organizations are: Scholars for Peace in the Middle East, "a grassroots community of scholars, who have united to promote honest, fact-based and civil discourse, especially in regard to Middle East issues" http://spme.org/ and Heterodox Academy, "a politically diverse group of social scientists, natural scientists, and other scholars who . . . share a concern about a growing problem: the loss or lack of 'viewpoint diversity' . . ." https://heterodoxacademy.org/

10 Cary Nelson, *Dreams Deferred: A Concise Guide to the Israeli-Palestinian Conflict and the Movement to Boycott Israel* (Bloomington: Indiana University Press, 2016) 27.

11 Quoted in Cary Nelson, "The Problem with Judith Butler: The Political Philosophy of the Movement to Boycott Israel," *Los Angeles Review of Books*, March 16, 2014.

12 "The Covenant of the Hamas Resistance Movement," English translation, *MEMRI*. http://www.memri.org/report/en/0/0/0/0/0/0/1609.htm

13 "Hassan Nasrallah: In His Own Words," *CAMERA*, July 26, 2006.

14 http://www.camera.org/index.asp?x_context=7&x_issue=11&x_article=1158 The Middle East Media Research Institute. www.memri.org

15 Neil J. Kressel, *"The Sons of Pigs and Apes," Muslim Antisemitism and the Conspiracy of Silence* (Dulles, VA: Potomac Books, 2012) 34–37.

16 Ibid., 26–33.

17   "Combating Holocaust Denial: Evidence of the Holocaust Presented at Nuremberg," United States Holocaust Memorial Museum. https://www. ushmm.org/wlc/en/article.php?ModuleId=10007271

CHAPTER 4 Media Slant and Rhetorical Frames

1   Jim A. Kuypers, *Partisan Journalism: A History of Media Bias in the United States* (Lanham: Rowman & Littlefield Publishers, 2015) 183.

2   George Cheney, Steve May, Debashsish Munshi, *The Handbook of Communication Ethics* (New York: Routledge, 2011) 193.

3   "SPJ Code of Ethics," Society of Professional Journalists. http://www.spj. org/ethicscode.asp

4   Art Swift, "Americans' Trust in Mass Media Sinks to New Low," Gallup, September 4, 2016. http://www.gallup.com/poll/195542/americans-trust-mass-media-sinks-new-low.aspx

5   PEW Research Center, "Trust and Accuracy," July 7, 2016. http://www.journalism.org/2016/07/07/trust-and-accuracy/

6   Jim A. Kuypers, *Press Bias and Politics, How the Media Frame Controversial Issues* (Westport, CN: Praeger, 2002) 14.

7   Stephen D. Cooper, "The Oppositional Framing of Bloggers," in *Doing News Framing Analysis*, Paul D'Angelo and Jim A. Kuypers, eds. (New York: Routledge, 2010) 135–155.

8   Honest Reporting, www.honestreporting.com and Committee for Accuracy in Middle East Reporting in America, www.camera.org

9   BBC Watch, https://bbcwatch.org/ and UK Media Watch, https://ukmediawatch.org/

10   "Deadly Attack on Israel-Egypt Border," BBC News, June 18, 2012. http://www.bbc.co.uk/news/world-middle-east-18483018

11   "Palestinian 'Attackers' Killed by Israeli Truck Driver," BBC News, June 17, 2012. http://www.bbc.co.uk/news/world-middle-east-18478829

12   "Four Palestinian attackers Killed by Israeli Troops," BBC News, January 8, 2016. http://www.bbc.com/news/world-middle-east-35259427; "London

Attack: Four Dead in Westminster Terror Incident," BBC News, March 23, 2017. http://www.bbc.com/news/uk-39359158

13 "Study: Reuters Headlines," *Honest Reporting*, July 14, 2003. http://honestreporting.com/study-reuters-headlines/

14 "BBC Complaints: Terror Attacks in Jerusalem and Tunisia Are 'Very Different,'" *BBC Watch*, November 8, 2015. https://bbcwatch.org/2015/11/08/bbc-complaints-terror-attacks-in-jerusalem-and-tunisia-are-very-different/

15 Bill Kovach and Tom Rosenstiel, *The Elements of Journalism: What Newspeople Should Know and the Public Should Expect* (New York: Three Rivers Press, 2007) 36.

16 George Lakoff, *Don't Think of an Elephant! Know Your Values and Frame the Debate* (White River Junction, VT: Chelsea Green Publishing, 2006) and George Lakoff and Mark Johnson, *Metaphors We Live By* (Chicago: University of Chicago Press, 1980).

17 Paul D'Angelo and Jim A. Kuypers, *Doing Framing Analysis: Empirical and Theoretical Perspectives* (New York: Routledge, 2010) 2.

18 Robert M. Enteman, "Framing, Media Bias, and Political Power," in Paul D'Angelo and Jim A. Kuypers, eds., *Doing Framing Analysis* (New York: Routledge, 2010) 331–355.

19 Jim A. Kuypers, *Partisan Journalism: A History of Media Bias in the United States* (Lanham, MD: Rowman & Littlefield Publishers, 2015); Tim Groseclose, *Left Turn: How the Liberal Media Bias Distorts the American Mind* (New York: St. Martins, 2011); Bernard Goldberg, *Bias: A CBS Insider Exposes How Media Distort the News* (Washington, D.C.: Regnery, 2001); Eric Alterman, *What Liberal Media? The Truth About Bias and the News* (New York: Basic Books, 2008); David Edwards and David Cromwell, *Guardians of Power: The Myth of the Liberal Media* (New York: Pluto Press, 2006).

20 Committee for Accuracy in Middle East Reporting, http://www.camera.org/search/?domains=camera.org&sitesearch=camera.org&q=thumbs+up&x=8&y=11

21 "BBC Writer Consistently Accurate and Impartial," BBC Watch, July 15,

2013. http://bbcwatch.org/2013/07/15/bbc-travel-writer-consistently-accurate-and-impartial/

22   Rafael Ahren, "Iran's Supreme Leader Backs 'Holy Intifada' to Destroy 'Cancer' Israel," *The Times of Israel*, February 21, 2017. http://www.timesofisrael.com/iran-leader-hails-holy-intifada-against-cancer-israel/

23   Stephen Reese, "Prologue—Framing Public Life, A Bridging Model for Media Research," in Stephen Reese, Oscar H. Gandy, and August E. Grant, eds., *Framing Public Life* (Mahwah, NJ: Lawrence Erlbaum, 2001) 11.

24   Michael J. Carter, "The Hermeneutics of Frames and Framing: An Examination of the Media's Construction of Reality" *SAGE Open*, April–June 2013, 1–12.

25   Paul D'Angelo and Jim A. Kuypers, *Doing Framing Analysis: Empirical and Theoretical Perspective*s (New York: Routledge, 2010) 1–2.

26   Jim A. Kuypers, *Press Bias and Politics: How the Media Frame Controversial Issues* (Westport, CN: Praeger, 2002) 24.

CHAPTER 5 Spotlight Fallacy: Frame of Only Conflict

1   Martin Luther King, Jr., *Martin Luther King, Jr.: The Last Interview: And Other Conversations,* (Brooklyn, NY: Melville House, 2017) 104–105.

2   "Israel Airlines' History: The 1980's", *EL AL.* https://www.elal.com/en/About-ELAL/About-ELAL/History/Pages/Decade-80.aspx

3   David Kashi, "El Al Airlines, the Safest Airline in the World; Is Also Worst On-Time Performer, *International Business Times*, February 20, 2014. http://www.ibtimes.com/el-al-israel-airlines-safest-airline-world-also-worst-time-performer-1556712

4   Arieh O'Sullivan, "Israeli Tech Uses Lasers to Protect Civilian Aircraft," *The Jerusalem Post*, October 6, 2011. http://www.jpost.com/Defense/Israeli-tech-uses-lasers-to-protect-civilian-aircraft

5   Jeff Jacoby, "What Israeli Security Could Teach Us," *The Boston Globe*, August 23, 2006. http://www.jeffjacoby.com/6733/what-israeli-security-could-teach-us

6   Isaac Ben-Israel, Oren Setter, Asher Tishler, "R&D and the War on Terrorism: Generalizing from the Israeli Experience," in A.D. James, ed., *Science and Technology Policies for the Anti-Terrorism Era* (Washington, D.C.: IOS Press, 2006) 51–63.

7   Karl Vick, "Why Israel Doesn't Care About Peace," *Time Magazine*, September 2, 2010. http://www.time.com/time/magazine/article/0,9171,2015789,00.html

8   *Time Magazine* cover, September 2, 2010. http://content.time.com/time/magazine/0,9263,7601100913,00.html

9   Jonathan Mark, "Media Watch: Time Says, 'Israel Doesn't Want Peace,'" *New York Jewish Week*, November 7, 2010. http://jewishweek.timesofisrael.com/media-watch-time-says-israel-doesnt-want-peace and Phyllis Chesler, "Time Magazine's Latest Blood Libel About Israel," *Arutz Sheva*, September 5, 2010. http://www.israelnationalnews.com/News/News.aspx/139492; Morton A. Kline, "ZOA Demands *Time Magazine* Apologize For Anti-Semitic/Cover/Article Entitled 'Why Israel Doesn't Care About Peace,'" *ZOA News*, September 13, 2010. http://zoa.org/2010/09/102755-zoa-demands-time-magazine-apologize-for-anti-semiticmisleading-coverarticle-entitled-why-israel-doesnt-care-about-peace/; Dvir Abramovich, "Time's Up: The Story That Shocked Israel," *Sydney Morning Herald*, September 15, 2010. http://www.smh.com.au/federal-politics/times-up-the-story-that-shocked-israel-20100915-15bzn.html

10   "No Time for Israel: An *Honest Reporting* In-Depth Analysis," http://honestreporting.com/a/time/index.html

11   Vick, "Why Israel Doesn't Care."

12   Ibid.

13   Obscuring the intentions of Hamas occurs frequently in mainstream press. See, for example, instances tracked by Lee S. Bender and Jerome R. Verlin, *Pressing Israel: Media Bias Exposed from A to Z*, (Philadelphia: Pavilion Press, 2012) 35–38.

14   Vick, "Why Israel Doesn't Care."

15 Noah Browning, "West Bank High Life Masks Deepening Economic Crisis," Reuters, US Edition, July 4, 2012. http://www.reuters.com/article/2012/07/04/palestinians-economy-idUSL6E8I488X20120704

16 Ibid.

17 Jim Zanotti, "U.S. Foreign Aid to the Palestinians," *Congressional Research Service,* December 16, 2016, 1.

18 Browning, "West Bank High Life."

19 David Kaufman, "Is Israel Using Gay Rights to Excuse its Policy on Palestine?" *Time Magazine,* May 13, 2011. http://www.time.com/time/world/article/0,8599,2070415,00.html

20 Martin S. Kramer, "'Gaza = Auschwitz,'" *Mosaic,* August 26, 2014. https://mosaicmagazine.com/observation/2014/08/gaza-equals-auschwitz/

21 Jayson Littman, "Letter to Israel from Gay Americans," *The Times of Israel,* February 28, 2013. http://blogs.timesofisrael.com/letter-to-israel-from-gay-americans/

22 Hebro.com http://www.myhebro.com/about-us/

23 Littman "Letter to Israel from Gay Americans."

24 Kaufman, "Is Israel Using Gay Rights."

25 Ibid.

26 Ibid.

27 Itay Blumenthal, "Tel Aviv Pride Parade Ends With Seaside Party," *YNet News,* June 9, 2017. http://www.ynetnews.com/articles/0,7340,L-4973529,00.html

28 Graham Smith, "Tel Aviv Trumps New York to Be Named World's Best Gay City," *UK Daily Mail,* updated January 24, 2012. http://www.dailymail.co.uk/news/article-2088319/Tel-Aviv-trumps-New-York-named-worlds-best-gay-city.htm

29 Christopher Muther, "Welcome to Tel Aviv: The Gayest City on Earth," *The Boston Globe,* March 17, 2016. https://www.bostonglobe.com/lifestyle/travel/2016/03/17/welcome-tel-aviv-gayest-city-earth/y9V15VazXhtSjXV-So9gT9K/story.html

30   "78 Countries Where Homosexuality is Illegal," *Erasing 76 Crimes*, updated May 19, 2017. https://76crimes.com/76-countries-where-homosexuality-is-illegal/

31   Sarah Shulman, "Israel and 'Pinkwashing,'" *The New York Times*, November 22, 2011. http://www.nytimes.com/2011/11/23/opinion/pinkwashing-and-israels-use-of-gays-as-a-messaging-tool.html

32   Jasbir Puar, "Israel's gay propaganda war," *The Guardian*, July 1, 2010. https://www.theguardian.com/commentisfree/2010/jul/01/israels-gay-propaganda-war

33   A Wider Bridge, http://awiderbridge.org/

34   Arthur Slepian, "An Inconvenient Truth: The Myths of Pink-Washing," *Tikkun*, July 3, 2012. http://www.tikkun.org/nextgen/an-inconvenient-truth-the-myths-of-pinkwashing

35   Michael Ordman, "Look How Israel Treats the Palestinian Arabs," *The Jerusalem Post*, July 16, 2011. http://www.jpost.com/printarticle.aspx?id=367029

36   Michael Ordman, *Good News From Israel*. http://verygoodnewsisrael.blogspot.co.il/

37   Michael Ordman, "Just Look At Us Now," *The Jerusalem Post*, January 4, 2015. http://www.jpost.com/Blogger/Michael-Ordman

38   Michael Ordman, "The Magic Touch," *The Jerusalem Post*, July 4, 2013. http://blogs.jpost.com/content/magic-touch

39   *No Camels, Israel Innovation News*, http://nocamels.com/about/

40   Kathryn Dura, "How Israeli Transportation Technologies Are Powering New York City Taxicabs," *No Camels*, June 13, 2017. http://nocamels.com/2017/06/israeli-car-technologies-driverless-safety/

41   *Israel 21C* https://www.israel21c.org/

42   "About" Israel 21C http://israel21c.org/about/

43   Cherryl Smith, "What Boycott? Major Musicians Rock Israel, *Honest Reporting*, December 8, 2013. http://honestreporting.com/what-boycott-major-musicians-rock-israel/

44   Liel Leibovitz, "The Rock Stars Guide to Eating, Praying and Loving in the High

Security State of Israel," *Tablet Magazine*, June 5, 2013. http://www.tabletmag. com/jewish-arts-and-culture/music/133855/rock-star-promoter-israel

45 Dave Itzkoff, "Despite Protests, Alicia Keys Says She Will Perform in Tel Aviv," *The New York Times*, May 31, 2013. http://artsbeat.blogs.nytimes. com/2013/05/31/despite-protests-alicia-keys-says-she-will-perform-in-tel-aviv/

46 PACBI (Palestinian Campaign for the Academic and Cultural Boycott of Israel), "Mark Almond Cancels Show in Israel," May 13, 2011. http://www. pacbi.org/etemplate.php?id=1596

47 "Santana Cancels Tel Aviv Concert," *I Googled Israel*, January, 28, 2010. http://igoogledisrael.com/2010/01/santana-cancels-tel-aviv-concert/

48 "Pixies Cancel Israel Shows," *Punk News*, June 7, 2010. http://www. punknews.org/article/38559/pixies-cancel-israel-shows

49 "Jon Bon Jovi Reveals He Would Love to Play in Israel," *IsraellyCool*, June 3, 2013. http://www.israellycool.com/2013/06/03/jon-bon-jovi-reveals-he-would-love-to-play-in-israel/

50 Salif Keita and Coumba Makalou, "Salif Keita forced to cancel Jerusalem Festival due to dangerous threats by BDS," *Creative Community for Peace*, August 22, 2013. http://www.creativecommunityforpeace.com/Articles. asp?AID=239

51 Daniel Lubetzky, "Anatomy of Activism: Paul McCartney and One Voice," *peaceworks.net*, September 27, 2008. http://blog.peaceworks.net/2008/09/ anatomy-of-activism-paul-mccartney-and-onevoice/

52 One approach was the *New York Times'* brief summary: "Despite Death Threats, McCartney Plans to Play," September 16, 2008. http://www.nytimes. com/2008/09/17/arts/music/17arts-DESPITEDEATH_BRF.html Another was *Newsweek's*, "A Paul McCartney Concert Puts Israel in a Tizzy," September 23, 2008. http://www.newsweek.com/paul-mccartney-concert-puts-israel-tizzy-89081

53 Omar Barghouti, in "Boycott, Divestment, Sanction Israel," *Enough News* uploaded July 27, 2010. https://www.youtube.com/watch?v=tnpilMYsRoI

54 "Full Transcript: Ambassador Prosor Highlights Anti-Israel Bias at the UN."

The Algemeiner, November 28, 2013. http://www.algemeiner.com/2013/11/28/
full-transcript-ambassador-prosor-highlights-anti-israel-bias-at-the-un/

55   Hillel Neuer, "The Demonization of Israel at the United Nations," in
Palestinian Manipulation of the International Community, Alan Baker,
ed., *Jerusalem Center for Public Affairs*, 2014. http://jcpa.org/demoniza-
tion_of_israel_at_the_united_nations/

56   Joshua Muravchik, *Making David Into Goliath: How the World Turned
Against Israel* (New York: Encounter Books, 2014) 66-72.

57   Gil Troy, *Moynihan's Moment: America's Fight Against Zionism as Racism*
(Oxford: Oxford University Press, 2013) 7.

58   "40th Anniversary of 'Zionism is Racism': Moynihan's Historic Speech," UN
Watch, November 10, 2015. https://www.unwatch.org/moynihans-moment-
the-historic-1975-u-n-speech-in-response-to-zionism-is-racism/

59   Troy, "Moynihan's Moment," 233–234.

60   "Excerpt from Kofi Annan's Report on UN Reform: In Larger Freedom,"
Global Policy Forum, March 21, 2005. https://www.globalpolicy.org/global-
taxes/48066-excerpt-from-kofi-annans-report-on-un-reform-in-larger-
freedom-.html

61   Irwin Colter, "The Tragic Farce of the Human Rights Council," *The National
Post*, March 6, 2014. http://nationalpost.com/goo/full-comment/irwin-
cotler-the-tragic-farce-of-the-un-human-rights-council/wcm/1297393a-
d8a4-4f28-999c-d3c6a8b02694?i1oc.referrer=https%3A%2F%2Fwww.google.
co.il%2F

62   Hillel Neuer, "The Demonization of Israel at the United Nations," in
Palestinian Manipulation of the International Community, Alan Baker,
ed., *Jerusalem Center for Public Affairs*, 2014. http://jcpa.org/demoniza-
tion_of_israel_at_the_united_nations/

63   Tova Lazaroff, "Clinton: UNHRC Bias Against Israel Undermines Its Work,"
The Jerusalem Post, February 28, 2011. http://www.jpost.com/Diplomacy-
and-Politics/Clinton-UNHRC-bias-against-Israel-undermines-its-work

64   "The UN and Israel: Key Statistics from UN Watch," *UN Watch*. https://

www.unwatch.org/un-israel-key-statistics/

65   "'Why does the UN obsess over Israel'—Nikki Hayley" YouTube, posted by UN Watch, February 15, 2017. https://www.unwatch.org/u-n-obsess-israel-nikki-haley/

CHAPTER 6 False Premise: Frame of Struggle Over Land

1   Khaled Abu Toameh, "The "Anti-Normalization" Campaign and Israel's Right to Exist," *Gatestone Institute International Policy Council*, August 8, 2016. https://www.gatestoneinstitute.org/8656/anti-normalization-israel

2   "The Israeli-Palestinian Conflict, Explained," *The Washington Post*, July 24, 2014. https://www.washingtonpost.com/posttv/world/the-israeli-palestinian-conflict-explained/2014/07/24/3895a6b6-1372-11e4-ac56-773e54a65906_video.html

3   "A Brief History of the Palestinian Conflict," student activity, Gaza history, *New York Times*, 2009. http://www.nytimes.com/learning/teachers/studentactivity/2009gazahistory.pdf

4   A Palestinian Arab state was possible in 1937 based on the San Remo Conference partition plan; in 1947 based on the UN partition plan; in 1967 based on Israel's offer, after winning the Six-Day war, of land in exchange for peace; in 2000 based on the Camp David Accords; in 2001 based on the proposals at the Taba Summit; or between 2006 and 2008 based on negotiations between the Israelis and the Palestinians. Lee S. Bender and Jerome R. Verlin, *Pressing Israel* (New York: Pavilion Press, 2012).

5   "History of Jerusalem: Timeline for the History of Jerusalem (4500 BCE–Present)," *Jewish Virtual Library*. http://www.jewishvirtuallibrary.org/timeline-for-the-history-of-jerusalem-4500-bce-present

6   Yoram Ettinger quoted in Hillel Fendel, "Jewish, Not Arab, Roots in Judea and Samaria," *Israel National News*, July 31, 2009. http://www.israelnationalnews.com/News/News.aspx/132671 Mark Twain, *The Innocents Abroad: or, The New Pilgrims' Program* (Kessinger Publishing, 2010). Ronn Torossian, "Judea and Samaria are Israel," *Front Page*, February 9, 2014 http://

www.frontpagemag.com/fpm/218379/judea-and-samaria-are-israel-ronn-torossian

7   Robert Deutsch, "Romans coins Boast 'Judea Capta'," *Archeological Center.* http://www.archaeological-center.com/en/monographs/m20/

8   Elon Gilad, "Why are Palestinians called Palestinians?," *Haaretz*, October 29, 2015. https://www.haaretz.com/israel-news/.premium-1.683062 "Israel: Origin of the name Palestine," *Jewish Virtual Library.* http://www.jewish-virtuallibrary.org/origin-of-quot-palestine-quot

9   Mike Lumish, "So, Just What is a 'Palestinian', Anyway," *The Times of Israel*, May 27, 2014. http://blogs.timesofisrael.com/so-just-what-is-a-palestinian-anyways/

10 Bernard Lewis, "The Palestinians and the PLO," *Commentary*, January 1, 1975. https://www.commentarymagazine.com/articles/the-palestinians-and-the-plo/

11 David Brooks, "A Brief History of Yasir Arafat: The PLO leader is a terrible administrator but a brilliant image crafter," *The Atlantic*, July/ August 2002. https://www.theatlantic.com/magazine/archive/2002/07/a-brief-history-of-yasir-arafat/302532/

12 Michael Curtis, *Jews, Antisemitism, and the Middle East* (New Brunswick, New Jersey: Transaction Publishers, 2013) chapter 4.

13 Efraim Karsh, "Arafat's Grand Strategy," *Middle East Forum*, Spring 2014. http://www.meforum.org/605/arafats-grand-strategy

14 Khaled Abu Toameh, "Why Palestinians cannot make peace with Israel," *Gatestone Institute*, July 13, 2015. https://www.gatestoneinstitute.org/6142/palestinians-peace-israel.

15 "Jewish history rewritten," *Palestinian Media Watch.* http://www.palwatch.org/main.aspx?fi=487 "UNESCO passes resolution denying Jewish ties to Jerusalem holy sites," *i24NEWS*, October 13, 2016. https://www.i24news.tv/en/news/international/127560-161013-unesco-due-to-pass-resolution-challenging-jewish-ties-to-jerusalem-holy-sites

16 "Jesus misrepresented as 'Muslim Palestinian'," *Palestinian Media Watch.*

http://palwatch.org/main.aspx?fi=505

17   William James and Jeffrey Heller, "A century on, UK's Jewish homeland declaration stirs celebration and mourning in Middle East," Reuters, November 2, 2017. https://www.reuters.com/article/us-britain-israel/a-century-on-uks-jewish-homeland-declaration-stirs-celebration-and-mourning-in-middle-east-idUSKBN1D2008

18   David Pratt, "Britain's bitter legacy," *The Herald*, October 29th, 2017. http://www.heraldscotland.com/news/15626149.Britain__39_s_bitter_legacy/

19   Noga Tarnopolsky, "A century later, the Balfour declaration still haunts the Middle East," *Los Angeles Times,* November 2, 2017. http://www.latimes.com/world/middleeast/la-fg-israel-britain-balfour-20171102-story.html

20   Ian Black, "The Contested centenary of Britain's 'calamitous promise'," *The Guardian*, October 17, 2017. https://www.theguardian.com/news/2017/oct/17/centenary-britains-calamitous-promise-balfour-declaration-israel-palestine

21   Dominic Sandbrook, "Britain's legacy of blood: How a British statesman paved the way for a Jewish state - and the countless deaths that followed after the creation of Israel," *Daily Mail,* November 3, 2017. http://www.dailymail.co.uk/news/article-5048567/How-British-statesman-paved-way-Jewish-state.html

22   Michael B. Oren, "Israel's 1967 Victory Is Something to Celebrate," *New York Times,* June 4, 2017. https://www.nytimes.com/2017/06/04/opinion/six-day-war-arab-israeli-anniversary.html

23   Mahmoud Abbas, "Britain must atone for the Balfour declaration – and 100 years of suffering," *The Guardian,* November 1, 2017. https://www.theguardian.com/commentisfree/2017/nov/01/arthur-balfour-declaration-100-years-of-suffering-britain-palestine-israel

24   Ian Black, "The Contested centenary."

25   Martin S. Kramer quoted in Clifford D. May, "The 100-year-old promise," *The Washington Times,* October 31, 2017. https://m.washingtontimes.com/news/2017/oct/31/israel-given-birth-thanks-to-international-efforts/

26   Martin S. Kramer. "The Forgotten Truth about the Balfour Declaration,"

Mosaic, June 5, 2017. https://mosaicmagazine.com/essay/2017/06/the-forgotten-truth-about-the-balfour-declaration/

27   Eli Rekhess, "The Evolvement of an Arab–Palestinian National Minority in Israel," *Israel Studies* 12, no. 3, 2007, 1–28.

28   Walter Laqueur and Barry Rubin, *The Israeli-Arab Reader, A Documentary History of the Middle East Conflict* (New York: Penguin Books, 1995) 17.

29   Fred M. Gottheil, "Arab immigration into pre-state Israel: 1922-1931," *Middle Eastern Studies* 9, no. 3, 1973.

30   Itamar Marcus, "Had There Been No Balfour Declaration, The PA Would Have Had to Invent It," *The Jerusalem Post,* November 2, 2017. http://www.jpost.com/Opinion/Had-there-been-no-Balfour-Declaration-the-PA-would-not-have-been-invented-513217

31   Efraim Karsh, "Turks, Arabs Welcomed the Balfour Declaration," *Middle East Forum*, Winter, 2018.

32   Walter Laqueur and Barry Rubin, *The Israeli-Arab Reader: A Documentary History of the Middle East Conflict* (New York: Penguin Books, 1995) 19–20.

33   "Israel: Freedom in the World 2016," *Freedom House*, 2016. https://freedom-house.org/report/freedom-world/2016/israel

34   Robert Zelnick, *Israel's Unilateralism: Beyond Gaza* (Stanford, CA: Hoover Institution Press, 2006) 9.

35   "The Security Fence," *European Institute of Public Administration.* http://eipa.eu.com/category/information-centre/defense-security/security-fence/

36   Nancy Hartevelt Kobrin, *The Banality of Suicide Terrorism, the Naked Truth about the Psychology of Islamic Suicide Bombing* (Washington, D.C.: Potomac Books, 2010).

37   Michael Bard, "West Bank security fence: background and overview," Jewish Virtual Library, updated February, 2017. http://www.jewishvirtuallibrary.org/background-and-overview-of-israel-s-security-fence

38   "In which BBC radio 4 insists on describing a fence as a wall," *BBC Watch*, March 2, 2017. https://bbcwatch.org/2017/03/02/in-which-bbc-radio-4-insists-on-describing-a-fence-as-a-wall/

39   William Booth and Sufian Taha, "A Palestinian's Daily Commute Through an Israeli Checkpoint," *The Washington Post*, May 25, 2017. https://www.washingtonpost.com/graphics/world/occupied/checkpoint/?utm_term=.8d8be89948f3 Daniel Pomerantz, *Honest Reporting*, *"Washington Post* Slams Israel, Ignores Ethics," May 28, 2017. http://honestreporting.com/washington-post-slams-israel-ignores-ethics-checkpoints

40   James Glanz and Rami Nazzal, "Smugglers in West Bank Open Doors to Jobs in Israel, and Violence," *The New York Times*, June 20, 2016. https://www.nytimes.com/2016/06/21/world/middleeast/west-bank-israel-palestinians-smugglers.html. Amos Harel, "Israel's Walls: Do They Work?" *Foreign Affairs*, February 17, 2017. https://www.foreignaffairs.com/articles/israel/2017-02-17/israels-walls

41   Kim Hjelmaard, "From 7 to 77: There's been an explosion in building border walls since World War II," *USA Today*, May 24, 2018. https://www.usatoday.com/story/news/world/2018/05/24/border-walls-berlin-wall-donald-trump-wall/553250002/

42   Jared Samilow, " The Manufactured Controversy of the Jerusalem Light Rail," *The Tower Magazine*, Issue 41, August 2016. http://www.thetower.org/article/the-manufactured-controversy-of-the-jerusalem-light-rail/

43   Joseph E. Katz, "A History of the Jews: A List of Expulsions for 2000 Years," *eretzyisroel.org.* http://www.eretzyisroel.org/~jkatz/expulsions.html

44   F.M. Loewenberg, "A Brief History of the Jewish Presence in Gaza," *The Jewish Magazine*, June 2013. http://www.jewishmag.co.il/176mag/jewish_gaza/jewish_gaza.htm

45   Robert Zelnick, *Israel's Unilateralism: Beyond Gaza* (Stanford, CA: Hoover Institution Press, 2006) 15.

46   Brian J. Hall, et al, "The Psychological Impact of Impending Forced Settler Disengagement in Gaza: Trauma and Posttraumatic Growth," *Journal of Traumatic Stress* 21, no. 1, 2008.

47   For example, *Reuters News Service*: "Opponents Citing Civil War: Sharon," ABC News, September 13, 2014. http://www.abc.net.au/news/2004-09-13/

opponents-inciting-civil-war-sharon/2042432

48   Jewish communities had been moved by the Israeli government before—from Sinai as part of the peace agreement with Egypt. In contrast, the Gaza move was undertaken because of a lack progress toward peace.

49   "Selective Quotes Distort Intent of Sharon's Gaza Withdrawal," *CAMERA*, October 18, 2004. http://www.camera.org/index.asp?x_context=7&x_issue=52&x_article=783

50   "The Disengagement Plan---General Outline," *Israel Ministry of Foreign Affairs*, April 18, 2004. http://www.mfa.gov.il/MFA/ForeignPolicy/Peace/MFADocuments/Pages/Disengagement%20Plan%20-%20General%20Outline.aspx

51   "Israel's Disengagement Plan, Renewing the Peace Process," *Israel Ministry of Foreign Affairs*, April 20, 2005. http://www.mfa.gov.il/mfa/foreignpolicy/peace/guide/pages/israels%20disengagement%20plan%20renewing%20the%20peace%20process%20apr%202005.aspx

52   Brian Knowlton, "Bush Supports Sharon's Plan to Withdraw From the Gaza Strip," *The New York Times*, April 14, 2004. http://www.nytimes.com/2004/04/14/international/middleeast/bush-supports-sharons-plan-to-withdraw-from-the-2004041492135886506.html

53   "The Disengagement Plan—General Outline."

54   "Poll: Israelis now see Gaza pullout as mistake," *Israel Today*, May 30, 2007. http://www.israeltoday.co.il/NewsItem/tabid/178/nid/12895/Default.aspx

55   Marissa Newman, "Herzog: Gaza disengagement was 'a mistake' for security," *The Times of Israel*, July 21, 2015. https://www.timesofisrael.com/herzog-gaza-disengagement-was-a-mistake-for-security/

56   "Preliminary Findings of a Survey of Israeli Jewish Attitudes on a Future Peace Agreement with the Palestinians," *Jerusalem Center for Public Affairs*, March 26, 2017.

57   "Rocket and Mortar Hits (launched from Gaza) 2001-2014," *SderotMedia.com.*

58   "Hamas Document of Principles and General Policies, 2017." https://www.

palwatch.org/main.aspx?fi=640&doc_id=20971

59   "Hamas Reiterates: armed wing not up for discussion in reconciliation talks," *Ma'an news agency,* October 8, 2017. https://www.maannews.com/Content.aspx?id=779284

60   Alex Margolin, "Media Uncovers Hamas Launch Sites in Populated Areas," *Honest Reporting,* August 6, 2014. http://honestreporting.com/media-uncovers-hamas-launch-sites-in-populated-areas/

61   Jeremy Havardi, *Refuting the Anti-Israel Narrative: A Case for the Historical, Legal and Moral Legitimacy of the Jewish State* (Jefferson, NC: McFarland, 2016) 29.

62   Mohamed Fadel Fahmy, "Egypt to open Gaza border crossing at Rafah," CNN, May 26, 2011. http://edition.cnn.com/2011/WORLD/africa/05/25/egypt.gaza.border.crossing/; Steven Erlanger, "Israel Closes All Gaza Border Crossings, Citing Palestinian Rocket Attacks," *The New York Times,* January 19, 2008. http://www.nytimes.com/2008/01/19/world/middleeast/19mideast.html; Khaled Abu Toameh, Ben Hartman, Ariel Ben Solomon, "Israel and Egypt Keep Gaza Strip Borders Shut," *The Jerusalem Post,* November 2, 2014. http://www.jpost.com/Arab-Israeli-Conflict/Gaza-border-crossings-closed-amid-rocket-fire-and-Egyptian-security-activity-380516

63   "Israel and occupied Palestinian territories," Amnesty International. https://www.amnestyusa.org/countries/israel-and-occupied-palestinian-territories/; Seumas Milne, "Gaza: this shameful injustice will only end if the cost of it rises," *The Guardian,* July 16, 2014. https://www.theguardian.com/commentisfree/2014/jul/16/gaza-shameful-injustice-israel-attacks-occupied-people; Pnina Sharvit-Baruch, "Is the Gaza Strip Occupied by Israel?," *Jerusalem Center for Public Affairs.* http://jcpa.org/wp-content/uploads/2012/02/Kiyum-sharvit-baruch.pdf

64   Operation Cast Lead lasted three weeks, from December 27, 2008 to January 18, 2009. It was preceded by the firing of thousands rockets into Israel from Gaza.

65   Yossi Klein Halevy, "The End of the Guilty Israeli," *Los Angeles Times,* March 2,

2008. http://articles.latimes.com/2008/mar/02/opinion/op-halevi2

66   Tawfik Hamid, "Why George Mitchell Failed," *The Jerusalem Post*, May 15, 2011. http://www.jpost.com/Opinion/Op-Ed-Contributors/Why-George-Mitchell-failed

67   Bassem Eid, "We Palestinians hold the key to a better future," *The Times of Israel*, February 12, 2015. http://blogs.timesofisrael.com/we-palestinians-hold-the-key-to-a-better-future/

68   Khaled Abu Toameh, "The "Anti-Normalization" Campaign and Israel's Right to Exist," *Gatestone Institute International Policy Council*, August 8, 2016. https://www.gatestoneinstitute.org/8656/anti-normalization-israel

69   Hamas, "Hamas Document of Principles and General Policies (2017)," *Palestinian Media Watch*, May 1, 2017. https://www.palwatch.org/main.aspx?fi=640&doc_id=20971 "The Covenant Of The Islamic Resistance Movement – Hamas," *MEMRI*, August 18, 1988. https://www.memri.org/reports/covenant-islamic-resistance-movement-%E2%80%93-hamas

70   "PLO Charter (1964)," *Palestinian Media Watch*. http://www.palwatch.org/main.aspx?fi=640&doc_id=8210 "Fatah Charter," *Palestinian Media Watch*, July 1, 2009. Note: Fatah's charter was originally written in 1971. https://www.palwatch.org/main.aspx?fi=640&doc_id=1160

71   *The Washington Post*, March 29, 1970 quoted in Paula R. Stern, "It's about Israel, stupid," *Jews Down Under*, October 16, 2014. https://jewsdownunder.com/2014/10/16/israel-stupid/

72   Edward Alexander and Paul Bogdanor, *The Jewish Divide over Israel: Accusers and Defenders* (New York: Transaction Publishers, 2006) 85.

73   Efraim Karsh, *Arafat's War: The Man and His Battle for Israeli Conquest* (New York: Grove Press, 2004) 58.

74   Itamar Marcus and Nan Jacques Zilberdik, "Abbas says all of Israel is "occupation"," *Palestinian Media Watch*, November 2, 2015. http://palwatch.org/main.aspx?fi=157&doc_id=16053

75   "Full text of Abbas's 2015 address to the UN General Assembly," *The Times of Israel*, September 30, 2015. http://www.timesofisrael.com/full-text-of-

abbas-2015-address-to-the-un-general-assembly/

76 "BBC WS history show claims Israel 'carved out of Palestinian land'," *BBC Watch*, August 23, 2017. https://bbcwatch.org/2017/08/23/bbc-ws-history-show-claims-israel-carved-out-of-palestinian-land/

77 M. Cherif Bassiouni and Shlomo Ben Ami, *A Guide to Documents on the Arab-Palestinian/Israeli Conflict: 1897–2008* (Leiden: Brill, 2009).

78 "Israel-Egypt Armistice Agreement," Israel Ministry of Foreign Affairs, February 24, 1949. http://www.mfa.gov.il/mfa/foreignpolicy/mfadocuments/yearbook1/pages/israel-egypt%20armistice%20agreement.aspx

79 "Israel PM Benjamin Netanyahu defiant on 1967 borders," BBC, May 24, 2011. http://www.bbc.com/news/world-middle-east-13515226; Boaz Atzili, "50 years after the Six-Day War, Israel's pre-1967 borders are still a hot topic. Here's why," *The Washington Post*, June 8, 2017. https://www.washington-post.com/news/monkey-cage/wp/2017/06/08/50-years-after-the-six-day-war-israels-pre-1967-borders-remain-important/?utm_term=.5caf9414a8ee Patrick Wintour, "Hamas presents new charter accepting a Palestine based on 1967 borders," *The Guardian*, May 1, 2017. https://www.theguardian.com/world/2017/may/01/hamas-new-charter-palestine-israel-1967-borders

80 "The Six-Day War: Precursor to War, Arab Threats against Israel," CAMERA. http://www.sixdaywar.org/content/threats.asp

81 Jonathan Adelman, "The Christians of Israel: A Remarkable Group," *Huffington Post*. https://www.huffingtonpost.com/jonathan-adelman/the-christians-of-israel_b_8055770.html. *Saturday People, Sunday People: Israel through the Eyes of a Christian Sojourner* (First Encounter Books, 2012) 226. "1948–1967: Jordanian Occupation of Eastern Jerusalem," CAMERA. http://www.sixdaywar.org/content/jordanianocuupationjerusalem.asp

82 "Article 24: 11 National Covenant of the Palestine Liberation Organization", *Israel Ministry of Foreign Affairs*, May 28, 1964. http://www.mfa.gov.il/mfa/foreignpolicy/mfadocuments/yearbook1/pages/11%20national%20covenant%20of%20the%20palestine%20liberation%20.aspx

83 "The Six-Day War: Precursor to War, Arab Threats against Israel."

84 Walter Laqueur and Dan Schueftan, *The Israeli-Arab Reader: A Documentary History of the Middle East Conflict* (New York: Penguin Books, 2016) 113.

85 Walter Laqueur and Barry Rubin, *The Israeli-Arab Reader: A Documentary History of the Middle East Conflict* (New York: Penguin Books, 1995) 409-410.

86 The original PLO charter from 1964 is identical to the 1968 charter except for article 24. "Palestinian National Charter of 1964," *Palestinian Media Watch*, 1968. http://www.palwatch.org/main.aspx?fi=640&doc_id=8210

Chapter 7 Double Standard Fallacy: Frame of Refugees

1 Ryan Bellerose, "Israel: The World's First Modern Indigenous State," *Israel National News*, January 14, 2014. http://www.israelnationalnews.com/Articles/Article.aspx/14377

2 Adrian Wolff, *Israel, a Chronology from Biblical to Modern Times* (2008). Paul Johnson, *A History of the Jews* (New York: Harper & Row, 1987).

3 Karen Brodkin, *How Jews Became White Folks and What That Says About Race in America* (New Brunswick, New Jersey: Rutgers University Press,1998).

4 Eric Goldstein, *The Price of Whiteness* (Princeton University Press, 2006). Jerome Karabel, *The Chosen, The Hidden History of Admission and Exclusion at Harvard, Yale, and Princeton* (Mariner Books, 2006). Michael Bryan Hart, *Introduction to Jews and Race* (Waltham, Massachusetts: Brandeis University Press, 2011).

5 Martin S. Kramer, *Ivory Towers on Sand, The Failure of Middle Eastern Studies in America* (Washington D.C.: Washington Institute for Near East Policy, 2001).

6 Zion refers to the Land of Israel and to Jerusalem.

7 Adrian Wolff, *Israel, a Chronology from Biblical to Modern Times* (2008). "History: Foreign Domination," *Israel Ministry of Foreign Affairs.* http://www.mfa.gov.il/MFA/AboutIsrael/History/Pages/HISTORY%20Foreign%20Domination.aspx Mitchell G. Bard. "History and overview of Acre;

Geography of Israel: Jaffa; Demographics of Israel: Population of Jerusalem," *Jewish Virtual Library,* 1998. *The Last Jews of Libya.* http://jewsoflibya.com/LibyanJews.html

8   Bellerose explains that according to these recognized standards for indigeneity (developed by anthropologist José R. Martínez-Cobo, special rapporteur of the Subcommission on Prevention of Discrimination and Protection of Minorities for the UN) Palestinians and all Arabs are indigenous to Arabia. One's place of indigeneity does not preclude one's rights of longstanding presence elsewhere.

9   Ryan Bellerose, "Are Jews Indigenous to the Land of Israel? Yes," *Tablet,* February 8, 2017. http://www.tabletmag.com/jewish-news-and-politics/224254/bellerose-aboriginal-people

10   Rachel Avraham, "Native American Tribal Support for the State of Israel," *United With Israel,* November 7, 2013. https://unitedwithisrael.org/native-american-tribal-support-for-the-state-of-israel/

11   Navajo Nation (2012). *President Shelly in Israel to Meet with Knesset, Agriculture Ministry, & Memorial Visit to Yad Vashem.* "Navajo President Ben Shelly Meets with Deputy Minister at Knesset, and Honors Survivors of Holocaust at Yad Vashem," *Kayenta Today,* December 13, 2012. http://www.kayentatownship-nsn.gov/blog/?p=4157

12   "WATCH: Why Does this Indigenous Man from New Zealand Stand with Israel?," *United With Israel,* October 16, 2017. https://unitedwithisrael.org/watch-why-does-this-polynesian-man-stand-with-israel/ "Indigenous Friends of Israel–Australia," *Jews Down Under,* July 10, 2017 https://jews-downunder.com/2017/07/10/indigenous-friends-israel-australia/

13   Ambassador Alan Baker, "The Jews: One of the World's Oldest Indigenous Peoples," Jerusalem Center for Public Affairs, August 2017. http://jcpa.org/article/jews-one-worlds-oldest-indigenous-peoples/

14   Elizabeth Redden, "Native American Studies Group Joins Israel Boycott," *Inside Higher Ed,* December 18, 2013. https://www.insidehighered.com/quicktakes/2013/12/18/native-american-studies-group-joins-israel-boycott

15   Jay Corwin, "Native American Academics Do Not Endorse the Boycott of Israeli Academics," *The Times of Israel,* December 25, 2013. http://blogs.timesofisrael.com/native-american-academics-do-not-endorse-the-boycott-of-israeli-academics/

16   Ran Aaronsohn, "Settlement in Eretz Israel—A Colonialist Enterprise? 'Critical' Scholarship and Historical Geography," *Israel Studies* 1, no. 2, 1996. This article appeared in the first year that *Israel Studies* was published and argued that a political agenda could be the only way to account for applying the term colonial to Israel. Irwin J. Mansdorf, "Is Israel a Colonial State? The Political Psychology of Palestinian Nomenclature," *Jerusalem Center for Public Affairs,* March 7, 2010. http://jcpa.org/article/is-israel-a-colonial-state-the-political-psychology-of-palestinian-nomenclature/

17   Ilan Pappe, "The value of viewing Israel-Palestine through the lens of settler-colonialism," *Washington Report on Middle East Affairs* 36, no. 3, 2017. Rashid Khalidi, *The Iron Cage: the Story of the Palestinian Struggle for Statehood* (Boston: Beacon Press, 2006). Joseph Massad, "Palestinian Identity: The Construction of Modern National Consciousness," *International Journal Middle East Studies* 32, no. 2, 2000. Joseph Massad, *The Persistence of the Palestinian Question* (New York: Routledge, 2006). Lorenzo Veracini, *Israel and Settler Society* (Ann Arbor, MI: Pluto Press, 2006). David Lloyd, "Settler Colonialism and the State of Exception: The Example of Palestine/Israel," *Settler Colonial Studies* 2, no. 1, 2012.

18   Eldad J. Pardo, "Palestinian Elementary School Curriculum 2016–17: Radicalization and Reviva of PLO Program," IMPACT-se, Hebrew University of Jerusalem, April 2017. http://www.impact-se.org/wp-content/uploads/PA-Curriculum-2017-Revised.pdf

19   *Academic Engagement Network.* http://academicengagement.org/ *The Third Narrative: Two States, Peace, and Justice for Israelis and Palestinians.* http://thirdnarrative.org/ "Scholars for Israel and Palestine," *The Third Narrative.* http://thirdnarrative.org/uncategorized/scholars-for-israel-and-palestine/ "Alliance for Academic Freedom," *The Third Narrative.* http://thirdnarra-

tive.org/get-involved/alliance-for-academic-freedom/

20   Gilead Ini, "Jewish Terrorism, Palestinian Terrorism, and a New York Times Double Standard," *CAMERA*, August 11, 2015. http://www.camera. org/index.asp?x_context=2&x_outlet=35&x_article=3078; "BBC's Double Standard," *Honest Reporting*, March 11, 2001. http://honestreporting.com/ bbcs-double-standard/; "A new BBC 'explanation' for its double standards on terror," *BBC Watch*, April 24, 2017. https://bbcwatch.org/2017/04/24/a-new-bbc-explanation-for-its-double-standards-on-terror/; Bret Stephens, "Palestine and Double Standards," *The Wall Street Journal*, August 4, 2014. https://www.wsj.com/articles/bret-stephens-palestine-and-double-standards-1407194971; Hunter Stuart, "How a Pro-Palestinian American Reporter Changed His Views on Israel and the Conflict," *The Jerusalem Post*, February 15, 2017. http://www.jpost.com/Jerusalem-Report/A-view-from-the-frontlines-480829

21   "The 1951 Convention relating to the Status of Refugees and its 1967 Protocol," *Refugee Legal Aids Information for Lawyers Representing Refugees Globally: Rights in Exile Programme.* http://www.refugeelegalaidinformation.org/1951-convention

22   Kimberly Curtis, "'Climate Refugee,' Explained" *UN Dispatch*, April 24, 2017. https://www.undispatch.com/climate-refugees-explained/ UNHCR urges governments: People fleeing war to be considered as refugees," UNHCR, December 2, 2016 http://www.unhcr.org/news/briefing/2016/12/584141ed4/ unhcr-urges-governments-people-fleeing-war-considered-refugees.html

23   "'Refugees' and 'Migrants'—Frequently Asked Questions (FAQs)," UNHCR, March 16, 2016. http://www.unhcr.org/afr/news/latest/2016/3/56e95c676/ refugees-migrants-frequently-asked-questions-faqs.html

24   UNWRA also recognizes Displaced Persons from the 1967 War. "Between 175,000 (Israel estimates) and 250,000 (Jordan estimates) Palestinians fled the West Bank for Jordan," Michael B. Oren, *Six Days of War, June 1967 and the Making of the Modern Middle East* (New York: Ballantine, 2002) 306.

25   "Palestine refugees," UNWRA. https://www.unrwa.org/palestine-refugees

26 "The United Nations and Palestinian Refugees," UNRWA, January 2007. https://www.unrwa.org/userfiles/2010011791015.pdf

27 Efraim Karsh, *Palestine Betrayed* (Yale University Press, 2010). Daniel Pipes, "From Time Immemorial, Reviewed," *Commentary*, July 1984. http://www.danielpipes.org/1110/from-time-immemoria

28 "Figures at a Glance," UNHCR, 2017. http://www.unhcr.org/en-us/figures-at-a-glance.html

29 Itamar Eichner, "UN spends times more on Palestinian refugees per person," *Ynet News*, August 27, 2017. https://www.ynetnews.com/articles/0,7340,L-5008515,00.htm

30 "Working at UNRWA,' UNRWA, 2017. https://www.unrwa.org/careers/working-unrwa; Asaf Romirowsky, "How UNRWA Supports Hamas," *In-Focus Quarterly*, Jewish Policy Center, Fall 2017. https://www.jewishpolicy-center.org/2007/08/31/how-unrwa-supports-hamas/

31 Karin Laub, "Plight of Palestinian refugees now spans 5 generations," AP News, April 23, 2017. https://www.apnews.com/bb1a0834a1774e9baaac6c941e9cc90e.

32 Ibid.

33 Mussa Hattar with Sarah Benhaida, "Palestinian refugees' dreams of returning home fade," *Yahoo News*, June 1, 2017. https://www.yahoo.com/news/palestinian-refugees-dreams-returning-home-fade-032237260.html

34 Asaf Romirowsky and Alexander H. Joffe, *Religion, Politics, and the Origins of Palestine Refugee Relief* (New York: Springer, 2013) 5.

35 Ben Dror Yemini, "The Arab Apartheid," (translation) *Elder of Ziyon*, May 16, 2011. http://elderofziyon.blogspot.com/2011/05/arab-apartheid-ben-dror-yemini-must.html

36 Khaled Abu Toameh, "Jordan: We do not want Palestinians," *Gatestone Institute*, September 12, 2015. https://www.gatestoneinstitute.org/6484/jordan-palestinians

37 "Not Welcome: Jordan's Treatment of Palestinians escaping Syria," Human Rights Watch, August 7, 2014. https://www.hrw.org/report/2014/08/07/not-welcome/jordans-treatment-palestinians-escaping-syria

38   "Lebanon: Seize Opportunity to End Discrimination Against Palestinians," Human Rights Watch, June 18, 2010. https://www.hrw.org/news/2010/06/18/lebanon-seize-opportunity-end-discrimination-against-palestinians

39   "The Situation of Palestinian Refugees in Lebanon," UNHCR, February 2016. http://www.refworld.org/pdfid/56cc95484.pdf

40   Abbey Sewell, "Palestinians in Lebanon less than half previous estimate, census shows," *Middle East Eye*, December 21, 2017. http://www.middleeasteye.net/news/palestinians-lebanon-less-half-previous-estimate-census-shows-1396725092

41   Yemini, "Arab Apartheid."

42   Toameh, "Jordan: We do not want Palestinians."

43   Khaled Abu Toameh, "Lebanon's Apartheid Laws," *Gatestone Institute*, June 21, 2013. https://www.gatestoneinstitute.org/3770/lebanon-apartheid-laws

44   Mohammed Daraghmeh, "Palestinian leader rejects deal on Syria refugees," Associated Press, January 10, 2013. https://www.yahoo.com/news/palestinian-leader-rejects-deal-syria-refugees-105551580.html

45   Yaffa Zilbershats and Nimra Goren-Amitai, "Return of Palestinian Refugees to the State of Israel," *The Metzilah Center for Zionist, Jewish, Liberal and Humanist Thought*, 2011.

46   Ibid., 52.

47   Ben Dror Yemini, "NGOs vs. Israel," *Middle East Quarterly*, Spring 2011. http://www.meforum.org/2919/ngos-vs-israel

48   Roz Rothstein and Roberta Seid, "BDS: What Who How?," *StandWithUs*. http://www.standwithus.com/news/article.asp?id=1949 "In Their Own Words," *Stop BDS*. http://www.stopbds.com/?page_id=48 Shirlee Finn, "From the river to the sea, Palestine will be free!," *Jews Down Under*, March 22, 2016. https://jewsdownunder.com/2016/03/22/river-sea-palestine-will-free/

49   Yemini, "Arab Apartheid."

50   Eldad J. Pardo, "Palestinian Elementary School Curriculum 2016-17: Radicalization and Reviva of PLO Program," (7) IMPACT-se, Hebrew University of Jerusalem, April 2017.

51   Ismail Zaydah, "Palestinian journalists frustrated with inability to cover PA corruption," *al-monitor,* April 22, 2008. https://www.al-monitor.com/pulse/originals/2017/01/israel-west-bank-hamas-benjamin-netanyahu-journalism.html "New Survey: 96% of Palestinians Believe Palestinian Authority is Corrupt," *The Tower,* May 24, 2016. http://www.thetower.org/3414-new-survey-96-of-palestinians-believe-palestinian-authority-is-corrupt/ Avi Issacharoff, Hamas spends $100 million a year on military infrastructure," *The Times of Israel,* September 8, 2016. http://www.timesofisrael.com/hamas-spends-100-million-a-year-on-military-infrastructure/?fb_comment_id=1033792160071811_103475877664181

52   Benny Morris, *1948, A History of The First Arab-Israeli War* (Yale University Press, 2008). Benny Morris, *The Making of Palestinian Refugees, Revisited* (Cambridge University Press, 2004).

53   Ibid., 399.

54   Ibid., 404.

55   Ibid., 396.

56   Ibid., 407–411.

57   Benny Morris, "Israel Had No 'Expulsion Policy' Against the Palestinians in 1948," *Haaertz,* July 29, 2017. https://www.haaretz.com/life/books/.premium-israel-had-no-expulsion-policy-against-the-palestinians-in-1948-1.5436863

58   "Arab responsibility for refugees," Palestinian Media Watch. http://palwatch.org/main.aspx?fi=567

59   Mohamad Torokman, "Ghostly exodus: Palestinian reenact 1948' Catastrophe'," NBC News, May 15, 2014. https://www.nbcnews.com/news/world/ghostly-exodus-palestinians-reenact-1948-catastrophe-n106236

60   Ibid.

61   Noah Browning, "Thousands of Palestinians Mark 65 Years Since Displacement," Reuters, May 15, 2013. https://www.reuters.com/article/us-israel-palestinians-nakba/thousands-of-palestinians-mark-65-years-since-displacement-idUSBRE94E0LF20130515

62   Martin Asser, "Obstacles to Arab-Israeli Peace: Palestinian Refugees," BBC, September 2, 2010. http://www.bbc.com/news/world-middle-east-11104284

63   Morris, "Israel Had No 'Expulsion Policy.'"

64   Asser, "Obstacles to Arab-Israeli Peace."

65   Avi Becker, "The Forgotten Narrative: Jewish Refugees from Arab Countries," *Jewish Political Studies Review*, 17:3-4, Fall 2005. *http://www.jcpa.org/jpsr/jpsr-beker-f05.htm*

66   Maurice M Roumani, *The Case of the Jews from Arab Countries, a Neglected Issue,* World Organization of Jews from Arab Countries; 2nd edition (Tel Aviv: World Organization of Jews from Arab Countries, 1978). Shulewitz, *The Forgotten Millions, The Modern Jewish Exodus from Arab Lands* (London: Bloomsbury Publishing, 1999). Francoise S. Ouzan and Manfred Gerstenfeld, *Postwar Jewish Displacement and Rebirth:* 1945–1967 (Leiden, The Netherlands: Brill, 2014). Itamar Levin, *Locked Doors: The Seizure of Jewish Property in Arab Countries* (Westport, Connecticut: Greenwood Publishing Group, 2001). Michael R. Fischbach, *Jewish Property Claims Against Arab Countries* (New York, Columbia University Press, 2008). *The Forgotten Refugees,* directed by Michael Gryszpan, The David Project and Isra TV, Israel, 2005. *Silent Exodus,* directed by Pierre Rehov, Middle East Studios, Israel, 2005. *Remember Baghdad,* directed by Fiona Murphy, Darthmouth Films, 2016. *Operation Mural, Casablanca 1961,* directed by Yehuda Kaveh, Israel and Switzerland, 2007. *El Hara,* directed by Margauz Fitoussi and Mo Scarpelli, France and Tunisia, 2017.

67   Shulewitz, *The Forgotten Millions.*

68   Jimena: Jews Indigenous to the Middle East and North Africa. http://www.jimena.org/ Point of No return: Jewish refugees from Arab and Muslim countries. http://jewishrefugees.blogspot.co.il/ Harif: Association of Jews from the Middle East and North Africa. http://harif.org/

69   Lyn Julius, *Uprooted: How 3000 Years of Jewish Civilization in the Arab World Vanished Overnight* (United Kingdom: Vallentine Mitchell, 2017).

70   Ben Sales, "Push for recognition of Jewish refugees from Arab lands seeks to

counterbalance Palestinian claims," Jewish Telegraphic Agency, September 4, 2012. https://www.jta.org/2012/09/04/news-opinion/israel-middle-east/push-for-recognition-of-jewish-refugees-from-arab-lands-seeks-to-counterbalance-palestinian-claims. Greer Fay Cashman, "Travails of Jews from Arab lands finally recognized after 66 years," *Jerusalem Post,* November 30, 2014. http://www.jpost.com/Israel-News/Politics-And-Diplomacy/Travails-of-Jews-from-Arab-Lands-finally-recognized-after-66-years-383262. Alan M. Dershowitz, "A Challenge to Opponents of Jewish Refugee Status," *Haaretz,* September 25, 2012. https://www.haaretz.com/opinion/alan-dershowitz-jewish-refugees-are-real-1.5168004

71   Mallory Browne, "Jews in Grave Danger in all Moslem Lands," *The New York Times,* May 16, 1948. [Note: "Moslem" was the conventional English spelling at the time.]

72   Samuel G. Freedman, "Are Jews Who Fled Arab Lands Refugees, Too?," *The New York Times,* Ocotober 11, 2003. http://www.nytimes.com/2003/10/11/arts/are-jews-who-fled-arab-lands-to-israel-refugees-too.html

73   Ya'akiv Meron, "Why Jews Fled the Arab Countries," *Middle East Forum: The Middle East Quarterly,* Volume 2: Number 3, September 1995. http://www.meforum.org/263/why-jews-fled-the-arab-countries

74   Country Profiles, *JIMENA.* http://www.jimena.org/jimena-country-by-country/0

75   "Fact Sheet: Jewish Refugees from Arab Countries," *Jewish Virtual Library.* http://www.jewishvirtuallibrary.org/jewish-refugees-from-arab-countries

76   Nathan Weinstock quoted in: Adi Schwartz, "The Inconvenient Truth About Jews From Arab Lands: They Were Expelled," *Forward,* June 1, 2014 http://forward.com/culture/199257/the-inconvenient-truth-about-jews-from-arab-lands/

77   "Jewish Refugees of The Middle East: An Unresolved Injustice," StandwithUs http://www.standwithus.com/booklets/JewishRefugees/

78   "Pogrom," *Oxford English Dictionary.* https://en.oxforddictionaries.com/definition/pogrom

79   David B. Green, "This day in Jewish History// 1934: A Rare Kind of Pogrom

Begins, in Turkey," *Haaretz*, June 5, 2014 https://www.haaretz.com/jewish/. premium-1934-a-rare-kind-of-pogrom-begins-in-turkey-1.5250809

80   "The Farhud," United States Holocaust Museum. https://www.ushmm.org/ wlc/en/article.php?ModuleId=10007277

81   "More about the Constantine pogrom, 1934," *Point of No Return: Jewish Refugees from Arab Countries*, August 12, 2014.http://jewishrefugees.blogspot. co.il/2014/08/more-about-constantine-pogrom-1934.html

82   "100th anniversary of a pogrom in Fez, Morocco," *Elder of Ziyon*, April 17, 2012 http://elderofziyon.blogspot.com/2012/04/100th-anniversary-of-pogrom-in-fez.html#.vsnat4x953y

83   Country Profiles, *JIMENA*.http://www.jimena.org/jimena-country-by-country/

84   Ron Prosor, The Middle East's Greatest Untold Story, *Huffington Post*. "https://www.huffingtonpost.com/ron-prosor/the-middle-easts-greatest-untold-story_b_1652777.html

85   "Proclamation of Independence," The Knesset, May 14, 1948. https://www. knesset.gov.il/docs/eng/megilat_eng.htm

86   Malka Hillel Shulewitz, *Forgotten Millions: The Modern Jewish Exodus from Arab Lands* (London: A&C Black, 2000) 45.

87   Bernard Lewis, "The Return of Islam," *Commentary*, January 1, 1976. https:// www.commentarymagazine.com/articles/the-return-of-islam/

88   John Pontifex, John Newton and Clare Creegan, "Persecuted and Forgotten: A report on Christians oppressed for their faith 2015-17 executive summary," Aid to the Church in Need.

89   "Jews Forced to Leave Muslim Lands," CBN News. http://www1.cbn.com/ content/jews-forced-leave-muslim-lands

90   Raymond Ibrahim, *Crucified Again: Exposing Islam's New War on Islam* (Washington, D.C.: Regnery, 2013).

91   Raymond Ibrahim, "World Ignores Christian Exodus from Islamic World," *Gatestone Institute*, August 6, 2014. https://www.gatestoneinstitute. org/4572/christian-exodus-islamic-world

92   Lela Gilbert, *Saturday People, Sunday People: Israel through the Eyes of a Christian Sojourner* (New York: Encounter Books, 2012) 238.

93   Ibid., 256.

94   Ayaan Hirsi Ali, *Infidel* (New York: Simon and Schuster, 2008). Ayaan Hirsi Ali, *Nomad* (London: Knopf, 2011). Zuhdi Jasser, *A Battle for the Soul of Islam: An American Muslim Patriot's Fight to Save His Faith* (New York: Threshold Editions, 2013). Raheel Raza, *Their Jihad Not My Jihad* (Possibly Publishing, 2014). Nonie Darwish, *Now They Call Me Infidel* (New York: Sentinel, 2006). Tawfik Hamid, *Inside Jihad* (Mountain Lake, MD: Mountain Lake Press, 2015).

95   Gilbert, *Saturday People, Sunday People*, x.

96   Jonathan Adelman, "The Christians of Israel: A Remarkable Group," *Huffington Post*. https://www.huffingtonpost.com/jonathan-adelman/the-christians-of-israel_b_8055770.html

97   "Behind the Headlines: Facts and Figures-Islam In Israel," Israel Ministry of Foreign Affairs, June 9, 2016. http://mfa.gov.il/MFA/ForeignPolicy/Issues/Pages/Facts-and-Figures-Islam-in-Israel.aspx

98   "A portrait of Jewish Americans: Chapter 1: Population Estimate," Pew Research Center, October 1, 2013. http://www.pewforum.org/2013/10/01/chapter-1-population-estimates/

99   "Israel is the 'only safe place' for Christians in Middle East, priest declares," *Catholic Online*, November 5, 2014. http://www.catholic.org/news/international/middle_east/story.php?id=57538&hc_location=ufi

100   "This Country is the Only Safe Haven for Christians in the Middle East," CBN News, July 22, 2016. https://www1.cbn.com/cbnnews/israel/2016/july/this-country-is-the-only-safe-haven-for-christians-in-the-middle-east

101   Ibrahim, "World Ignores Christian Exodus."

CHAPTER 8 Bandwagon Fallacy: Frame of the Neighborhood Bully

1   Bob Dylan, "Neighborhood Bully," Recorded 1983, Special Rider Music, *Infidels*. https://bobdylan.com/songs/neighborhood-bully/

2   Gabe Friedman, "Unearthing Bob Dylan's Forgotten Pro-Israel Song," *Haaretz*, May 24, 2016. https://www.haaretz.com/jewish/news/1.721200

3   ABC World News, "Cease fire with Israel and Hezbollah," YouTube, 2006. https://www.youtube.com/watch?v=aVc2JYTqQjU

4   Dore Gold, "From 'Occupied Territories' to 'Disputed Territories'," Jerusalem Center for Public Affairs, January 16, 2002. http://www.jcpa.org/jl/vp470.htm

5   Victor David Hanson, "Occupation hypocrisy: Gaza vs. Cyprus," *The Washington Times*, August 13, 2014. https://www.washingtontimes.com/news/2014/aug/13/hanson-occupation-hypocrisy/

6   Nima Shirazi, "No surprise Bob Dylan is visiting the 'neighborhood bully,'" *Mondoweiss*, April 13, 2011. http://mondoweiss.net/2011/04/no-surprise-dylan-is-visiting-the-neighborhood-bully/

7   Anthony Vareisa, *The Bob Dylan Albums: A Critical Study* (Montreal: Guernica Editions, 2002) 164.

8   Shirazi, "No Surprise Bob Dylan."

9   Cary Nelson, "Am I a Zionist?," *The Jerusalem Post*, October 25, 2014. http://www.jpost.com/Opinion/Am-I-a-Zionist-379801

10   Noah Beck, "Pessin Affair Exposes Connecticut College Anti-Semitism," *The Jerusalem Post*, February 13, 2016. http://www.jpost.com/Opinion/Pessin-affair-exposes-Connecticut-College-anti-Semitism-443747

11   Amanda Borschel-Dan, "Target of Anti-Israel Witch Hunt Stands Up for Freedom of Speech," *The Times of Israel*, April 17, 2015. https://www.timesofisrael.com/target-of-anti-israel-witch-hunt-stands-up-for-freedom-of-speech/

12   Andrew Pessin and Doron S. Ben-Atar, eds., *Anti-Zionism on Campus: The University, Free Speech, and BDS* (Bloomington: Indiana University Press, 2018). See also: Rafael Medoff, "Tsunami of Anti-Israel and Anti-Semitic Activity Emerges on Campuses Across US," *Scholars for Peace In the Middle East*, October 31, 2017. http://spme.org/boycotts-divestments-sanctions-bds/boycotts-divestments-and-sanctions-bds-news/anti-bds/tsunami-

anti-israel-anti-semitic-activity-emerges-campuses-across-us/24330/; Scott Jaschik, "2 Events Unsettle Jewish Students at Brown," *Inside Higher Ed*, March 21, 2016. https://www.insidehighered.com/news/2016/03/21/two-events-unsettle-jewish-students-brown-university; Jeremiah Poff, "Gender Studies is Hotbed for Anti-Israel BDS Activism Among Faculty: Report," *College Fix*, November 1, 2017. https://www.thecollegefix.com/post/38479/

13   Michael B. Oren, *Six Days of War: June 1967 and the Making of the Modern Middle East* (New York: Ballantine, 2002) 162–164.

14   "The Six-Day War: Precursors to War, Arab Threats Against Israel," *CAMERA*. http://www.sixdaywar.org/content/threats.asp

15   Joshua Muravchik, *Making David into Goliath: How the World Turned Against Israel* (New York: Encounter Books, 2014) 13–15.

16   Ibid., chapters 4 and 5.

17   Mark Langfan, "Abbas: Paymaster of 1972 Munich Massacre Terrorists," *Arutz Sheva*, April 10, 2013. http://www.israelnationalnews.com/Articles/Article.aspx/13916

18   Daniel L. Byman, "The 1967 War and the Birth of International Terrorism," *Brookings*, May 30, 2017. https://www.brookings.edu/blog/markaz/2017/05/30/the-1967-war-and-the-birth-of-international-terrorism/

19   "Watch: Former Fatah Official, 'Do We Need to Hijack Your Planes to Make You Care?'," *Haarertz*, February 8, 2016. https://www.haaretz.com/middle-east-news/watch-former-fatah-official-do-we-need-to-hijack-your-planes-to-make-you-care-1.5401752

20   "The Khartoum resolutions," Israel Ministry of Foreign Affairs, September 1, 1967. http://www.mfa.gov.il/mfa/foreignpolicy/peace/guide/pages/the%20khartoum%20resolutions.aspx

21   Muravchik, *Making David into Goliath,* 52.

22   Paul Delaney, "Arafat Has Plea for Arab Nations," *The New York Times*, January 24, 1988. http://www.nytimes.com/1988/01/24/world/arafat-has-plea-for-arab-nations.htm

23   Jonathan Schanzer "Palestinian Uprisings Compared," *Middle East Quar-*

terly, Summer 2002, 27–37. http://www.meforum.org/206/palestinian-uprisings-compared

24   Karen A. Arenson, "Columbia Debates a Professor's 'Gesture'," *The New York Times*, October 19, 2000. http://www.nytimes.com/2000/10/19/nyregion/columbia-debates-a-professor-s-gesture.html

25   Ruth Wisse, *Jews and Power* (New York: Schocken Books, 2007) 137.

26   Tim Harding, "The David and Goliath Fallacy," *The Logical Place*, June 18, 2013. https://yandoo.wordpress.com/2013/06/18/the-david-and-goliath-fallacy/

27   The 16 Countries are Algeria, Bangladesh, Brunei, Iran, Iraq, Kuwait, Lebanon, Libya, Malaysia, Oman, Pakistan, Saudi Arabia, Sudan, Syria, United Arab Emirates, and Yemen.

28   "Israeli Resilience," *The Jerusalem Post*, June 12, 2016. http://www.jpost.com/Opinion/JPOST-EDITORIAL-Israeli-resilience-456562; Marissa Newman, "Day after Terror Attack, Congregants Return to Pray at Har Nof Synagogue," *The Times of Israel*, November 19, 2014. https://www.timesofisrael.com/congregants-return-to-synagogue-for-first-prayers-after-attack/

29   Associated Press, "The Latest: Peace 'Quartet' Urges Restraint in Jerusalem," *Daily Mail*, July 23, 2017. http://www.dailymail.co.uk/wires/ap/article-4720144/The-Latest-Israeli-troops-raid-home-Palestinian-attacker.html

30   "US Urges Restraint after Teenagers Bodies Found," *The Telegraph*, June 30, 2014. http://www.telegraph.co.uk/news/worldnews/middleeast/israel/10937116/US-urges-restraint-after-teenagers-bodies-found.html; Louis Charbonneau, "U.N. Uurges Israeli Restraint in Hunt for Teens, Warns of Violence," Reuters, June 24, 2014. https://www.reuters.com/article/us-palestinian-israel-un/u-n-urges-israeli-restraint-in-hunt-for-teens-warns-of-violence-idUSKBN0EY2LS20140624

31   Andrew Markus, "Little Choice for a Defiant Israel," *The Age*, July 15, 2006. https://web.archive.org/web/20070311000828/http://www.theage.com.au/text/articles/2006/07/14/1152637865649.html

32   Ellen Knickmeyer, "2006 War Called a 'Failure' for Israel," *The Washington*

Post, January 31, 2008. http://www.washingtonpost.com/wpdyn/content/article/2008/01/30/AR2008013000559.html; Yossi Melman, "Was the Second Lebanon War Indeed a Failure?," *The Jerusalem Post,* July 23, 2016. http://www.jpost.com/Jerusalem-Report/AN-UNAPPRECIATED-WAR-457455; Yossi Melman, "Analysis: Was the Second Lebanon War a Success?," *The Jerusalem Post,* July 12, 2016. http://www.jpost.com/Arab-Israeli-Conflict/Analysis-Was-the-Second-Lebanon-War-a-success-460129

33   Michael Elliott, "The Way Out: . . . of this Mess: The Six Keys to Peace in the Middle East," *Time Magazine,* vol. 168, no. 5, July 31, 2006.

34   Tamar Liebes, "Our war/their war: Comparing the *intifadeh* and the gulf war on U.S. and Israeli television," *Critical Studies in Mass Communication* 9, no. 1, 1992.

35   ABC World News, *Cease Fire.*

36   Marvin Kalb and Carol Saivitz, "The Israeli-Hezbollah War of 2006: The Media as a Weapon in Asymmetrical Conflict," *The International Journal of Press/Politics,* July 1, 2007. http://journals.sagepub.com/doi/abs/10.1177/1081180x07303934

37   Cherryl Smith, "The Disappearing Ongoing Terror Wave," *Honest Reporting,* October 12, 2015. http://honestreporting.com/the-disappearing-ongoing-terror-wave/

38   Kalb and Saivitz, "The Israeli—Hezbollah War."

39   Benjamin Weinthal, "B'Tselem's Gaza War Statistics Under Fire," *The Jerusalem Post,* August 20, 2014. http://www.jpost.com/Operation-Protective-Edge/BTselems-Gaza-war-statistics-under-fire-by-right-wing-Israeli-groups-371590

40   Simon Plosker, "Synagogue Terror Attacks: Top Headline Fails," *Honest Reporting,* November 18, 2014. http://honestreporting.com/synagogue-terror-attack-top-headline-fails/

41   Ari Soffer, "CNN Apologizes for 'Israel Shoots Palestinians' Headline," *Arutz Sheva,* November 18, 2014. http://www.israelnationalnews.com/News/News.aspx/187614

42   "Five Palestinians killed 'after attacking Israelis'," BBC, February 14, 2016. http://www.bbc.com/news/world-middle-east-35574604

43   Kareeem Khadder, "4 Palestinians Shot Dead in Alleged Knife Attacks on Israeli Forces," CNN, January 8, 2016. http://edition.cnn.com/2016/01/08/middleeast/palestinian-israeli-knife-attack-shootings/index.html

44   Josh Feldman, "MSNBC's Ayman Mohyeldin Corrected On-Air After Suggesting Dead Palestinian Terrorist Wasn't Armed," *Mediaite*, October 15, 2015. https://www.mediaite.com/tv/msnbcs-ayman-mohyeldin-corrected-on-air-after-suggesting-dead-palestinian-terrorist-wasnt-armed/#ooid=o2bnU3eDq-m_nFIz9BrrfhQn_jYQrXe

45   Matti Friedman, "An Insider's Guide to the Most Important Story on Earth," *Tablet*, August 26, 2014. http://www.tabletmag.com/jewish-news-and-politics/183033/israel-insider-guide

46   Matti Friedman, "What the Media Gets Wrong About Israel," *The Atlantic*, November 30, 2014. https://www.theatlantic.com/international/archive/2014/11/how-the-media-makes-the-israel-story/383262/

47   Mark Lavie, *Broken Spring: An American-Israeli Reporter's Close-up View of How Egyptians Lost Their Struggle for Freedom* (Jerusalem: Gefen, 2014). "Matti Friedman Hits Back at AP, and So Do I," *Broken Spring*, September 19, 2014. https://brokenspring.wordpress.com/2014/09/19/matti-friedman-hits-back-at-ap-and-so-do-i/

48   Tom Gross, "The Media Aims Its Missiles," *The Jerusalem Post*, August 2, 2006. http://www.jpost.com/Opinion/Op-Ed-Contributors/The-media-aims-its-missiles

49   Friedman, "What the Media Gets Wrong."

50   Marcus Sheff, "A Decade Since the Battle of Jenin, 'The Myth of Jeningrad'," *The Jerusalem Post*, April 19, 2012. http://www.jpost.com/Opinion/Columnists/A-decade-since-the-battle-of-Jenin-the-myth-of-Jeningrad

51   "The Palestinian Account of the Battle of Jenin," *MEMRI*, April 23, 2002. https://www.memri.org/reports/palestinian-account-battle-jenin

52   Tom Gross, "Jeningrad: What the British Media Said," Tom Gross MidEast

Media Analysis, May 13, 2002. http://www.tomgrossmedia.com/Jeningrad. html; Ian Black, "Israel Faces Rage over 'Massacre'," The Guardian, April 17, 2002. https://www.theguardian.com/world/2002/apr/17/israel2; "Jenin Camp Situation 'Horrendous'," BBC News, April 15, 2002. http://news.bbc. co.uk/2/hi/middle_east/1930295.stm

53   Sheff, "A Decade Since."

CHAPTER 9 Faulty Analogy: Frame of the Cycle of Violence

1   Bassem Eid, "Palestinians Need Real Support, Not Self-serving BDS," *The Times of Israel*, May 8, 2017. http://blogs.timesofisrael.com/palestinians-need-real-support-not-self-serving-bds/

2   Ewan MacAskill, "Israel Vows Revenge After Boys Are Stoned to Death," *The Guardian*, May 10, 2001. https://www.theguardian.com/world/2001/may/10/israel

3   "'Stoning to Death' of Israeli Youths Fuels Tension," ABC News, May 9, 2001. http://abcnews.go.com/International/story?id=81112&page=1

4   MacAskill, "Israel vows revenge."

5   Ibid.

6   "Both Sides Condemn Killing of 2 Israeli Boys," CNN, May 9, 2001. http://www.cnn.com/2001/WORLD/meast/05/09/mideast.02/

7   Yoav Appel, "Two Israeli Teen-Agers Killed," *The Washington Post*, May 9, 2001. http://www.washingtonpost.com/wp-srv/aponline/20010509/aponline105912_000.htm

8   Although they are underreported in US and UK media, these celebrations and honors are routine: Ben Cohen, "Palestinian Leader Mahmoud Abbas' Fatah Movement Praises Har Adar Terrorist as 'Martyr'," *Algemeiner*, September 26, 2017. https://www.algemeiner.com/2017/09/26/palestinian-leader-mahmoud-abbas-fatah-movement-praises-har-adar-terrorist-as-martyr/; "Glorifying Terrorists and Terror," *Palestinian Media Watch*. http://palwatch.org/main.aspx?fi=448; "With Publication of High School Finals Results, Palestinian Authority Press Notes Deaths of Students Who

Carried Out Stabbing Attacks, Stresses: 'Dying As a Martyr Is the Path of Excellence and Superiority'," *MEMRI*, July 13, 2016. https://www.memri. org/reports/publication-high-school-finals-results-palestinian-authority-press-notes-deaths-students-who; "Palestinian Authority and Fatah Glorify Terrorist Dalal Al-Mughrabi and the Contribution of Other Female Martyrs and Prisoners to the Palestinian Cause," *MEMRI*, March 12, 2018.https:// www.memri.org/reports/palestinian-authority-and-fatah-glorify-terrorist-dalal-al-mughrabi-and-contribution-other

9   Suzanne Goldenberg, "Rush Hour Car Bombing Signals New Cycle of Violence in Israel," *The Guardian*, November 23, 2000. https://www.the-guardian.com/world/2000/nov/23/israel; Tarik Kafala, "Cycle of Violence Gains Momentum," BBC, January 25, 2002.http://news.bbc.co.uk/2/hi/middle_east/1776265.stm

10   MacAskill, "Israel Vows Revenge."

11   The phrase "expansion of Jewish settlements" and the word "settlement" are most often used by media as a way of talking about renovations to existing apartments or about new apartments built in existing Jewish neighbor-hoods over the green line. Groundbreaking for the first new settlement in 20 years, meaning the first new Jewish community over the green line (in Israeli controlled Area C) occured in June, 2017. Raf Sanchez, "Israel Breaks Ground on First New Settlement in 20 Years," *The Telegraph*, June 20, 2017. https://www.telegraph.co.uk/news/2017/06/20/israel-breaks-ground-first-new-settlement-20-years/.

12   Sherri Mandell, *Blessings of a Broken Heart* (New Millford, CT: Toby Press, 2003) and *The Road to Resilience: From Chaos to Recovery* (New Millford, CT: Toby Press, 2015).

13   The Koby Mandell Foundation, http://www.kobymandell.org.

14   "One Family Overcoming Terror," OneFamily. http://www.onefamilyto-gether.org/about-us/. "United Hatzalah of Israel," United Hatzalah. https://israelrescue.org/

15   Ishaan Tharoor, "The Problem of Gaza: An Endless Cycle of Violence," *Time*

Magazine, November 21, 2012. http://world.time.com/2012/11/21/no-peace-in-gaza-an-endless-cycle-of-violence/. "Killings in Jerusalem Raise Fears of a New Cycle of Violence," *The Economist*, October 7, 2015. https://www.economist.com/news/middle-east-and-africa/21671969-now-discussion-new-intifada-premature-killings-israel-raise-fears-new-cycle. Karen Bruilliard, "In Israel, Resignation to the Cycle of Violence," *The Washington Post*, November 19, 2002. https://www.washingtonpost.com/world/middle_east/in-israel-resignation-to-the-cycle-of-violence/2012/11/19/df250048-328d-11e2-bfd5-e202b6d7b501_story.html?utm_term=.c1ae75b7a746

16 Conal Urquhart, "Israel and Hizballah Step Back From the Brink After Tit-for-Tat Attacks," *Time Magazine*, January 28, 2015; Stephen Farrel, "Hamas Vows to Hit Back in Israel's Tit for Tat War," *Sunday Times* (UK), September 11, 2003 https://www.thetimes.co.uk/article/hamas-vows-to-hit-back-in-israels-tit-for-tat-war-ckofcolnmzs. http://time.com/3685763/hizballah-israel-retaliation/; "Tit for Tat," *The Economist*, October 18, 2001. https://www.economist.com/node/825471

17 Micah Halpern, "Explosive Charge: Israel is Not Part of 'the Cycle of Violence'," *Forward*, March 17, 2017. https://forward.com/opinion/366374/explosive-charge-israel-is-not-part-of-a-cycle-of-violence/

18 David A. Jaeger and M. Daniele Paserman, "Israel, the Palestinian Factions, and the Cycle of Violence," *American Economic Review*, vol. 96, no. 2, May 2006, 45–49.

19 "Hamas is Expert at Driving Media Agenda 'British commander tells U.N. debate'," UN Watch, October 20, 2009. https://www.unwatch.org/issue-208-british-hero-military-expert-tells-u-n-idf-moral-army-history-warfare/.

20 Halpern, "Explosive Charge."

21 David A. Jaeger and M. Daniele Paserman. "An Empirical Analysis of Fatalities in the Palestinian-Israeli Conflict," *American Economic Review*, 2008 98:4

22 Ibid.

23   Ibid.

24   Alexei Abrahams, Eli Berman , Prabin Khadka , Esteban F. Klor, and John Powell, "*Not* a Cycle of Violence: An Episodic Analysis of the Israel-Gaza Conflict," February, 2018. https://scholars.huji.ac.il/sites/default/files/eklor/files/cycles_february_2018.pdf

25   Ibid.

26   Hamas Covenant http://avalon.law.yale.edu/20th_century/hamas.asp Hamas Policy Document, *MEMRI.* https://jij.org/news/new-hamas-charter/

27   Jeffrey Goldberg, "What Would Hamas Do If It Could Do Whatever It Wanted?," *The Atlantic,* August 4, 2014. https://www.theatlantic.com/international/archive/2014/08/what-would-hamas-do-if-it-could-do-whatever-it-wanted/375545/

28   "Mahmoud Al Zahar reveals Hamas' genocidal agenda—shocking!" YouTube, November 22, 2012. https://www.youtube.com/watch?v=oKgupoduYRo. Al Zahar made this statement in 2010. In 2018, referring to the Gaza violence on Israel's border that is routinely called "protests" by the media, Al Zahar said, "So when we talk about 'peaceful resistance' we are deceiving the public." MEMRI TV, "Senior Hamas Official, Mahmoud Al-Zahhar on Gaza Protests: This is Not a Peaceful Protest, It is Supported by Our Weapons," clip 36573, May 13, 2018. https://www.memri.org/tv/senior-hamas-official-mahmoud-zahhar-on-gaza-protests-this-is-not-peaceful-resistance

29   "Proclamation of Independence," Knesset, May 14, 1948. https://www.knesset.gov.il/docs/eng/megilat_eng.htm

30   "Code of Ethics and Mission," IDF. https://www.idf.il/en/minisites/code-of-ethics-and-mission/

31   Like the earlier studies that were focused on patterns of violence rather than episodes, Abrahams et al "find no evidence episodes with counter-retaliations (i.e., cycles of violence) induce or deter subsequent violence." Abrahams, et al, "*Not* a Cycle of Violence"

32   Daniel Pomerantz, "Iran Attack: It All Started When Israel Fired Back," *Honest Reporting,* February 11, 2018. http://honestreporting.com/iran-

attack-it-all-started-when-israel-fired-back/

33   "Militants killed in Israeli air strikes on Gaza", BBC, October 29, 2011. www. bbc.com/news/world-middle-east-15506823.

34   Melanie Phillips, "The BBC Airbrushes Out Palestinian Terror Attacks—Again," *Daily Mail*, October 30, 2011. http://phillipsblog.dailymail. co.uk/2011/10/the-bbc-airbrushes-out-palestinian-terror-attacks-again. html

35   Pomerantz, "Iran Attack."

36   Karen Yourish and Josh Keller, "The Toll in Gaza and Israel, Day by Day," *The New York Times*, August, 2014. https://www.nytimes.com/interactive/2014/07/15/world/middleeast/toll-israel-gaza-conflict.htmhtt

37   "Over a year since Operation Cast Lead: A Summary of Statistics," *Sderot Heritage Party*, January 22, 2009. http://sderotmedia.org/over-a-year-since-operation-cast-lead-a-summary-of-statistics/2217/

38   Max Fisher, "Israel, Gaza, and the Patterns of the Past," *The Washington Post*, November 19, 2012. https://www.washingtonpost.com/news/worldviews/wp/2012/11/19/israel-gaza-and-the-patterns-of-the-past/?noredirect=on&utm_term=.696ac2acc677

39   Jaeger and Paserman, "An Empirical Analysis."

40   *New York Times* Editorial Board, "The Cycle of Violence in Israel," *The New York Times*, October 15, 2015.

41   Louise Richardson, *What Terrorists Want: Understanding the Enemy, Containing the Threat* (New York: Random House, 2006) chapter 1.

42   Alex P. Schmid, "The Revised Academic Consensus Definition of Terrorism," *Terrorism Research Initiative*, 2011, vol. 6, no. 2. http://www.terrorismanalysts.com/pt/index.php/pot/article/view/schmid-terrorism-definition/html

43   Richardson, *What Terrorists Want*, 4–6.

44   Boaz Ganor, "Defining Terrorism—Is One Man's Terrorist Another Man's Freedom Fighter?," International Institute for Counter-Terrorism, January 1, 2010. https://www.ict.org.il/Article/1123/Defining-Terrorism-Is-One-Mans-Terrorist-Another-Mans-Freedom-Fighter#gsc.tab=0

45   "International Coverage of TA Terror Attack Refer to 'Shooting,' But Not Terrorists," *YNet,* June 9, 2016. https://www.ynetnews.com/articles/ 0,7340,L-4813964,00.html.

46   "BBC Misleads—Again," *The Jerusalem Post,* June 20, 2017. https://www. jpost.com/Opinion/BBC-misleads-again-497443

47   "What we Investigate: Terrorism," FBI. https://www.fbi.gov/investigate/ terrorism; "Terrorism," *Crown Prosecution Service.* https://www.cps.gov. uk/terrorism

48   Philip Jenkins, *Images of Terror: What We Can and Can't Know About Terrorism* (New York: Aldine de Gruyter, 2003) 19–20.

49   "Reuters Admits Appeasing Terrorists," *Honest Reporting,* September 21, 2004. http://honestreporting.com/reuters-admits-appeasing-terrorists-2/. Steven Stotsky, "More Terror Bias NPR," *CAMERA,* May 23, 2006. http:// www.camera.org/article/more-terror-bias-at-npr/; Tuvia Book, "The Missing Word: How BBC Reports Terror Attacks in Israel Without Using the Word 'Terror'," *The Times of Israel,* April 15, 2017. http://blogs.timesofisrael. com/the-missing-word-how-bbc-reports-terror-attacks-in-israel-without-using-the-word-terror/.

50   Eid, "Palestinians need real support."

51   Ibid.

52   Steve Visser, Andrew Carey, and Abeer Salman, "West Bank, Jerusalem Violence Flares After Recent Calm," CNN, September 17, 2016. https://edition. cnn.com/2016/09/16/middleeast/west-bank-violence/index.html

53   Ibid.

54   Steven Erlanger, "Anger in a Palestinian Town Feeds a Cycle of Violence," *The New York Times,* January 19, 2016. https://www.nytimes.com/2016/01/20/ world/middleeast/anger-in-a-palestinian-town-feeds-a-cycle-of-violence. html?_r=0

55   Ibid.

56   Tamar Pileggi, "Dafna Meir Fought Back Fiercely, Her Teen Killer Says," *The Times of Israel,* June 19, 2016. http://www.timesofisrael.com/dafna-meir-

fought-back-fiercely-her-teen-killer-says/

57   "A Fatal Israeli-Palestinian Flaw," *LA Times*, March 14, 2011. http://articles. latimes.com/2011/mar/14/opinion/la-ed-settlements-20110314

58   "Israel–Palestine: Tit-for-Tat?," *LA Times*, March 24, 2011. http://opinion. latimes.com/opinionla/2011/03/israel-palestine-tit-for-tat.html

59   Ibid.

60   Conal Urquhart and Ewen Macaskill, "Israel Warns of 'Aggressive' Response to Jerusalem Blast," *The Guardian*, March 23, 2011. https://www. theguardian.com/world/2011/mar/23/israel-warns-over-jerusalem-blast?INTCMP=SRCH

61   Ashley Fantz, "Why Are So Many Civilians Dying in Hamas-Israel War?," CNN, August 6, 2014. https://edition.cnn.com/2014/08/04/world/meast/gaza-israel-why-civilian-deaths/index.html

62   "Kashmir Fast Facts," CNN, March 25, 2018. https://edition.cnn.com/2013/11/08/world/kashmir-fast-facts/index.html.

63   Yourish and Keller, "The Toll in Gaza and Israel."

64   Nick Cumming-Bruce, "Death Toll in Syria Estimated at 191,000," *The New York Times*, August 22, 2014. https://www.nytimes.com/2014/08/23/world/middleeast/un-raises-estimate-of-dead-in-syrian-conflict-to-191000.html

65   Andrew Rafferty, "The War in Afghanistan: By the Numbers," NBC News, August 22, 2017. https://www.nbcnews.com/politics/politics-news/war-afghanistan-numbers-n794626

66   Fantz, "Why Are So Many Civilians Dying."

67   "Gaza Crisis: Toll of Operations in Gaza," BBC, September 1, 2014. http://www.bbc.com/news/world-middle-east-28439404

68   Adam Taylor, "The Lopsided Death Tolls in Israeli-Palestinian Conflicts," *The Washington Post*, July 11, 2014. https://www.washingtonpost.com/news/worldviews/wp/2014/07/11/the lopsided-death-tolls-in-israel-palestinian-conflicts/?noredirect=on&utm_term=.f75d11ccec78

69   Richard Kemp, "Gaza's Civilian Casualties: The Truth Is Very Different," *Gatestone Institute*, August 3, 2014. https://www.gatestoneinstitute.org/4570/

gaza-civilian-casualties; Philip Klein, "Five Reasons Why Comparing Israeli and Palestinian Death Totals Is a Misleading Way to Judge the Conflict," *Washington Examiner,* July 16, 2014. https://www.washingtonexaminer.com/ five-reasons-why-comparing-israeli-and-palestinian-death-totals-is-a-misleading-way-to-judge-the-conflict; Evelyn Gordon, "What Raqqa Says about Gaza's Death Toll," *Commentary,* October 27, 2017. https://www.commentarymagazine.com/foreign-policy/middle-east/raqqa-says-gazas-death-toll/

70   Sam Harris, "Sam Harris: 'Why Don't I Criticize Israel?'," *Tablet,* July 30, 2014. http://www.tabletmag.com/scroll/180808/sam-harris-why-dont-i-criticize-israel#undefined.

CHAPTER 10 Poisoning the Well: Frame of the World's Worst

1   Howard Jacobson, "Howard Jacobson: Let's See the Criticism of Israel for What It Really Is." *Independent,* February 18, 2009.

2   Cherryl Smith, "The Quiet and the Hamas Sides of the Street," *American Thinker,* November 19, 2012. http://www.americanthinker.com/blog/2012/11/ the_quiet_and_the_hamas_sides_of_the_street.html#ixzz4RILZyWEW.

3   Stand With Us, San Francisco Chapter. http://www.standwithus.com/ chapters/san%20francisco/;

4   Cnaan Liphshiz, "Protesters Chant 'Hamas, Jews to the Gas' in Antwerp," *Jewish Telegraphic Agency,* November 11, 2012. https://www.jta.org/2012/11/19/ news-opinion/world/protesters-chant-hamas-jews-to-gas-in-antwerp; Micki Weinberg, "Wave of Anti-Semitic Rallies Hits Cities Across Germany," *The Times of Israel,* July 21, 2014. https://www.timesofisrael.com/wave-of-anti-semitic-rallies-hits-cities-across-germany/.

5   "Maps Erase Israel," *Palestinian Media Watch.* http://palwatch.org/pages/ allmaps.aspx

6   "American and Israeli Jews: Twin Portraits from PEW Research Center Surveys," January 24, 2017. http://www.pewforum.org/essay/american-and-israeli-jews-twin-portraits-from-pew-research-center-surveys/

7   Alan M. Dershowitz, *The Case For Israel* (Hoboken: Wiley, 2003) 222.

8   Alan M. Dershowitz, "Israel: The Jew Among the Nations," in Alfred E. Kellerman, Kurt Siehr and Talia Einhorn, eds., *Israel Among the Nations* (Leiden: E.J. Brill, 1998) 129.

9   See Melanie Phillips, *The World Turned Upside Down: The Global Battle over God, Truth, and Power* (New York: Encounter Books, 2010); Bernard-Henri Levy (Trans., Stephen B. Kennedy), *The Genius of Judaism* (New York: Random House, 2017) chapter 1; Phyllis Chesler, *The New Anti-Semitism* (Jerusalem: Gefen, 2015).

10   Alan M. Dershowitz, "Pink Anti-semitism Is No Different from Brown Anti-semitism," *Algemeiner*, February 26, 2013. https://www.algemeiner. com/2013/02/26/pink-anti-semitism-is-no-different-from-brown-anti-semitism/

11   Peter Yeung, "Ramadan 2016: Israel 'Cuts Off Water Supply to West Bank' During Muslim Holy Month," *Independent*, June 15, 2016. https://www. independent.co.uk/news/world/middle-east/ramadan-2016-israel-water-west-bank-cuts-off-a7082826.html

12   Adam Levik, "Contrary to Indy Charge Israel increased water supply to Palestinian during Ramadan," *UK Media Watch*, June 16, 2016. https:// ukmediawatch.org/2016/06/16/contrary-to-indy-charge-israel-increased-water-supply-to-palestinians-during-ramadan/.

13   Dov Lieber, "Daily Mail Epic Geography Fail: UK Paper Claimed Israel Flooded Gaza's Major West Bank Cities," *The Jerusalem Post*, February 24, 2015. https://www.jpost.com/Israel-News/Daily-Mail-epic-geography-fail-UK-paper-claimed-Israel-flooded-Gazas-major-West-Bank-cities-392057

14   "Ten Worst UN Actions, 2018," *UN Watch*, December 23, 2018. https://www. unwatch.org/top-10-worst-un-actions-2018; "10 Most Insane UN Anti-Israel Actions of 2017," UN Watch, December 20, 2017. https://www unwatch.org/ top-10-insane-u-n-anti-israel-actions-2017/; "The UN and Israel: Key Statistics from UN Watch," *UN Watch*, August 23, 2016. https://www.unwatch. org/un-israel-key-statistics/

15   Judah Ari Gross, "UN Ranks IDF Emergency Medical Team as 'No. 1 in the

World,'" *The Times of Israel*, November 13, 2016. http://www.timesofisrael. com/un-ranks-idf-emergency-medical-team-as-no-1-in-the-world/

16   Jacob Balme, "US–Israel Academic Collaboration Increases Dramatically," *Israel on Campus Coalition*, December 8, 2016. https://www.iccgw. org/2016/12/us-israel-academic-collaboration-increases-dramatically

17   Cary Nelson, "The New Assault on Israeli Academia (and Us)," *Fathom*, Spring, 2014. http://spme.org/boycotts-divestments-sanctions-bds/new-assault-israeli-academia-us/18485/

18   William A. Jacobson, "University Statements Rejecting Academic Boycott of Israel," *Legal Insurrection*, December 22, 2013. https://legalinsurrection. com/2013/12/indiana-wash-u-st-louis-gwu-northwestern-cornell-reject-academic-boycott-of-israel/

19   Phillips, *The World Turned Upside Down*, 365.

20   Jackson Diehl, "Israel's Spying Vulture—and Killer Shark," *The Washington Post*, January 5, 2011. http://voices.washingtonpost.com/postpartisan/2011/01/israels_spying_vulture--and_ki.html

21   Taylor Hom, "Israeli 'Spy' Captured in Sudan," ABC News, December 10, 2012. https://abcnews.go.com/Blotter/israeli-spy-captured-sudan/story?id=17926788

22   "You'd Be Surprised By How Many Animals Are Arrested for Being Israeli Spies," *Albawaba News*, January 26, 2016. https://www.albawaba.com/loop/you%E2%80%99d-be-surprised-how-many-animals-are-arrested-being-israeli-spies-798032

23   Babak Dehghanpisheh, "Egypt Shark Attacks Spur Conspiracy Theories," *Newsweek*, August 12, 2010. http://www.newsweek.com/egypt-shark-attacks-spur-conspiracy-theories-68901

24   Yair Rosenberg, "The Top Five Most Hilarious Anti-Semitic Conspiracy Theories," *Tablet*, May 19, 2016. https://www.tabletmag.com/jewish-life-and-religion/202716/anti-semitic-conspiracy-theories

25   Inna Lazareva, "Israeli 'spy dolphin' caught off Gaza coast," *The Telegraph*, August 19, 2015. https://www.telegraph.co.uk/news/worldnews/middleeast/

israel/11813322/Israeli-spy-dolphin-caught-off-Gaza-coast.html

26 Khaled Abu Toameh and Herb Keinon, "Report: Abbas Accuses Israel of Using Wild Boars Against Israel," *The Jerusalem Post*, November 22, 2014. https://www.jpost.com/Arab-Israeli-Conflict/PA-chief-warns-against-resorting-to-religious-war-382499

27 "Blood Libel: A False, Incendiary, Claim Against Jews." Anti-Defamation League. https://www.adl.org/education/resources/glossary-terms/blood-libel

28 Mark G. Yudof and Ken Walzer, "Majoring in Anti-Semitism at Vassar," *The Wall Street Journal*, February 17, 2016. https://www.wsj.com/articles/majoring-in-anti-semitism-at-vassar-1455751940; Cinnamon Stillwell, "In New Low, Scholars Defend Medieval Blood Libel Against Israel," *Middle East Forum*, 2016. https://www.meforum.org/5895/puar-revives-blood-libel

29 Robin Emmott and Dan Williams, "Abbas says some Israeli rabbis called for poisoning Palestinian Water," Reuters, June 23, 2016. https://ca.reuters.com/article/topNews/idCAKCN0Z91J8#pq=ed5Emt

30 Raphael Israeli, *Poison: Modern Manifestations of a Blood Libel* (Lanham: Lexington Books) 2002.

31 Yair Rosenberg, "Abbas Tells EU Parliament the Israeli Rabbis Called to Poison Palestinian Water," *Tablet*, June 23, 2016. https://www.tabletmag.com/scroll/206162/abbas-tells-eu-parliament-that-israeli-rabbis-called-to-poison-palestinian-water

32 Michael J. Totten, "The Myth of Jewish-Only Roads," *Commentary*, December 5, 2010. https://www.commentarymagazine.com/culture-civilization/religion/judaism/the-myth-of-jewish-only-roads/

33 Simon Plosker, "*Washington Post*'s, Richard Cohen: 'Jewish-Only Roads,'" *Honest Reporting*, March 28, 2017. http://honestreporting.com/washington-posts-richard-cohen-jewish-only-roads/; "'Jewish Only Road' Falsehood Corrected," *CAMERA*, January 5, 2010, https://www.camera.org/article/jewish-only-road-falsehood-corrected/

34 Richard Landes, "Pallywood: A History," *The Augean Stables*, http://www.

theaugeanstables.com/reflections-from-second-draft/pallywood-a-history/

35 Pierre Rehov, Middle East Documentaries, http://www.pierrerehov.com/

36 Richard Landes, "The al-Dura Case," *The Augean Stables*. http://www.theaugeanstables.com/al-durah-affair-the-dossier/al-durah-faqs/

37 Nidra Poller, "The Muhammad al-Dura Hoax and Other Myths Revived," *Middle East Quarterly*, Fall 2011, vol. 11, September, 2011. https://www.meforum.org/articles/2011/the-muhammad-al-dura-hoax-and-other-myths-revived; Phillippe Karsenty, "We Need to Expose the Muhammad al-Dura Hoax" *Middle East Quarterly*, Fall 28, vol. 15, September, 2008. https://www.meforum.org/articles/2008/philippe-karsenty-we-need-to-expose-the-muhamma

38 Google's academic search engine, GoogleScholar, turns up thousands of academic books and papers using the formulation Israel-Palestine or Palestine-Israel besides those that refer to an Israel-Palestine conflict.

39 Ismael Khaldi, *A Shepherd's Journey: The Story of Israel's First Bedouin Diplomat* (Khawlid, Israel: Ishmael Khaldi, 2010) 117–118.

40 Stuart Winer, "Abbas Pledges: There Will Be No Israelis in Palestine," *The Times of Israel*, July 30, 2013. http://www.timesofisrael.com/abbas-says-there-will-be-no-israelis-in-palestine/

41 Simon Tomlinson, "World of Walls," *Daily Mail*, August 21, 2015. http://www.dailymail.co.uk/news/article-3205724/How-65-countries-erected-security-walls-borders.html

42 "I Know What Apartheid Was, and Israel Is Not Apartheid, Says S. African Parliament Member," *The Jerusalem Post*, August 25, 2015. https://www.jpost.com/Israel-News/Politics-And-Diplomacy/I-know-what-apartheid-was-and-Israel-is-not-apartheid-says-S-African-parliament-member-413101

43 Tshediso Mangope, "I'm a South African Activist Who Used to Fight Against Israel—Until I Went There," *Tower Magazine*, Issue 45, December, 2016. http://www.thetower.org/article/im-a-south-african-activist-who-used-to-fight-against-israel-until-i-went-there/.

Acknowledgements

I wish to thank the many people whose encouragement helped me immensely while I worked on this book—those who read and responded to drafts, those with whom I talked over the topics of the book, and those who are the ongoing supporters of my writing and of me.

The book exists because of my great publisher at RVP Press, René van Praag, whose enthusiasm for *Framing Israel* was immediate, and because of Astrid Bosch, who meticulously and artfully did the layout and design.

I am grateful to Simon Plosker at Honest Reporting, who cheered on the project from its beginning, to my talented research intern from the MASA Program Sydney Fenton, and to David Stein Potache for his well-suited cover photo.

My heartfelt appreciation goes to Sylvia Vivrette, James Vivrette, Debra Haber, Sonja Kaubisch, Diana Loera Laris, Sheryl I. Fontaine, Ellen Moss, Lynn Grants, Ira Levy, Loretta Breuning, Cinnamon Stillwell, Bea Lieberman, Trudy Zuckermann, Ury Weiss, Lila Navi, Wendy Fielding, Nancy Hartvelt Cobrin, Avi Levy, Jessica Geva, Beverly Lewin, Monica Broido, Helen Katznelson, Bella Rubin, Anna Kissin Shechter, Helen Sarid, Ilana

Shiloh, Miriam Mandel, Raquelle Azran, Vicki Abolafia-Fabricant, Ayala Amir, Israel Kimchi, Jin Kimchi, and the Kimchi family, to my wonderful partner Jerry, and as always to my son Jeremy Zev, my bright light.